DAVID RATTRAY'S
Guidebook to the
ANGLO-ZULU WAR
BATTLEFIELDS

DAVID RATTRAY'S
GUIDEBOOK TO THE
ANGLO-ZULU WAR BATTLEFIELDS

by

David Rattray FRGS

and

Dr Adrian Greaves FRGS

in conjunction with

The Anglo-Zulu War Historical Society

LEO COOPER

First published in Great Britain in 2003 by
LEO COOPER
an imprint of
Pen & Sword Books Ltd
47 Church Street
Barnsley
South Yorkshire
S70 2AS

ISBN 0 85052 922 0

A CIP catalogue record for this book is
available from the British Library

Printed and bound in Singapore by
Kyodo Printing Co (S'pore) Pte Ltd

CONTENTS

How To Use This Guide and Useful Information

The purpose of this guidebook is to enable both independent and guided visitors to the Anglo-Zulu War battlefields to understand and explore each site. Helpful advice is given with regard to locations and route-finding. An individual map that includes hints and points of interest, with modern amenities superimposed, illustrates each battlefield. The guide will also be of use to enthusiasts of the Zulu War as the text and maps contain new material.

The *Battlefield Guidebook* includes many useful suggestions for visitors travelling on their own but we would always recommend that an experienced guide is well worth the cost. If travelling alone, ensure your vehicle always has sufficient fuel, and that you have refreshments and a modern road map due to the isolated location of some of the battlefields and sites.

Useful addresses

The Anglo Zulu War Historical Society (AZWHS)
Woodbury House, Woodchurch Road
Tenterden, Kent
TN30 7AE
United Kingdom

Tel: (UK) 01580 764189   Web Site: www.anglozuluwar.com

Fugitives' Drift Lodge
Tel: (SA) 034 642 1843   Web Site: fugdrift@trustnet.co.za

Part One

A General Background
to the Anglo-Zulu War of 1879

The Overtures to War

If we are to have a fight with the Zulus, I am anxious that our arrangements should be as complete as it is possible to make them. Half-measures do not answer with natives. They must be thoroughly crushed to make them believe in our superiority. General Thesiger, July 1878 – shortly to become Lord Chelmsford

During the sixty-four-year reign of Queen Victoria the red-jacketed British soldier was engaged in a similar number of campaigns throughout the British Empire fighting for his Queen and country. Of all these conflicts, it was the Anglo-Zulu War that most seized the popular imagination, mainly because of a series of serious British defeats during the first half of 1879. Further political disaster followed with the death of the heir to the Napoleonic dynasty, Louis Napoleon, the exiled Prince Imperial, who volunteered to fight with the British in Zululand. Famous British regiments soon found themselves fighting their former friend, King Cetshwayo of the Zulus and his most ferocious and feared army. On 22 January 1879 1,329 officers and men of Lord Chelmsford's Central Column, the main body of his three-pronged invasion force, would be killed. Not since the Indian Mutiny in 1857 had such total and humiliating losses been reported to an incredulous British public.

Confederation – The Excuse for War

At the time of the Anglo-Zulu War, Britain was using the proven policy of Confederation as a means of successfully administering her numerous colonies. In South Africa this involved merging a number of neighbouring colonies under British control to bring the area's trade, defence and colonial law all under one central and stable administration. Each colony would run its own military system, supervised and led by British officers, which relieved Britain of the expensive responsibility for maintaining military garrisons in the colonies. At the time this policy appeared to be the solution to the problem of uniting Britain's southern African colonies into a self-financing confederation.

The discovery in October 1867 of diamonds in the Boer Orange Free State saw thousands of prospectors from all over the world converge on South Africa. In 1871, after several years of chaos and with obvious wealth still to be won, Britain annexed the whole area to the British Crown, including Basutoland. The total cost to the Crown was £90,000, paid in the form of compensation. Lord Carnarvon appointed Sir Bartle Frere as High Commissioner to South Africa and Governor of the Cape in 1877.

The Conspiracy Deepens
In its origins, the Zulu War was of special interest in the history of South Africa because the crushing of King Cetshwayo and his fighting men was seen, accurately or inaccurately, as the solution to the problem of knitting together the European colonies into a workable confederation. Sir Henry Bartle Frere and his Secretary for Native Affairs, Sir Theophilus Shepstone, both favoured military intervention against the Zulus. They encouraged the belief that King Cetshwayo possessed an army of 50,000 warriors, which was poised to invade the developing British colony of Natal. Their views about the Zulus were shared by Major General Frederic Thesiger, shortly to become Lord Chelmsford following the death of his father and recently appointed as Commander in Chief of British forces in South Africa. It was generally believed that a quick campaign was all that was needed; the British Army had wide experience gained during several years suppressing black insurrections and King Cetshwayo would quickly be obliged to understand that Queen Victoria ruled much of Africa and, further, relationships between the British and Boer communities could be strengthened. All this could be achieved once the Zulu Army that 'threatened' both communities was defeated.

In reality the situation was very different. The Zulus had been faithful allies of the British for many years and, although they had not engaged in warfare during the previous twenty-two years since the Battle of Ndondakusuka (between Cetshwayo and his brother), they were, nevertheless, highly trained. The Zulus' determination to defend their country was to produce the most unexpected result.

At the time very few people in Britain even knew their army was undertaking an invasion of Zululand. As far as the press was concerned, the deteriorating situation in Zululand was considered to be insignificant and only one of the London newspapers sent a correspondent to cover it. Understandably, newspaper editors were focused on Afghanistan where, in the event, the British had some severe difficulties.

Then, all of a sudden, Charles Norris-Newman of *The Evening Standard* reported the astonishing British defeat at Isandlwana, a name never heard of before. Newspaper correspondents were rapidly despatched to South Africa to report on the disaster and its consequences. From this point onwards the news from South Africa was to dominate the British press.

During the next six months England sent a great number of reinforcements to Lord Chelmsford in South Africa, and Zululand was then invaded for a second time. There were many more engagements, and further Zulu victories included Hlobane Mountain, Ntombe River and the death of the Prince Imperial of France, who was the heir and last hope of the Napoleonic Dynasty. The Zulu Army, though, was effectively crushed after the battles of Khambula, Gingindlovu and Ulundi.

We speak of disaster and failure and inglorious warfare only as regards those who made the war and undertook its management. Our brave soldiers acted as bravely as ever men acted in any war; implicitly obeying orders which they knew must end in failure, marching calmly into the jaws of death, enduring hardships innumerable without complaint and entering into the conflict of battle with genuine enthusiasm, notwithstanding the fact that the sympathies of the many were not in the cause.

Edwin Hodder, Heroes of Britain, Cassell 1880

A soldier of the 24th Regiment
from *Records of the 24th* 1892

Army Life

Life in Britain during the 1870s was a struggle against massive unemployment, poverty and widespread malnutrition. Tuberculosis, cholera, influenza, whooping cough, scarlet fever, measles and a variety of lesser infectious diseases caused the major health problems of the population. By 1879 life expectancy for the working classes was as low as thirty-eight years, only the wealthy having any hope of reaching their mid-fifties.

Domestic sanitation, piped water and sewage disposal were gradually improving general health. In the meantime, life in 1879 was dominated by the spectre of disease. Syphilis was also widespread, both at home and abroad and among the army the condition was normally recorded by military doctors under the vague heading of 'other diseases'.

Don't despair – enlist!

By the mid 1870s unemployment and all its social effects had reached terrifying proportions. For young unemployed men, enlistment in the Army was always there as the last resort. It is hardly surprising that the majority of recruits came from backgrounds of squalor and wretchedness. Even those young men who had survived the numerous common childhood diseases would often be suffering from poor physique. The average height of an army recruit had fallen over the previous ten years to a skinny 5 foot 4 inches. The prospect of eating regularly was an enormous attraction, as the recruiting sergeants knew only too well.

'...an all for a shillin'a day...'

During the reign of Queen Victoria there were sufficient recruits to make conscription unnecessary. Taking the Queen's shilling, and all it stood for, was a legally binding contract. Recruiting sergeants also frequented public houses and taverns where unemployed young men collected, although any recruit who had been drunk at the time of his 'enlistment' could be released from the commitment. Recruits were normally 'sworn in' within twenty-four hours. They would then be medically examined before joining an under-strength regiment or being sent abroad.

It was not unknown for men to enlist under a false name. One famous Zulu War Victoria Cross recipient joined the army to avoid personal problems; Private 1395 John Fielding VC of the 2nd 24th (2nd Warwickshire) Regiment won his medal at Rorke's Drift under the alias of Williams. When he returned home with his

Private Fielding VC.
*Courtesy of Major Martin Everett,
24th Regimental Museum, Brecon*

Victoria Cross, he re-established his friendship with the young lady in question, now the mother of his baby, and married her.

Army pay was poor and from the daily shilling official deductions maintained the soldier's poverty. A married soldier could have part of his pay paid to his wife or family. The widow of a soldier killed in action or who died of disease on campaign could expect no official help other than charity; only in 1881 was any form of widow's pension instituted. Even so, by the time of the Zulu War army life was attractive enough for conscription to be unnecessary. An increasing proportion of soldiers consisted of short-service recruits with a liability for just six years' active service, followed by a further six years in the reserves.

Letters from soldiers in the Zulu War reveal that they had little or no idea why they would be fighting. The soldiers'information came largely from rumour and hearsay; after all, there was no military reason why the men should be informed. Their main ambition appeared to be to survive in order to go home as soon as possible. On campaign, their life centred on staying as dry and comfortable as possible while keeping out of trouble. Much was made at the time of the brutality of the Zulus, but within the British Army flogging was still regularly practised; out of some 20,000 soldiers who took part in the campaign, records reveal that 545 were flogged, with twenty-five lashes being the norm. The practice had been outlawed in peacetime but remained lawful on active service.

Flogging can never be done away with in wartime in the English army unless some equally efficient punishment can be discovered.

Colonel Bray Précis of Information concerning Zululand

At the time of the Zulu War dysentery, enteric fever and tuberculosis also posed serious problems for the soldiers, especially in a hot climate such as that of South Africa. Tuberculosis spread rapidly when its hosts, both humans and cattle, lived in squalid and overcrowded conditions. The disease was spread by coughing and spitting, drinking contaminated milk and from contact with polluted water, grass, animal feed and soil. Enteric fever resulted from unhygienic living conditions and dysentery was spread from contaminated water supplies. Such diseases were prevalent during the Zulu War.

Dysentery is not very common, but the occurrence of bloody urine is very frequent in both man and animals, and tapeworm exists to such an extent that almost every second person you meet with has worms of some sort.

Dr Jones' Report on the Climate and Diseases of Natal & Zululand
Appendix to the Army Medical Department's Report 1878

The Officers

British officers invariably represented the wealthy or land-owning class and, on average, they were taller and generally fitter than their men. The Cardwell reforms of 1870 changed the composition of the army and abolished the practice of officers purchasing commissions, yet most of the officers who fought and died in the Zulu War had already purchased their commissions prior to the reform. The cost of a commission was beyond all but the wealthy and, furthermore, independent means were required for officers to meet their expensive mess bills and pastimes such as hunting and riding. In addition, officers were expected to display a high level of fitness, loyalty, team spirit and physical bravery. By the time of the Zulu War, many officers had adopted a more paternal attitude towards their men; they were more concerned for their men's welfare and many readily assisted with the vital task of letter writing and reading.

The 24th (2nd Warwickshire) Regiment of Foot
It was a coincidence that both battalions of this regiment were to serve together in the Zulu War. By 1879 the very experienced 1st Battalion were battle-hardened after four years'campaigning in the 9th Frontier War in the eastern Cape Colony. They and one company of the recently arrived 2nd Battalion were destined to face the Zulu attack at Isandlwana where almost all the men and officers involved would be killed.

On 1 April 1873 Brecon in Wales became the regimental depot of the 24th, but most recruits for the local 2nd Battalion came from the English counties bordering Wales, especially from Monmouthshire, which was then an English

county. Monmouthshire became part of Wales in 1974. Other recruits came from Brecknock, Cardigan and Radnor. Having seen continuous service in various Mediterranean garrisons for the eight years prior to arriving in South Africa on 4 February 1875, the 1st Battalion's link with Wales was tenuous.

On 1 February 1878 the 2nd Battalion, with 24 officers and 849 other ranks, sailed from Chatham in Kent for South Africa in HM troopship *Himalaya*. They were reinforcements for the British force being assembled in South Africa and by the time of the Zulu War the majority of the 2nd Battalion were English, the next highest proportion Irish, with fifteen per cent from Wales. Due to the location of its depot, the 24th (2nd

24th Officer. *On Active Service*, Lloyd.

The Zulu People. *Adrian Greaves collection*

Warwickshire) Regiment changed its title to The South Wales Borderers in 1881. It was King Shaka (1780-1828) who trained the then fledgling tribe of Zulus in total warfare; he ordered the use of short stabbing spears rather than throwing spears; he also developed and taught the 'horns of the bull' tactic of surrounding and then destroying an enemy.

By 1818 Shaka's army had grown to nearly three thousand. He consolidated his position and watched while other Bantu tribes engaged in totally destructive warfare against each other. Shaka thereafter ruled unchallenged. His army grew to over twenty thousand trained warriors and was based in a heartland that extended from the Indian Ocean to the Drakensberg and from the Pongola River in the north to the Tugela River in the south. The effects of Shaka's military activities extended his influence still further and by 1822 his clan had grown into an empire, the influence of which extended as far west as the Kalahari Desert, north to the shores of Lake Malawi and south to the Eastern Cape.

By early 1824 Shaka knew of the handful of white men living at Port Natal and to satisfy his curiosity he sent them an invitation to visit his royal homestead at kwaBulawayo (at the place of killing). The invitation was accepted and the party, carrying a large number of gifts, consisted of Lieutenant Francis George Farewell, Henry Francis Fynn, John Cane, Henry Ogle, Joseph Powell and Thomas Halstead; James King and Nathaniel Isaacs later joined them.

After various displays and feasts, Farewell and Fynn finally met with Shaka and during one of their meetings they persuaded Shaka to grant trading rights for the Farewell Trading Company. The party returned to Port Natal but without Fynn who remained at Shaka's request – not as a hostage, but to enable Shaka to learn more of the white men. Fynn was residing at the royal kraal when an attempt was made on Shaka's life. He was stabbed through his left arm and ribs by an unknown assailant and lay at death's door for a week. During this time Fynn cleaned and bandaged the wound and generally cared for Shaka, who quickly recovered. Shaka was encouraged to believe that members of the distant Qwabe tribe had made the attempt; two impis were dispatched to seize the Qwabe cattle and destroy their kraals. The settlers' position was assured and Shaka allegedly made an agreement granting Farewell nearly four thousand square miles of land around Port Natal.

During 1826 Farewell and Fynn accompanied Shaka's army of over twenty thousand warriors[1] on an expedition against the Ndwandwe clan. The result was a near total slaughter of the Ndwandwe, an event that distressed even Farewell and Fynn, though Shaka was delighted with the sixty thousand captured cattle.

Shaka's rule was total until 1827 when his mother, Nandi, suddenly died. He ordered stringent regulations to be enforced in order that everyone should share his grief. Thousands of people, Fynn tells us, were put to death and the carnage was such that Shaka's half-brothers, Dingane and Mhlangana, agreed that Shaka must die. They waited until the army was on campaign and stabbed Shaka to death during a meeting with his senior indunas (counsellors). His body was unceremoniously buried in a pit weighted down with stones. Many years later, the site was purchased by a farmer and today Shaka's grave lies somewhere under Cooper Street in the small town of Dukuza (formally Stanger) north of Durban.

Farewell's traders had previously enjoyed Shaka's protection but with his death, their future looked uncertain. They attempted to consolidate their position by enlarging their small fort. Their fears were not realized as the new king, Dingane, duly informed them that they were welcome to continue trading. In 1829 Farewell, the principle founder of Port Natal and not yet forty years old, was killed by the Qwabe Chief Nqetho. At the age of thirty years, Dingane settled into a life of luxury and security. He reduced the size of the Zulu Army and military discipline slackened somewhat. Miscreants, however, were still summarily executed.

In February 1838 a Boer leader, Piet Retief, had led a party of trekkers across the Drakensberg to seek permission from Dingane to settle the area. Retief and his men duly arrived at Dingane's kraal only to be done to death. Dingane immediately sent his warriors to destroy the unsuspecting Boer families and in a night of massacre 541 women, children and servants were slaughtered. The Boers made two attempts at exacting revenge; the first failed, but the second resulted in a Boer victory at Blood River in 1838. Following this battle,

Zulu Warriors at the time of the Zulu War. *Adrian Greaves collection*

Modern-day visitors to the Memorial at Blood River.

Adrian Greaves collection

A Zulu Warrior (modern day) with the classic stabbling spear of the Zulu War period.

Adrian Greaves collection

Dingane withdrew his army and regrouped his forces to rebuild his capital to the north. Although defeated in battle, Dingane still possessed large numbers of Boer guns, cattle and horses and he spent the following months consolidating his position.

Meanwhile, the Boer trekkers were crossing the Drakensberg in ever-increasing numbers and began settling on the central plateau. They named the area the 'Free Province of New Holland in South East Africa' and its main residential area became known as 'Pietermaritzburg' after the Boer leaders Retief and Maritz. The British formally occupied Port Natal and re-named it 'Durban' after Sir Benjamin D'Urban, Governor of the Cape Colony. They negotiated a truce with Dingane and then abandoned the port to the Boers. Dingane was later murdered by his own people, having been defeated by an army of Zulus under the command of his brother Mpande, assisted by these Boers.

After Dingane's death Mpande became King and many tribes that had been displaced in these earlier years began to move back to Zululand, only to discover the Boers were settling their lands in increasing numbers. The Boer Volksraad decreed that these 'surplus'[2] black people, now homeless, were to be rounded up and moved to a black homeland well away from the Boer farms in Natal. Towards the end of 1841 the British heard of the plan, forbade the Boer action and, re-seizing Durban, despatched sufficient administrators to govern Durban.

In 1843 Natal became a British colony and in 1845 was annexed into the Cape. Reluctantly the Boer Volksraad acquiesced. The Boers had over-reached themselves and, by provoking the British, duly lost sovereignty over much of their recently settled lands. European settlers continued to arrive, but the biggest change to the area since the Boers crossed the Drakensberg came with the dredging of Durban Harbour. From this single engineering feat Durban rapidly prospered as Pietermaritzburg declined.

Mpande's rule of the Zulus was fair but firm according to Zulu custom and peace followed. As Mpande aged, two heirs apparent began to emerge from his sons; Prince Cetshwayo and Prince Mbuyazi, and the senior men of Zululand began to gravitate towards the man of their choice. The two brother princes were now in their early twenties and led the uThulwana and amaShishi regiments respectively. Cetshwayo was a traditionalist and hankered after the regal days of Shaka, whereas Mbuyazi was more inclined to intellectual matters, though equally powerful. In 1856 neither had acquired any battle experience, though both sought to become king.

Resolution was to come through bloody conflict, perhaps the worst seen or recorded in African history. Near Ndondakusuka hill on the Tugela River, Cetshwayo's twenty thousand warriors, the uSuthu, were pitted against Mbuyazi's *iziGqoza* army, which numbered some thirty thousand. The battle lasted no more than an hour with Mbuyazi's army being heavily defeated. Cetshwayo ordered the total slaughter of the iziGqoza and only a handful escaped.

In order to strengthen his grip further Cetshwayo courted friendship with the British, whereupon Theophilus Shepstone, later to be knighted, and Secretary for Native Affairs, went to Mpande and suggested that, in the name of Queen Victoria, Cetshwayo be appointed heir apparent. Mpande accepted on behalf of the Zulus, though Cetshwayo was aware that his future now depended, to a degree, on British support. Mpande died in 1872 after thirty-two relatively peaceful years on the Zulu throne, a reign marred only by his two sons' battle on the Tugela. Mpande was the only Zulu king in this period to die of natural causes.

Cetshwayo was in his mid-forties when he became king and he immediately sought British approval. Shepstone agreed and in a farcical ceremony on 1 September 1873 Cetshwayo was crowned King of the Zulu nation in the name of Queen Victoria. He established his royal homestead near the present day Ulundi. An astute and intelligent man, he now ruled a united nation although he faced dealing with the Boer people who were streaming into the wedge of Zululand known as the 'disputed territory' to the north of Rorke's Drift. Cetshwayo inherited this problem from his father, Mpande, who had been in an invidious position because of the support the Boers had previously given him. Nevertheless, his army was at its most powerful and he believed he had a friend in Queen Victoria.

Because Zululand possessed sufficient available land for settlement and a ready source of labour, the British needed it to be included in any confederation; it would also alleviate the threat that the British believed the Zulus constituted to peace in the region. However, the Zulus' autocratic king had the ability to muster an army of forty thousand warriors who would never agree to a surrender and dissolution of Zululand merely to facilitate British economic development. In order to find an excuse to invade Zululand, officials spread rumours of a bloodthirsty and defiant Zulu Army plotting to invade Natal. This ploy was highly successful and spread unease among the white settlers who believed war with the Zulus was inevitable. Cetshwayo appeared to be unaware of this subversive undercurrent and continued to believe he enjoyed good relationships with the British. For the Zulus time was running out.

By the time the Zulu War began, successive Zulu kings had efficiently controlled the development of Zulu society and ensured a comparatively healthy and prosperous population. Anthony Trollope travelled through southern Africa and parts of Zululand during 1877 just as European hysteria was mounting; yet he viewed the Zulus as being perceptive and living in sympathy with their time and environment.

I have no fears myself that Natal will be overrun by hostile Zulus, but much fear that Zululand should be overrun by hostile Britons. Anthony Trollope South Africa 1878

Zulu Tactics

Pre Shaka, tribal confrontation, known as 'giya', was more of a ritual process than combative. In such a confrontation, the young men involved would take up opposing sides, some forty to fifty yards apart, and hurl abuse with only the occasional spear being thrown. Giya usually lasted about two hours before the two sides separated and returned to their respective home areas. Shaka changed the process into one that was ruthless and deadly; this was demonstrated when he mobilized his highly trained and efficient force against the neighbouring Buthelezi tribe, later to become an important part of the Zulu nation.

The Zulus originally used the *Impondo Zenkomo* for hunting. These tactics had stood the test of time; it was Shaka who developed them to defeat a human foe; the British invading force was about to experience its efficiency for the first time.

Tactics Pre Shaka
The ritual 'giya' formation:

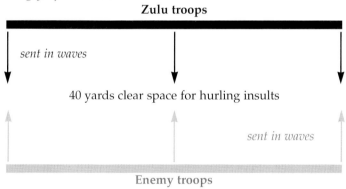

Shaka Battle Tactics
The 'horns of the bull' (Impondo Zenkomo)

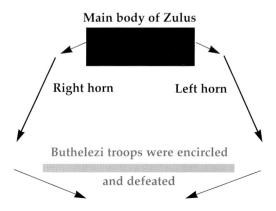

A Zulu Chief's white shield.
Adrian Greaves collection

Zulu spear and knobkerrie.
Adrian Greaves collection

Zulu Weapons

The Zulus' cowhide shields were the most visible part of a warrior's armoury and were made by specialist shield-makers. The colour of the hide was important. In the time of Shaka the combination of colour and patches was carefully selected, the differences between each regiment's colour being detailed and specific; the whiter the shield, the more senior was its owner. By the time of the Zulu War, the practice was less strictly observed, although married regiments carried predominantly white or red shields while those of unmarried regiments were black or a combination of black and white.

The full Zulu War shield was the isiHlangu, which covered the warrior from his face to his feet and was at least two feet six inches wide. During the civil war of the 1850s Cetshwayo had introduced a smaller variant called the umbumbulozo at three feet six inches long and two feet wide. It was soon discovered that this shield was much lighter and easier to use. Both shields were carried, even within the same regiment, although the umbumbulozo may have been most popular with younger more adventurous warriors. The shields were strengthened by a single stick, fastened to the back by a double row of hide strips threaded through slits carefully cut in the shield. It was held by a small handle. All regimental shields were the property of the king rather than the individual; they were kept in special raised stores out of the way of ants and rodents. By the time of the British invasion, Zulu warriors had learned that by soaking their shields in water and then inclining them at forty-five degrees, they could deflect Martini-Henry rounds at distances of more than 200 yards. Zulu bodies were rarely found beyond 200 yards from a British firing line even though fire was often commenced at between 400 and 600 yards, a fact initially established by British officers following investigations carried out following the Battle of Gingindlovu.

By the time of the British invasion of Zululand, Zulu weapons consisted of traditional spears and obsolete European rifles. The stabbing spear, or Ikwa, which originated at the time of Shaka, had a blade some eighteen inches long

King Cetshwayo. *Ron Sheeley collection*   **Sir Bartle Frere.** *Ron Sheeley collection*

and two and a half inches wide, set into a wooden shaft 2 feet 6 inches long. It was Shaka who realized the ineffectiveness of hurling the longer throwing spears at the enemy, only to have them gathered up and thrown back in retaliation. Shaka drilled his soldiers in shock tactics that involved a mass charge and close quarter combat – culminating in under-arm stabbing to the death. Throwing spears were still common in 1879 and most had a blade of about five or six inches with the iron shank visible for several inches before being set into the wood. They were particularly useful against British soldiers whose aim at close range deteriorated under a shower of spears.

Only skilled smiths who lived along the White Mfolozi River and in the Nkandla forests were entrusted with the manufacture of stabbing spears. They collected the iron ore from surface deposits and smelted it in clay forges with the aid of skin bellows. The blades were hammered into shape, tempered with fat, and sharpened on special flat stones before being set into wooden shafts. Each shaft would then be glued with strong vegetable glues and bound with wet cane fibres. A tube of hide, cut from a calf's tail, was rolled over the join and allowed to shrink. These weapons were strong and well designed for the purpose of killing.

Warriors were responsible for their own weapons, but the King initially received the spears in bulk from those clans that made them, distributing them to warriors who had distinguished themselves. Most warriors also carried clubs or knobkerries, the iWisa, which were simple polished sticks with a heavy bulbous head. Zulu boys carried them for everyday protection and their possession at all times became second nature.

By the time of the British invasion, the Zulu Army possessed a large variety of guns. An English trader, John Dunn, had imported some 16,000 of these and sold them on to King Cetshwayo at a huge profit. It is believed that Cetshwayo had 20,000 guns at his disposal. The majority of these were obsolete military firearms manufactured at Potsdam, Danzig, Tulle, Manchester (many proofed in London, hence being known as 'Tower muskets') and in America, all dumped on the unsophisticated 'native market'. More modern types were available, particularly the percussion Enfield, and a number of Chiefs, including Prince Dabulamanzi and Chief Sihayo of Rorke's Drift, had collections of quality sporting guns. Most Zulus were untrained in the use of firearms and their firing was highly inaccurate; various accounts of Zulu War battles note both the indiscriminate use of their firepower and general inaccuracy. After Isandlwana large numbers of Martini-Henry rifles fell into Zulu hands; many were shortly to be used to good effect against the British at Khambula and Ulundi.

The Annexation of the Transvaal

When in 1838 the Boers first crossed the Drakensberg Mountains into Natal, they initially remained south of the Tugela River, the natural border of Zululand, before a small number moved across the Zulu border. By the mid-1870s Boer settlers again began surreptitiously moving into Zululand and these incursions were opposed by the Zulus with increasing vigour. One area of heightened tension lay between the Buffalo and Blood rivers immediately north of Rorke's Drift.

The Zulu king, Cetshwayo, was growing increasingly agitated by Boer farmers encroaching into that part of Zululand (the disputed territory north of Rorke's Drift) and claimed by the Boers to be part of the Transvaal so that it fell outside British jurisdiction after Natal was proclaimed a British colony. Although Cetshwayo's father had accepted the Boers in return for their support, Cetshwayo viewed them with grave suspicion, whereas he had long regarded the British as his friends.

Sir Bartle Frere neatly deferred the problem by constituting an independent Boundary Commission to adjudicate, once and for all, on title to the disputed territory. King Cetshwayo was consulted and he readily agreed to abide by the Commission's decision. The Commission's principal members consisted of Michael Gallwey, a barrister who, at the age of thirty-one, had become the Attorney General of Natal in 1857, Lieutenant Colonel Anthony Durnford R.E., who had served in South Africa for many years, and John Shepstone, brother and deputy of the Secretary for Native Affairs. Piet Uys, a farmer who had lost relatives to Dingane's impis, Gert Rudolph, the Boer Landdrost of Utrecht, and Henrique Shepstone who served on his father's staff in Pretoria, represented the Boers.

The Boundary Commissioners concluded that the Boers never acquired and the Zulus never lost dominion over the disputed territory and that it still belonged to Zululand. The Commission further agreed that the developing Boer settlement at Utrecht must also be surrendered. The Boundary Commission results were eventually delivered to Frere in July 1878.

Thwarted, Frere kept the decision a secret. On 28 July a minor incident occurred which Frere used to generate widespread anti-Zulu sentiment. Two of Chief Sihayo's sons crossed the river into Natal to capture two of their father's adulterous wives. The women were duly returned across the border at Rorke's Drift and put to death (clubbed, shot or strangled – various accounts) in sight of the Mission Station. The incident received officially orchestrated publicity throughout Natal in order to inflame public opinion against King Cetshwayo.

Rebuffed by the Boundary Commission, Frere knew that publication of the Commission's findings would seriously antagonize the Boers who might have to surrender their farms in Zululand. Frere knew the Boers could well retaliate against Britain by resorting to military action against British-controlled Natal – and even involve Holland and Germany at a time when Britain faced war against Afghanistan and relationships with Russia were deteriorating.

Reading Ultimatum to Zulu Chief Natal Side of Drift Lower Tugela 11th Dec /78

Ultimatum Tree. *Adrian Greaves collection*

<u>**THE MAIN REQUIREMENTS OF THE ULTIMATUM:**</u>

Conditions to be fully met within twenty days

1. The surrender to the British of the Swazi Chief, Mbelini, (for cattle raiding).
2. The surrender of Chief Sihayo's two sons (for crossing the river border into Natal, abducting and them murdering two of Sihayo's adulterous wives) plus a fine of 500 cattle.
3. A fine of 100 cattle for having molested two British surveyors, Deighton and Smith, at a border crossing.

Conditions to be fully met within thirty days

1. A number of prominent Zulus were to be surrendered for trial (no names were specified).
2. Summary executions were forbidden.
3. The Zulu Army was to disband.
4. The Zulu military system was to be abandoned.
5. Every Zulu was to be free to marry.
6. Missionaries were to be re-admitted to Zululand without let or hindrance.
7. A British resident official was to oversea Zulu affairs.
8. Any dispute involving a European was to be dealt with under British jurisdiction.

The Ultimatum

To Frere a British military victory over the Zulus was a certainty; a Zulu defeat would placate the Boers, deter other black nations and free up a valuable source of labour for British and Boer commercial activities. Frere ordered his General Commanding British Forces in South Africa, the Hon. Frederic Thesiger, to prepare his forces for an immediate war against the Zulus. Meanwhile, he decided that the Boundary Commission's findings were best dealt with by ignoring them.

On 9 October an incident occurred which Frere was able to use to his advantage. A local chief, Mbilini Ka Mswati, (who was not a Zulu but a Swazi freebooter living in Northern Zululand), attacked immigrant Boers and local tribesmen in the disputed area and stole herds of their cattle. Frere was already composing an ultimatum to the Zulus and the raid by Mbilini formed the first item in the draft ultimatum. At about the same time a Zulu border patrol had encountered two British surveyors, Smith and Deighton, working on the Natal side of the border; the Zulus temporarily detained the surveyors. These incidents reinforced Frere's determination to act against the Zulus. Eventually, on 11 December 1878, Zulu chiefs were summoned to the site of a shady fig tree on the Natal bank of the Tugela River to learn the result of the Boundary Commission's deliberations. John Shepstone represented the British officials, while King Cetshwayo sent three of his

The first British invasion of Zululand. Colonel Glyn's Force crossing the Buffalo River Valley near Rorke's Drift. *Illustrated London News, 1879*

1. Cliff, 200 ft. high; 2. Waterfall; 3. Lieutenant-Colonel Russell's Mounted Infantry; 4. Major Dartnell's Natal Mounted Police and Volunteers; 5. The 2nd Company, 1st Battalion, of 24th Regiment; 6. N Battery, 5th Brigade, Royal Artillery (Lieutenant-Colonel Harness, R.A.).

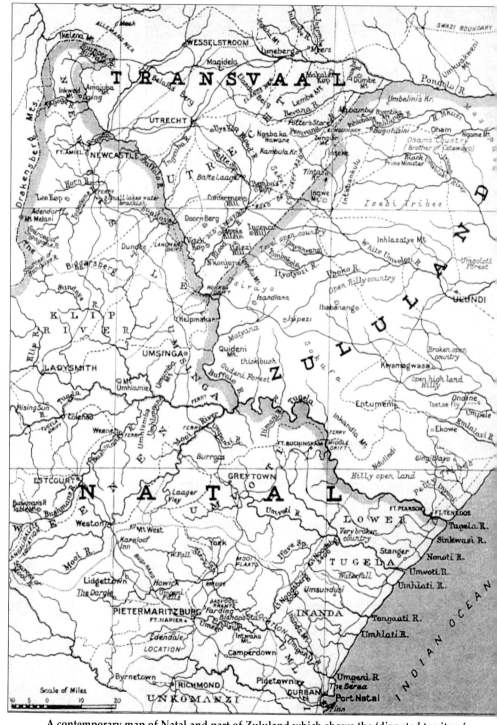

A contemporary map of Natal and part of Zululand which shows the 'disputed territory'
north of Rorke's Drift.

senior indunas, together with eleven chieftains, to listen to the findings.

At the first meeting the findings of the Boundary Commission were read out by Shepstone, while Mr Fynney, the Border Agent, translated them to the Zulu deputies. The findings were in the Zulus' favour and they were relieved at the terms. The meeting then adjourned and reassembled in the afternoon when the ultimatum was read by Shepstone and translated, sentence-by-sentence, again by Mr Fynney. The astonished Zulus then set off to report the crushing terms of the ultimatum to their king.

Knowing the Zulus would and could not comply with the ultimatum, the British invasion force was already advancing towards the borders of Zululand.

Colonel Wood, who would command the British Northern Column of the invasion, requested a meeting with the Transvaal Boers to gain their support in the forthcoming war. The Boers had initially informed Wood that they would support the British with several thousand armed riders, but when the Boers discovered that the Boundary Commission had already found against them they became resentful and withheld their support. In the end, only a handful of Boers took part, including Piet Uys whose father and brother had been killed by the Zulus in an earlier campaign against Dingane.

Logistics and Supplies
By 1879 there was still no established system of transport within the British Army. Lord Chelmsford's invasion force amounted to an estimated total of 16,500 fighting men, 985 wagons with some 10,000 oxen, 60 mule carts, 450

The Zulu War – some difficulties of the campaign. *The Graphic*

Troops on their way to the Front, experiencing transport difficulties. *The Graphic*

mules and 870 horses. The invasion itself was a simple task when compared with the task of supplying this force with food and water for men and animals. There were extensive stockpiles of tins of bully beef, 200lb bags of locally grown corn and wooden crates of hardtack army biscuits. Sufficient tentage had to be transported for all the officers' and troops' mess rooms, hospitals, mobile bakeries, engineering equipment, ammunition and medical supplies. The lengthy list of supplies included items such as axes, blankets, kettles, lanterns, shovels, tools, lifting jacks, stretchers, ropes and waterproof sheets. Chelmsford's staff calculated that the total weight of these stores would amount to nearly two thousand tons; much of it was destined to fall into Zulu hands at Isandlwana.

The task fell to Commissary General Strickland and his staff of less than twenty officers. Having assembled sufficient stores, creating an effective transport system was the next problem. The total number of wagons per infantry battalion amounted to seventeen, including one HQ wagon; a battery of artillery was allocated ten wagons and a squadron of mounted infantry had four. The overall responsibility for transport fell on the appointed Transport Officer, one per invading column, assisted by a sub-conductor for every ten wagons.

The average soldier was probably more concerned with the availability of his daily rations and bottled beer. His daily entitlement was a minimum of 1lb. of fresh meat, $1\frac{1}{2}$ lb of fresh bread or its equivalent in biscuits, plus fresh vegetables and fruit or lime juice and sugar in lieu. Medicinal rum was also available, but only if authorized by the accompanying medical officer.

Chelmsford knew that victory depended on the Zulus attacking prepared positions where they would face his awesome firepower. He accordingly gave priority to the implementation of regulations relating to the availability of ammunition. Each artillery battery of two guns carried 68 rounds for every gun, together with 12 rockets; additional reserves were to be readily available in accompanying carts and wagons. Rifle ammunition was calculated at 270 rounds per soldier, 70 in the possession of each man and 200 in clearly identifiable ammunition wagons. All column commanders had received written instructions that 'a commanding officer would incur a heavy responsibility should required supplies fail to arrive in time, through any want of foresight and arrangement on his part'.

By 11 January, when the invasion began, Chelmsford had achieved an almost impossible task. Sufficient supplies and transport to sustain his campaign had been assembled.

Soldiers with Martini-Henry rifles and bayonets. On Active Service, *Lloyd,*

British Fire Power

In 1879 the Martini-Henry rifle was the backbone of British firepower. After several modifications, the Martini-Henry Mark II, as used in the Zulu War, was 4 ft 1½" in length and weighed 9 lbs. It fired a black powder 0.45"calibre, 480 grain, centre fire Boxer cartridge in a flat trajectory, which gave it considerable stopping power.[4]

The rifle was sighted up to 1,000 yards, but only in a marksman's hands was it accurate beyond 300 yards. The average sighting for volley firing was 600 yards and a well-trained infantryman could, theoretically, fire off twelve rounds per minute, although five rounds was more likely. Each rifle was issued with an equi-angular bayonet with three hollow-ground faces. Fitted to the end of a Martini-Henry, it gave its handler an imposing reach and was most effective against black foes. Another bayonet was designed especially for the Martini-Henry and was known as the Sword Bayonet. This was also carried in the Zulu War by sergeants in Line Regiments and by the 60th Regiment, and eventually replaced the socket bayonet.

> When 'arf of your bullets fly wide in the ditch,
> Don't call your Martini a cross-eyed old bitch;
> She's human as you are – you treat her as sich
> An'she'll fight for the young British soldier.
>
> Rudyard Kipling, 'The Young British Soldier'

The Martini-Henry did, though, have serious drawbacks. On field-tests in the UK as late as 1878 it was noted that 'Barrels heat with quick firing which may prove a serious drawback to rapidity of fire. A barrel cannot be touched after five or six rounds on some occasions. A leather shield attached to the fore-end may be found a necessary addition'.

Although some modifications and improvements were made, the barrels still grew hot with rapid fire and the kick remained fearsome. This was less to do with the weapon itself but rather the black powder propellant. After about twenty rounds the barrel became fouled with residue, which reduced the bore slightly. This was enough to make the rifle kick fiercely. Bruised shoulders and cheeks, torn firing fingers and bloody noses were often the result and much of the poor marksmanship observed during the Zulu War may well have been caused by young recruits flinching when they fired.

Only frequent cleaning could reduce the problem and that was clearly impossible in the heat of battle. The Boxer cartridges also caused occasional problems; the thin rolled cartridge brass gave way and stuck to the chamber while the ejectors tore off the iron rim. The soldier then had to remove the

A Martini-Henry rifle and bayonet recovered from Isandlwana battlefield. *Adrian Greaves collection*

empty case with a knife or try and knock it out with the cleaning rod – which was three inches too short. The cartridge was also found wanting in other respects. If carried for any length of time in an ammunition pouch, rounds became deformed, causing the bullets to loosen and to shed black powder. They were also notoriously prone to dampness.

Shoulder-to-shoulder firing created its own perils; a volley would produce thick acrid smoke, which obscured the enemy, stung the eyes and parched the throat. A pause was required to allow the smoke to disperse before another volley could be fired.

...and we followed suit, firing volleys by sections in order to prevent the smoke obscuring the enemy, and we had repeatedly to cease fire to allow the smoke to clear off, as some young aspirants out of hand paid little attention to section firing.

He concluded,

One lesson we learnt in our fight was, that with the Martini-Henry, men must fire by word of command either by individuals, or at most, by sections: independent firing means, in firing in twenty seconds, firing at nothing; and only helped our daring opponents to get close up under cover of our smoke. Officers had to be everywhere, and to expose themselves to regulate the fire within bounds, and I feel sure that for the future only volleys by sections will be fired.

Lieutenant Wilkinson of the 3rd Battalion 60th Rifles

Nevertheless, the rifle was a real man-stopper. The soft lead slug flattened on impact causing massive tissue damage and shock to its victim.

Rifles and ammunition taken by the Zulus after their victory at Isandlwana were subsequently used against the British and, if the Zulus had mastered the use of the rifle's leaf sight, there would probably have been many more casualties. By the end of the War, in which the Martini-Henry had been subjected to heat, heavy rain, mud, dust and rough handling, it had emerged as a solid and reliable arm. The average cost to the government of each Martini-Henry rifle, including bayonet and cleaning kit, was £14 1s. 8d.

The Royal Artillery had six 7-pound rifled muzzle-loading guns, two of which were used at Isandlwana. These were originally designed for mountain warfare and were therefore considered to be ideal weapons for Zululand. They were towed by three pairs of horses and were highly manoeuvrable, although it was quickly discovered they were prone to overturning on rocky ground. These guns could fire their explosive shells to a maximum range of 3,000 yards, whereas the shrapnel rounds or case shot were used at close range. The Royal Artillery was also equipped with Hales rockets that could not be aimed accurately and their main purpose was to alarm Zulu Warriors by the shrieking sound of the rockets in flight.

BRITISH INVASION ROUTES INTO ZULULAND

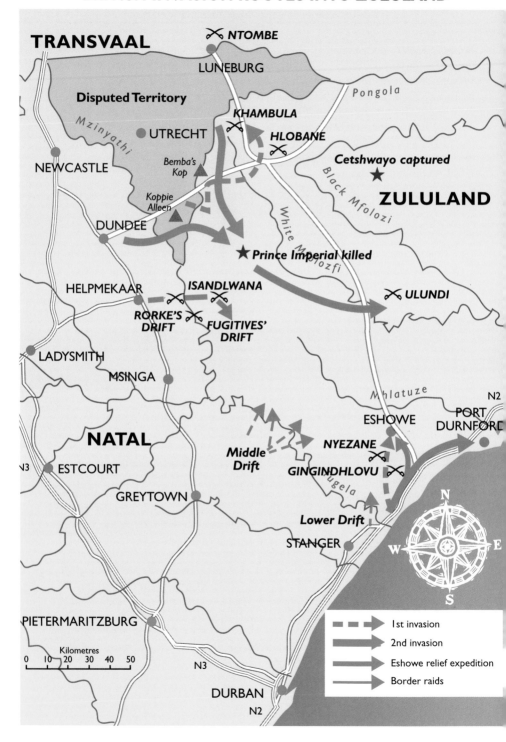

British Strategy in Zululand

Once Sir Bartle Frere had committed Lord Chelmsford to an offensive campaign against Zululand, three large independent columns were prepared and assembled ready for the invasion, which was scheduled to take place on 11 January 1879. They were: Colonel Pearson's Coastal Column consisting of 1,800 white troops and 2,000 black troops; Colonel Glyn's Central Column with 1,600 white troops and 2,500 black troops, which was the main attacking column, and the Northern Column commanded by Colonel Wood VC, with 1,700 white troops and 300 black troops. There were another two small columns, one with 1,400 white troops and 400 black troops under Colonel Rowlands VC whose role was to police the north near Luneburg and to keep an eye on the increasingly rebellious Transvaal Boers and prevent the Swazis in the north from getting involved; Brevet Colonel Durnford commanded the

Lord Chelmsford's invasion route from Helpmekaar.

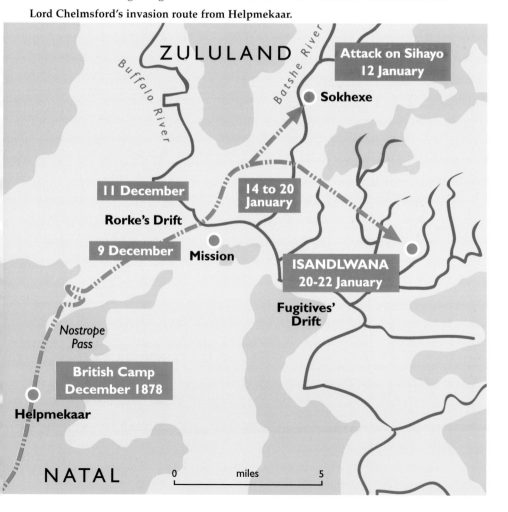

Colonel Anthony Durnford RE
Mackinnon & Shadbolt, 1880

Mrs Glyn
Ron Sheeley collection

Lieutenant Colonel Richard Glyn
Ron Sheeley collection

other column, which was to act as a rearguard to the Natal border to prevent a Zulu incursion and had a theoretical strength of 3,000 blacks. In reality, its effective strength amounted to 500, of which half were the elite and very loyal (to Durnford) Natal Native Horse[5] and a small Rocket Battery commanded by Major Russell RA. Lord Chelmsford's strategy of invading Zululand with three independent columns was devised to discourage the Zulus from outflanking any one column or, more seriously, retaliating against a defenceless Natal before he could inflict defeat on the Zulus'main force. The invasion was to be spearheaded by the 24th (2nd Warwickshire) Regiment; both battalions were enthusiastic at the prospect of leading the Central Column in operations against the Zulus.

Lord Chelmsford's Plan

Lord Chelmsford firmly believed that the Zulus would not stand and fight. In order to ensure that the Zulu Army would be brought to battle, Chelmsford devised a three-pronged invasion that would advance on the Zulu capital, Ulundi. Each 'prong'or column was thought to be strong enough to engage and defeat the Zulu Army. The actual tactic was remarkably similar to the Zulu tactic of the 'horns of the bull'and the irony of its use by the British would not have escaped King Cetshwayo and his advisers.

Chelmsford's chosen invasion date in early January 1879 was deliberate, as it would coincide with the Zulu harvest. In addition, the spring rains were late, thus delaying the Zulu harvest and, on advice from his staff, he presumed the Zulus would be unprepared for a lengthy campaign during this intensive harvest period. From January until early April the rivers forming the Natal boundary with Zululand were expected to be in full flood and would thus

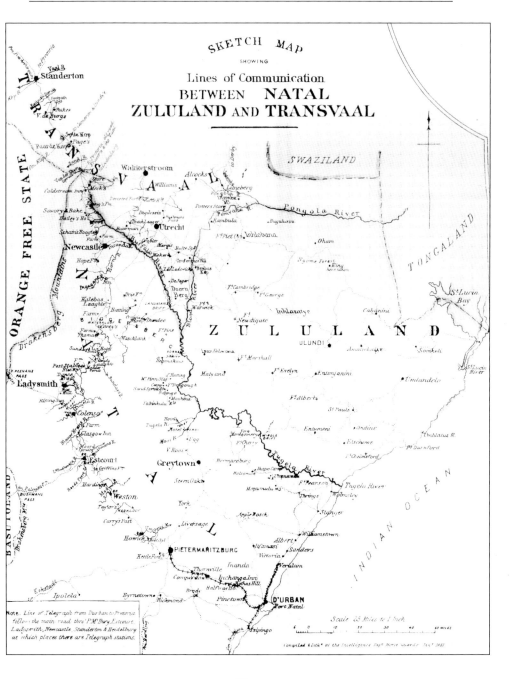

provide Natal with a natural defence against Zulu attacks. Chelmsford also relied on natural grazing for the invasion force's numerous oxen and horses, the lack of which would hamper an invasion during the later dry season.

Owing to the rocky terrain of Zululand and the ponderous progress of ox-drawn supply wagons, the British invasion force would be very slow moving. Nevertheless, a measured advance towards Ulundi permitted both reconnaissance of uncharted Zululand and allowed the destruction of Zulu crops and villages as his invasion force advanced.[6]

Zulu Strategy
Faced with the British invasion of Zululand, King Cetshwayo's strategy was to inflict a decisive defeat on the British. King Cetshwayo's army was well trained but, apart from older warriors who had fought at Ndondakusuka 22 years earlier, totally inexperienced in actual warfare. Knowing the British possessed overwhelming firepower, King Cetshwayo instructed his generals not to engage the British in entrenched positions but to interrupt their supply lines or attack them in the open. He reasoned that, starved or trapped, the invaders would be forced to withdraw from Zululand.

The Zulu king knew that if the British invasion force could be trapped he could force the British to sue for peace. Unfortunately his generals often thought they knew better and, after the Zulu success at Isandlwana, most Zulu attacks were against defended positions and were repulsed. Military operations were usually controlled from a remote vantage point, although one of their generals would be ready for dispatch into the battle to rally the warriors if an assault faltered, as occurred at Isandlwana.

Zulu tactics were based on the encircling 'horns of the bull' whereby the encircling flanks of the younger, fitter warriors would surround the enemy, while the main body, made up of experienced warriors, would bear the brunt of the attack. The main features of the attack were speed and precision. The force would advance at a steady jogging pace and complete the final attack at a run. Once among the enemy, the short stabbing spear, popularly known by the British soldiers as the assegai, was most effective. The Zulus possessed antiquated firearms, probably as many as twenty thousand rifles having been sold to the Zulus by unscrupulous traders.

Set-piece tactics were effectively used by the Zulus who were skilled at creating feints with one horn to confuse the enemy. Such a tactic was shortly to succeed spectacularly against the British at Isandlwana.

On 17 January the Zulu Army formed up to undergo ritual purification before the coming conflict. That same day they began leaving their base on the Mahlabatini Plain; moving slowly to conserve energy, they moved the sixty miles (100 km) towards a deep valley just five miles (8 km) from the

Zulu Chief.

dominating rock outcrop known as Isandlwana. It is widely believed that King Cetshwayo had ordered his army not to cross into Natal; certainly he was acting on the defensive and made several futile attempts to negotiate with the British before they invaded.[7]

Until that time no British settler or traveller had ever been harmed by the Zulus.

British Tactics

Lord Chelmsford fully expected an early victory over the Zulu Army. His officers and most of their troops were experienced in African warfare and his main fears were that the Zulus would not fight or that his campaign would deteriorate into a series of 'hit and run' skirmishes as had been his experienced in the Eastern Cape Colony against the amaXhosa. Chelmsford had been warned by a number of Boer leaders experienced in Zulu affairs that he faced a powerful adversary.

The standard battle tactic employed by the British in South Africa was a combination of reconnaissance and ruthless skirmishing. In rough country, both the infantry and mounted troops would engage the enemy, the infantry by volley fire and the mounted troops attacking them in flight. In the unlikely event that the Zulus would appear in any number, the British were trained to form a square or entrench their position, thus drawing the Zulus into the range of their overwhelming firepower. Well-aimed rifle volley fire by calm and experienced troops supported by rockets, artillery and, later in the campaign, Gatling guns, would, in Chelmsford's opinion, ensure the swift defeat of the enemy.[8]

The Second Invasion and Destruction of Zululand

After the first invasion had been repulsed, the British re-invaded Zululand on 6 April 1879. They were better equipped, in greater strength and tactically aware of the fighting skills of the Zulus. The second invasion met with limited Zulu resistance and was brought to a close with the final battle at Ulundi. The Zulu Army was, thereafter, in disarray and their nation never recovered from the war. The war had cost the British Treasury more than five million pounds of British taxpayers' money, and the army lost seventy-six officers and 1,007 Imperial soldiers. About 10,000 Zulus had been killed and many more were maimed on the various fields of battle. The Zulu Empire had lasted for sixty-three years.

References

1 Fynn, who was prone to exaggeration, recorded this figure.

2 Dodds, Glen, *The Zulus and Matabele*, Arms and Armour 1998.

3 Blue Books C. 1883,19. or *Zulu Battle Piece Isandlwana*, Sir Reginald Coupland, 1948, Collins.

4 Greaves. Adrian, *Isandlwana*, Cassell, 2001.

5 The term 'Natal Native Horse', as used here to describe the Edendale Contingent, is technically incorrect although it has been used historically in official documents and by most historians. The NNH was formally established in 1906. See *The Volunteer Regiments of Natal and East Griqualand* by Hurst, 1945.

6 Chelmsford's Memo to Major General Crealock 12 April 1879.

7 An account by a Zulu deserter recorded by the Hon. William Drummond, a Zulu-speaking staff officer on the HQ Staff, states that Cetshwayo ordered his army to drive the British back to the Drakensberg Mountains. This could possibly explain the actions of the Zulu reserve that crossed the border to attack Rorke's Drift. See *The Red Soldier*, Ball Paperbacks, Johannesburg, 1977.

8 Greaves. Adrian, *Isandlwana*, Cassell, 2001.

Part Two

The Actions of the Columns

THE CENTRAL COLUMN

The Central Column (No 3 Column) originated in Pietermaritzberg. The column was made up of 4,709 officers and men, 303 wagons and carts and 1,507 oxen. This column, which was accompanied by Lord Chelmsford and his staff, moved from Pietermaritzberg to Greytown, across the Tugela River at the Tugela Ferry and then on to the Biggarsberg Plateau at Helpmekaar. Here Lord Chelmsford fortified a position that was to be his springboard for this column's invasion of Zululand. He had left small garrisons at fortified positions along the way.

Helpmekaar

Overview

Helpmekaar, meaning 'help-one-another' in Afrikaans (usually spelt Helpmakaar by the British), today consists of a local police station and a small cluster of mostly deserted buildings. At the time of the Zulu War it was the main supply depot for Lord Chelmsford's Central Column. It is situated on the top of the long Biggarsberg plateau that runs from Pomeroy, north of Greytown, to Dundee and, being only ten miles (16 km) from the Zulu border, it was the ideal location for such a depot. Most of the survivors from the Battle of Isandlwana escaped to Helpmekaar. Following the defeat at Isandlwana and the defence of Rorke's Drift, Helpmekaar received numerous wounded soldiers. Due to the heavy rains, unhygienic conditions and lack of medical supplies lost at Isandlwana, many of the troops suffered appalling illness and disease. Those who died of their injuries or disease subsequent to these actions on 22 January 1879 are buried in the dilapidated cemetery behind the police station.

HELPMEKAAR TO ISANDLWANA

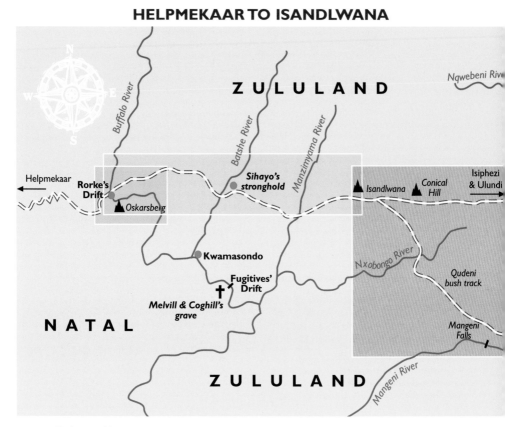

Points of interest

➤ *Site of British camp.* This whole area was given over to storage and would have contained several hundred tents and a considerable numbers of horses and oxen. Being flat and level, it was an ideal site for the British to accumulate their vast quantity of supplies for the Central Column prior to the invasion of Zululand. Following the British defeat at Isandlwana, the 5th Company Royal Engineers under Captain Parke-Jones built an entrenched laager. The fort was manned throughout the Zulu War by a variety of units, including the 24th and 2/4th Regiments.

➤ *British cemetery.* This cemetery contains the graves of those who died of illness or disease following the events of 22 January. Due to its inaccessibility, the cemetery is usually overgrown and in a state of disrepair. It can be found behind the modern police station, access is by the farm gates either side of the buildings.

➤ *Site of Helpmekaar fort.* The outline of the fort can still be seen on the ground.
➤ *Nostrope Pass* (along the road to Rorke's Drift but signposted 'Noustroop'). From here one has a spectacular view of the Buffalo River – it was the border between British Natal and Zululand – and into Zululand with the distant peak of Isandlwana. From this point the British would have had their first view of Zululand and Isandlwana. When taking the Nostrope Pass to Rorke's Drift, be aware that this road descends a very steep hill with a number of hairpin bends. In wet weather this road should only be attempted in 4WD vehicles.

Location: Helpmekaar is situated on the **R33** between Greytown and Dundee. It is also the landmark for the connecting road to Rorke's Drift via the Nostrope Pass. (Marked as 'NOUSTROOP' on the road sign).

How to find it: *From Durban and Greytown* – Take the **R33** north from Greytown through Keate's Drift, Tugela Ferry and Pomeroy towards Greytown. Helpmekaar is a further 10 miles (16 km) from Pomeroy.
From Dundee – Take the **R33** towards Greytown for 22 miles (38 km). When the road sign 'Helpmekaar' is reached, follow the directions onto a dirt road that immediately leads into the small settlement; park near the police station. The cemetery is situated behind the police station. The old fort is situated on the hill next to the police station.

Distinguishing features: Only the sign on the **R33** to the police station at Helpmekaar and the low hill beside it give any indication of its location. The area of the British camp is south (to the right) of the Helpmekaar to Rorke's Drift road before it drops down the escarpment. The land is now farmed and there is no trace of the camp.

A modern view of the British Cemetery at Helpmekaar. *Adrian Greaves collection*

Contemporary Helpmekaar. *Illustrated London News.*

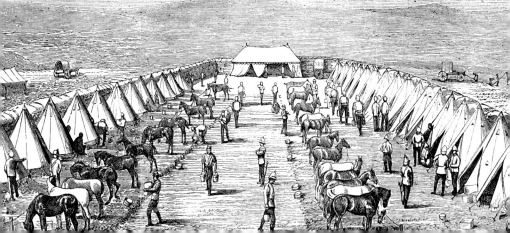

Helpmekaar in 1879 after the Battle of Rorke's Drift. *Killie Campbell Library, Durban*

Participants

Imperial: The whole Central Column passed through Helpmekaar. On 22 January, the position was manned by three companies of the 2/24th Regiment who were due to proceed to Rorke's Drift later that day. As they approached their beleaguered colleagues at Rorke's Drift, they saw the Mission Station on fire and, three miles (5 km) from the fighting, about-turned and marched back to Helpmekaar, which they then prepared to defend in anticipation of a Zulu attack. *Zulus:* There was no Zulu attack on Helpmekaar.

Recommendations

• The neglected British cemetery is worth a visit before driving on to Rorke's Drift.
• The drive down the Nostrope Pass towards Rorke's Drift is spectacular – be very careful in the wet.

The Central Column invades Zululand

Having descended from the plateau, the Central Column, under the command of Colonel Richard Glyn, waited on the Natal bank of the Buffalo River at Rorke's Drift for the British ultimatum to expire. The column consisted of

Helpmekaar after the battles of Rorke's Drift and Isandlwana. *Killie Campbell Library, Durban*

some 4,709 men, 303 wagons and carts and 1,507 oxen.[1] The backbone of this force consisted of both the 1st and 2nd battalions of the 24th (2nd Warwickshire) Regiment. The Royal Artillery had six 7-pounder rifled muzzle-loading guns, two of which were used at Isandlwana.

The British attack on Sihayo's Stronghold

The crossing of the river into Zulu territory began on 11 January 1879. As a first move the following day, Chelmsford attacked the homestead of the Chieftain Sihayo kaXongo Ngobese, whose people were ensconced in 'Sihayo's stronghold', a huge, horseshoe-shaped gorge of sandstone flanking the east bank of the Batshe River. This is clearly visible from a viewpoint half way along the Rorke's Drift to Isandlwana road as it descends into the Batshe Valley.

The stronghold nestled up against a great blood-red cliff face, beneath which lies a jumble of house-sized boulders. Here on 12 January 1879 Chelmsford's force, consisting mainly of NNC men, supported by the 24th Regiment, easily defeated Sihayo's people. This action met with only a token resistance by its few Zulu occupants as most of the warriors were already at Ulundi preparing for battle; it left thirty warriors dead, for the British loss of two men of the NNC killed and seventeen men wounded. It was here that Lieutenant Harford famously put the rare beetle into a matchbox at the height of the battle. It is thought that this minor victory was sufficient to strengthen Chelmsford's haughty approach to the Zulu War. Sihayo's village, Sokhexe, was burned and an over-confident Lord Chelmsford proceeded deeper into Zululand, crossed the Manzimyama River and set up his next major

SIHAYO'S STRONGHOLD

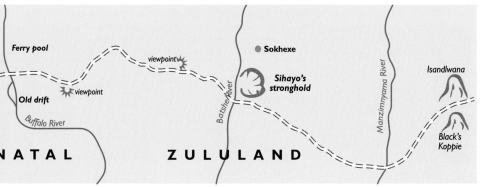

temporary camp at Isandlwana on 20 January.

> *I am in great hopes that the news of the storming of Sirayo's [Sihayo's] stronghold and the capture of so many of his cattle, about 500, may have a salutary effect in Zululand and either bring down a large force to attack us or else produce a revolution in the country.* Lord Chelmsford, 12 January 1879

Note that the road from Rorke's Drift to Isandlwana only approximates to the route that Chelmsford took. The old track is still visible from the air, and when the new road was constructed great care was taken not to damage the old wagon track, which ran from the Manzimyama River onto the saddle of Isandlwana. The new road runs from the Manzimyama River to the north of Isandlwana Mountain.

The hidden Ngwebeni Valley from where the Zulu Army surprised the British at Isandlwana. *Adrian Greaves collection*

A contemporary drawing of Isandlwana before the attack. *Adrian Greaves collection*

Isandlwana was thought to be a good position because of its elevation above the plain, its provision with water and wood and defendable features. Chelmsford set up a huge, sprawling, tented camp on the eastern slope of the hill. He failed to entrench this camp and failed to draw his wagons into a defensive arrangement.

It appears that Chelmsford and his staff believed that the Zulu threat, if there was one, would come from the direction of Ulundi, fifty-five miles to the east of Isandlwana. Accordingly, his scouting thrust was directed into that region, led by Major John Dartnell, commanding the Natal Mounted Police. When Dartnell reported to Chelmsford on 21 January that he had come upon a Zulu force that was too big for him to fight without reinforcements, Chelmsford assumed Dartnell was in touch with the main Zulu Army. He immediately resolved to split the column at Isandlwana and march out with Colonel Glyn and over half the column to reinforce Dartnell before dawn on 22 January.

Lieutenant Smith-Dorrien (95th Regt) was immediately sent to Rorke's Drift to summon Lieutenant Colonel Durnford and his column that had just arrived there from the Middle Drift on the Tugela River. Durnford was ordered forward to support Chelmsford's advance to engage Chief Matshana KaMondise's people who were active in the region – there is no primary evidence that he was ordered to support Lieutenant Colonel Henry Pulleine, now in command of the camp at Isandlwana. This controversy is typical of the saga of Isandlwana.

Leaving Pulleine with vague instructions to remain on the defensive, Chelmsford departed Isandlwana before first light to meet up with Dartnell. At about 8 a.m. British scouts on the heights north of Isandlwana detected a movement of Zulu forces from the north-east. This was reported to Pulleine, who ordered his men to leave their breakfasts and form up in a skirmishing line to face the threat; he also sent a note to inform Chelmsford. At this critical time, Durnford and his men reached Isandlwana on their way to engage Matshana. Isandlwana was about to take its place in history.

Pulleine's last message. *Courtesy of Major Martin Everett, 24th Regimental Museum, Brecon.*

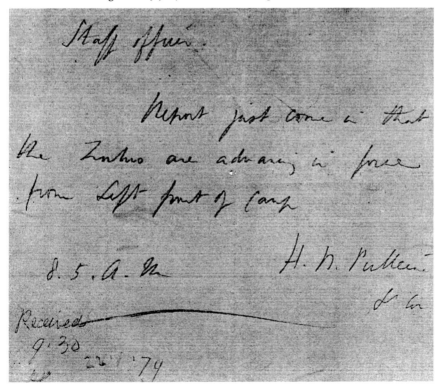

Mangeni Falls, 20-22 January 1879

Overview

The area of the Mangeni Falls and gorge forms the furthest part of the battlefield of Isandlwana. In 1879 the area, some 12 miles (20 km) to the south-east of Isandlwana, was controlled by Chief Matshana KaMondise (Matyana) and included the Hlazakazi and Magogo hills and the Qudeni Bush. On the 21 January 1879 Chelmsford received reports suggesting that the Zulu Army was approaching his position from the direction of Ulundi. He dispatched a large reconnaissance force towards Mangeni under Major Dartnell to ascertain the situation. Dartnell endeavoured to engage Matyana's skirmishers, who refused to be drawn. After darkness fell, the Zulus lit hundreds of campfires across the hills, which induced Dartnell to believe that the main Zulu Army was in that region.

Dartnell immediately requested reinforcements; Chelmsford reacted by sending half his force – not realizing that the main Zulu Army was already camped only 6 miles (10 km) to his north-east. It was at Mangeni that Chelmsford received reports that Isandlwana was under attack, but owing to the fact that the British at Isandlwana did not strike their tents, the distant view through the heat haze suggested that the camp was intact. Chelmsford presumed that, had an attack occurred, the British were in sufficient numbers to win the day easily.

It was only at about 3pm that Chelmsford decided to return to Isandlwana to ascertain events for himself. He took with him a small escort; en route he met Commandant Hamilton-Browne who, having watched the defeat of the camp from a safe distance, tried to persuade Chelmsford that the camp was lost. While the two officers discussed the situation, Commandant Lonsdale arrived from Isandlwana and confirmed the British defeat.

Chelmsford ordered his scattered force around Mangeni to assemble for the 12-mile march back to Isandlwana; they arrived one mile from the camp in darkness.

Zulu boys at Mangeni Falls where Chelmsford lunched on 22 January. Milne's Hill is in the background. *David Rattray collection*

Plan of British patrols on 21 and 22 January between Isandlwana and Mangeni

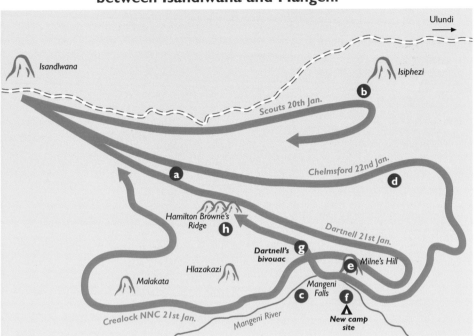

Points of interest

a The route between Isandlwana and Mangeni is approximately the route taken by Chelmsford's force on both 21 and 22 January.

b Site of Chelmsford's proposed camp for the night of 22 January.

c Site of Chelmsford's lunchtime position.

d First hill used by Lieutenant Milne to view Isandlwana.

e Second hill used by Lieutenant Milne to view Isandlwana.

f The revised new camp site.

g Dartnell's bivouac site on the night of 21 January.

h Hamilton-Browne's ridge where he observed the Zulu attack on Isandlwana.

Chelmsford ordered the artillery to fire several shells into the camp to dislodge any Zulu occupants. Major Black and two companies of men then seized the Stony Hill (Black's Koppie) south of the saddle, which was strewn with smashed wagons. The Zulus had long since departed, having looted the camp.

The Mangeni Falls are situated in a most spectacular piece of country and will provide the visitor with a good idea of the difficulties of distance and communication that Chelmsford faced. Points to note on this excursion are the prominent conical hill that Lieutenant Milne RN climbed with a telescope and from where he relayed reassuring messages to Chelmsford.

Of considerable significance is the drive back from Mangeni to Isandlwana; one gets a perfect view of the escarpment that concealed the Zulu Army to the north-east of Isandlwana, of Conical Hill, and a magnificent Zulu perspective of Isandlwana from the east.

Participants
Lord Chelmsford in command.
Imperial: 22 January. Four of the six Royal Artillery guns of N Battery, six companies of the 2/24th, Mounted Infantry and Pioneers.
Colonial: 21 January. Natal Mounted Police, Natal Mounted Volunteers and sixteen companies of the NNC under Major Dartnell
Zulus: Zulu skirmishers of Chief Matshana KaMondise.

Location: 12 miles (20 km) to the south-east of Isandlwana battlefield.

How to find it: From the Isandlwana battlefield proceed east for approximately two miles (3 km) just beyond the very prominent Conical Hill, turn right – take the next turn to the left (after approximately 1 mile (1,6 Km) and stay on that road for about ten miles (16 km), which follows the great flat-topped Hlazakazi Mountain on your right. Having passed the next conical hill (Milne's Hill) on your left, proceed half a mile into the valley beyond, cross the stream and immediately turn right across the causeway. The water is usually shallow and can easily be crossed on foot or by private car. Continue for about 300 yards along the track until the waterfall can be seen on the right. Taking care, park and walk to the lip of the gorge. Note, this route is not signposted.

Route: See the directions to the battlefield at Isandlwana.

Distinguishing features: After driving from the battlefield at Isandlwana for 12 miles (20 km), a prominent conical hill to the left of the road becomes very obvious. The road then crosses the stream that leads to the waterfall.

Recommendations
• The falls are relatively isolated and it is wise to hire an experienced guide.
• There are no facilities at the falls. A 4WD vehicle is most suitable to get close to the falls, and remember, great care must be taken near the edges of the gorge and waterfall due to the sheer drop to the valley below.

Isandlwana, 22 January 1879

Lord Chelmsford's plan
Having received intelligence that the Zulu Army was within a day's march of the Central Column, and buoyed up by the successful skirmish at Sihayo's homestead, Lord Chelmsford was anxious to engage the Zulus lest they should slip past this force

and cross into Natal. Apart from Durnford's No. 2 Column at Rorke's Drift, Natal and its civilian population were otherwise relatively defenceless. Chelmsford readily accepted these intelligence reports at face value and, thinking that the opportunity of battle was imminent, he split his force in order to engage the Zulus as quickly as possible.

Battle account

By 21 January the Central Column of the British invasion force was camped at Isandlwana. Having consolidated his position and having amassed the supplies needed for his advance into Zululand, Lord Chelmsford intended to move towards iSiphezi Mountain and Ulundi. During the previous days Chelmsford had received intelligence reports that the Zulu Army was approaching his position from Ulundi. He dispatched a large reconnaissance party under Major Dartnell towards the Mangeni Falls to investigate the Zulus. During the day Dartnell reported seeing numerous Zulu scouting parties and after dark he saw countless Zulu cooking fires across the hills to his front. He accordingly requested further reinforcements from Chelmsford, who mistakenly believed that Dartnell had found the Zulu Army. Lord Chelmsford left the Isandlwana camp before dawn on 22 January with over half the force at Isandlwana. His intention was to meet up with and support Dartnell in the south-east.

Chelmsford left the camp in the command of Brevet Lieutenant Colonel Pulleine with five companies of the 1st Battalion 24th (2nd Warwickshire) Regiment, one company of the 2nd Battalion 24th (2nd Warwickshire) Regiment, two guns of the Royal Artillery and some 600 members of the NNC, a total force of over 1,700 men. Pulleine's orders were to defend the camp while at the same time he was to expect an order to move to the next campsite at Mangeni. The camp was undefended in spite of written orders to the contrary; various officers had expressed their concern at the camp's vulnerability, including Major Dunbar and Lieutenant Melvill of the 24th Regiment.

Do the staff think we are going to meet an army of schoolgirls? Why in the name of all that is holy do we not laager?

Captain Duncombe to Commandant Hamilton-Browne
A Lost Legionary in South Africa.

At 8.05 a.m. Pulleine received information from his pickets on the rim of the plateau that there was Zulu activity to the north-east, and ordered the combatant troops out in a defensive line some 800 yards beyond the outer edge of the tented camp. The line ran along the crest of a low ridge, forming a quarter circle subtending the north-east of the Isandlwana position. The men were deployed in skirmishing order, to stand between three and five yards apart in front of the camp. Two 7-pounder guns (N Battery, 5th Brigade) of the Royal Artillery were placed on the centre of the line.

British positions and direction of Zulu attack at Isandlwana

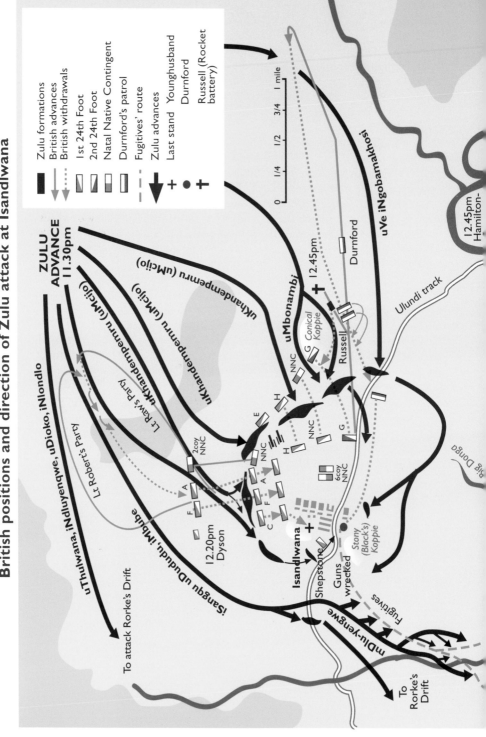

The battlefield from iNyoni where Zulu Chiefs controlled the battle.
Adrian Greaves collection

Durnford's Donga.
Adrian Greaves collection

Isandlwana from the direction of the Zulu attack. *Adrian Greaves collection*

At about 10am parties of Zulus were seen looking down on the Isandlwana camp from the Nqutu plateau to the north. This concerned Pulleine who believed the Zulu Army was still approaching from Ulundi in the east. Before leaving Isandlwana to support Dartnell near Mangeni, Chelmsford had ordered Colonel Durnford and his mounted black troops to move towards Mangeni from Rorke's Drift where he had been held in reserve. By 10.30 a.m. Durnford and his mounted men reached Isandlwana, just as the Zulus appeared to move away from the plateau. The Zulus were in sufficient numbers to cause the experienced Durnford great concern; he dispatched two of his mounted troops to go up the plateau to assess the situation. Durnford then moved off towards the east, apparently to protect Chelmsford's flank in the south-east, past the prominent conical hill and onto the plain beyond, followed by his rocket battery under Major Russell RA. Captain Essex was in his tent writing letters when he heard of the Zulus' approach. He took his binoculars and revolver but

...did not trouble to put on my sword, as I thought nothing of the matter and expected to be back in half an hour to complete my letters.

Captain Essex, Evidence to the Isandlwana Inquiry.

About five and a half miles north-east of the camp one of the patrols on the plateau stumbled upon the unimaginable: the main Zulu Army, in strength between 23,000 and 25,000 men, was lying in a great hidden valley, the Ngwebeni. While the British focus was the region to the south-east, the Zulus were already in the north-east and the Zulu attack, stimulated by a volley fired by the patrol, immediately started from the north.

The Zulu force, superbly disciplined and under the command of the chieftains Ntshingwayo ka Mahole Khoza and Mavumengwana ka Ndlela Ntuli, swiftly emerged from the hidden valley, deploying into the tactic of the 'horns of the bull'. The first inkling the British force at Isandlwana had of their coming crisis was when they saw a large force of Zulus descend from the plateau and destroy the Rocket Battery under the command of Major Russell at 'The Notch'. More Zulus then descended off the plateau, engaging Colonel Durnford on the plain below, and they began to push Durnford's men obliquely back towards Isandlwana. Durnford made a stand in a dry watercourse east of the camp, known thereafter as 'Durnford's Donga'.

The two guns of the Royal Artillery were then limbered up and from the front line accurately fired several shells into the Zulus who were pinned down by Durnford on the far side of the donga. This was the left horn of the Zulu Army. The main Zulu force then became visible on the heights to the north and north-east of the camp.

A large wing of the Zulu Army (the right horn) moved down the valley which extends north-west from a point north of Isandlwana, and the British forces up on the ridge fired into them, eliciting little or no response. These warriors then turned south, threatening the road back to Rorke's Drift.

Overlooking Isandlwana, the Zulu commanders stood on the great bluff of rocks known as iNyoni; from this vantage point they directed the movement of Zulu forces. When the 'horns of the bull' were in position, the centre or chest of the main Zulu Army descended into the killing field. Within half an hour the whole Zulu force had deployed towards the British front line. Due to the distance of the British firing line from the camp, it is unlikely that the camp commander, Colonel Pulleine, could even see his men's position or predicament.

There was something of an impasse when the Zulu force came up against the concentrated Martini-Henry rifle fire of disciplined British troops. The Zulus sustained heavy casualties in the depression below the British firing line, but they bravely held their position.

Zulu warriors began to edge their way around the south of Durnford's position in the 'donga', thus threatening 'G' Company 2/24th which, having detached from the southern extremity of the British firing line to assist Durnford, got caught in the open and was swiftly destroyed. Durnford retired to a position to the right (south) of the Isandlwana camp and made a determined last stand near the north-eastern base of the 'Stony Koppie' (Black's Koppie).

A bugler sounded 'The Retire', whereupon a tactical withdrawal of the line began towards the camp. It failed, and the retreat became a rout when the soldiers were forced to fight through the chaos in the camp, the tents of which had not been struck. Some British soldiers fought their way in small pockets down what is today known as the 'Fugitives' Trail', and the last stand of the 24th was probably fought on the banks of the Manzimyama River at least a mile south-west of Isandlwana.

Before we knew where we were they came right into the camp, assegaing everybody right and left. Everybody who then had a horse turned to fly. The enemy were going at a kind of fast half-walk and half-run. On looking round we saw that we were completely surrounded and the road to Rorke's Drift was cut off.

Lieutenant Smith-Dorrien, 25 January. Letter to his father.

At least one company of men, believed to be C Company of the 1/24th under the command of Captain Reginald Younghusband, made their last stand high up on the shoulder of the Isandlwana hill. The last man to die on the British side is thought to have taken up a position in the cave at the base of the crag above Younghusband's position where he is believed to have held off the Zulus for some considerable time. Within half an hour the Zulus breached the

Isandlwana

Saving the Guns –22 January 1879

Artist, Jason Askew, Anglo-Zulu War Historical Society

British defences, forced Colonel Durnford's survivors back towards the camp and completed their encirclement. Within a further half an hour, the camp and its survivors were completely surrounded then destroyed. Only about sixty or so whites survived, including five Imperial officers. A survivor, Lieutenant Henry Curling RA, commented on the bravery of the British soldiers,

They behaved splendidly in this fight. They were all killed in the ranks as they stood. Not a single man escaped from the companies that were placed to defend the camp. Indeed, they were completely cut off from any retreat and could not do so, as we did, gallop through the Zulus. When I last saw them, they were retreating steadily but I believe a rush was made and they were all killed in a few minutes.
Lieutenant Curling RA. Letter to his mother.

In the closing moments of the battle Lieutenant Melvill, Adjutant of the 1/24th, made an epic ride to save the Queen's Colour of his battalion. He rode for over five miles through attacking Zulus across boulder-strewn, bush-clad, broken country down to the Buffalo River. He and Lieutenant Coghill were both killed high up on the lip of the gorge on the Natal side of the river, having saved each other's lives but having lost the Queen's Colour to the waters of the flooded river in a gallant attempt to get the Colour to the Natal bank.

Both Coghill and Melvill were honoured with posthumous Victoria Crosses 28 years later in 1907.

I can't understand it, I left a thousand men here.
Lord Chelmsford, on returning to Isandlwana that same night.

Participants
Imperial: Commanded by Brevet Lieutenant Colonel H. Pulleine 1/24th (Warwickshire) Regiment.
N Battery 5th Brigade Royal Artillery, 5th Field Company Royal Engineers, 5 companies of the 1st Battalion 2/24th (Warwickshire) Regiment, G company of the 2nd Battalion 2/24th (Warwickshire) Regiment plus detachments from other companies of the 2nd Battalion 2/24th (Warwickshire) Regiment, the 90th Foot, the Army Service Corps, Army Hospital and Army Pay Corps. Detachments of the Mounted Infantry, Natal Volunteer Corps from the Natal Carbineers, Newcastle Mounted Rifles and the Buffalo Border Guard.
Colonial: 3rd Regiment NNC, Natal (black) Pioneer Corps.
Total force: 67 Officers. 1,707 men.
Casualties: 52 officers and 806 white troops plus an estimated 500 supporting black troops.
Zulu: The total Zulu fighting force is estimated at 25,000. They were

commanded by Chieftains Ntshingwayo ka Mahole Khoza and Mavumengwana ka Ndlela Ntuli and included 13 full amabutho (regiments). Casualties. The Zulu losses have been assessed between 1,500 and 3,000.

Location: The nearest towns are Dundee 30 miles (50 km) and Nqutu 14 miles (24 km). It is 10 miles (16 km) from Rorke's Drift.

How to find it:

Route 1. **From Helpmekaar on Route 33. Good, dry weather conditions only.**
Take the dirt road signposted to Rorke's Drift. After descending the steep pass, continue for two miles (3.6 km) to the junction; turn right towards Rorke's Drift. Half a mile (1km) from the Mission Station, turn left towards Isandlwana, cross the Buffalo River at the actual Drift from where the British invaded Zululand and continue for five miles (8 km) to the T-junction. Turn right towards the battlefield. Isandlwana will now come into view from this road. Continue into the village of Isandlwana and proceed to the Orientation Centre for your tickets before entering the Battlefield.

Route 2. **From Dundee - All weather.**
From Dundee, take the **R33** towards Greytown for 9 miles (14 km). Turn left onto the gravel road marked 'Rorke's Drift'. Proceed for 26 km. Turn left at the Isandlwana sign, cross the Buffalo River at the site of the old Drift into Zululand. This road is clearly marked with signboards. Turn right at the T-junction and continue into the village of Isandlwana. Proceed to the Orientation Centre for your tickets before entering the Battlefield.

Route 3. **Route 68 From Babanango to Nqutu. All weather.**
When eight miles (12 km) from Nqutu, take the signposted dirt road to Isandlwana. This road follows the route of the attacking Zulu Army and descends onto the battlefield from the Nqutu Plateau. As the road drops down on to the plain, the Conical Hill will be immediately to the front with Isandlwana to the right. Follow the road into Isandlwana village and proceed to the Orientation Centre for your tickets before entering the Battlefield.

Distinguishing features: An isolated battlefield dominated by the Isandlwana outcrop covering a wide area. A vehicle is necessary to reach all points of interest and it is essential to take enough food and drink, as there are no shops. The Isandlwana Orientation Centre sells maps, books and souvenirs only.

Isandlwana

The Death of Private W. Griffiths VC
22 January 1879

Artist, Jason Askew, Anglo-Zulu War Historical Society

BRITISH CAMP AT ISANDLWANA

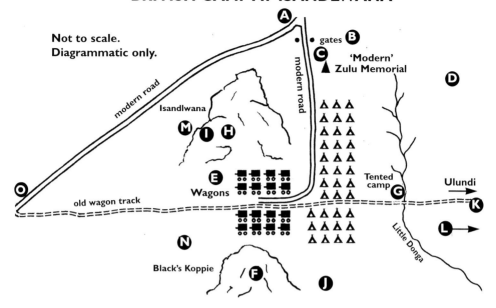

Points of interest in suggested order

A Orientation Centre. Report here to pay your battlefield entrance fee.

B Entrance gate to battlefield.

C The Zulu Memorial – erected in 1999 replicating a Zulu Warrior's Isiqu necklace.

D The Royal Artillery Memorial – erected in 1999. It is close to the actual site of the two guns on the 'knuckle' of the British firing line. (Note; leave your vehicle at the Zulu memorial site.)

E The Wagon Park (modern day car park). Site of the column's supply wagons and oxen that were due to return to Rorke's Drift for further supplies. It is also the site where the British survivors of the battle tried, unsuccessfully, to form into defensive groups to break through the Zulu encirclement.

F Black's Koppie – named after Major Black who, in the dark, led a bayonet charge to the top when Chelmsford returned to Isandlwana.

G Memorials erected by military units, schools and friends of the dead.

H Younghusband's Cairn – where C Company made their stand before trying to rejoin the other 24th Regiment's survivors in the area of the Wagon Park.

I Cave of last defender – probably a member of C Company. Follow the path from Younghusband's Cairn.

J Carbineers Memorial and approximate site of Colonel Durnford's death. Durnford was later re-buried at Pietermaritzburg.

K Durnford's Donga – where Durnford held the Zulu left horn until it outflanked his position. This point can easily be reached on foot from the car park; just follow the obvious track to the site; or by vehicle, drive back out of the battlefield and then follow the right fork behind Conical Hill, take the next fork to the right which takes you up to the donga. At the donga, Durnford's men held the south side of the modern road for a distance of about 100 yards. They were forced to retreat back to the camp when their ammunition ran low. At the same time the Zulu left horn began to outflank them.

L Direction to the Mangeni Falls. This is 12 miles (20 km) from Isandlwana but on a good gravel road. See the Mangeni Falls section for details.

M Site of Captain Shepstone's grave and those of his men. The area is marked by a collection of cairns and is best approached on foot directly from the car park. The graves and cairns lie in scrub some 500 yards from the car park. (Usually overgrown and in bushes.)

N Start of the Fugitives' Trail – see separate section for details.

O Original 'donga' crossing point used by British. It is immediately to the left of the road when approaching Isandlwana. It is here that the Zulu advance blocked the British escape route from Isandlwana back to Rorke's Drift and overwhelmed Lieutenant MacDowell's sappers.

Recommendations:
- Employ a reputable guide to obtain maximum benefit.
- Allow a full day to see the whole battlefield.
- Wear stout shoes and take clothing for inclement conditions.
- Spray legs and ankles against ticks if walking around in long grass.

This battlefield is famous for its cairns – marking the graves of men who were buried where they fell. The British bodies were not buried for many weeks and, in the case of the 24th Regiment, not for many months. The 24th had specifically requested that they alone should be permitted to bury their own dead. In the meantime the bodies were subjected to the ravages of scavengers, the weather and packs of dogs, many of which had actually belonged to the British invasion force. Zulu bones were probably interred with those of the British – this is strangely appropriate. As late as March 1880 complaints were still being made of bones protruding from graves around Isandlwana, so later that month Lieutenant M. O'Connell of the 60th Rifles was dispatched back to Isandlwana with a large burial party and ordered to complete the burials; any bones found on or near the surface were collected up in tarpaulin sheets and when a sufficient number had been collected, they were duly buried and a fresh cairn was built. O'Connell concluded that 'a few stray bones will be found at Isandlwana for many years to come'. They still appear frequently and are always re-buried with care and attention.

Apart from the new Zulu memorial, there is no evidence today of where the Zulu dead were buried. The small chapel behind St. Vincent's Church is where the missionaries re-interred Zulu bones that were discovered post-battle.

Isandlwana after the battle. *Adrian Greaves collection.*

Zulu memorial at Isandlwana.
Adrian Greaves collection

Authors with Trooper Pollard's medal – first name on the memorial at Isandlwana.
Adrian Greaves collection

The Fugitives' Trail, 22 January 1879

Overview

The Fugitives' Trail is an extension of the Isandlwana battlefield. The trail, which is poorly marked and difficult to follow, starts at the site of the wagon park on the saddle between Isandlwana and Black's Koppie and follows the fugitives' escape route for some five miles (8 km) to Fugitives' Drift. The river crossing was formerly known as Sothondose's Drift after Chief Sothondose, a chief who lived on the Natal side of the Buffalo River and who had jurisdiction over the immediate area in 1879. Completing the trail is a remarkable experience that brings home the realities and desperation of the fugitives' plight.

The trail must only be undertaken by the fit and well prepared, for the route itself is very rough and stony with several deep gullies that need to be crossed. The trail is poorly marked and no one should undertake the trek unless they have an experienced guide. It is very easy to get seriously lost, as the trail is criss-crossed with cattle trails that lead nowhere. The climax of the trail is the crossing of the Buffalo River. Do not consider this unless you are guided. Even when the river is running at a low level, the current can be very strong and the

Recently discovered cairn and grave on the Fugitives' Trail.
Adrian Greaves collection

Tourists pause along the Fugitives' Trail.
Adrian Greaves collection

crossing point is immediately above several dangerous rapids. Finally, on crossing the river, the trail enters a private game reserve and permission must be obtained.

The safe solution for anyone seeking to undertake the trail is to arrange the walk with a reputable guide or via Fugitives' Drift Lodge who will arrange a guide, transport and any safety equipment for the river crossing.

Battle account

Zulus seemed to be behind, before, and on each side of us, and as we hurried on we had to leave poor fugitives crying and begging us not to leave them.

Trooper W. Barker Natal Carbineers.

The scene across the British position at Isandlwana, as stabbing Zulus fought hand to hand with desperate soldiers, was unimaginably terrifying. Panic and rout had replaced calm British discipline; it was every man for himself amid the chaos. With the British force so heavily outnumbered, some of the 24th Regiment, probably about 150 soldiers, made a gallant stand at the wagon park. When that position collapsed, surviving clusters of them then fought back-to-back as they slowly tried to follow the earlier fugitives; some managed to get as far as the banks of the Manzimyama stream but all were overwhelmed.

With the exception of Lieutenant Curling, who vainly tried to save the artillery guns, no British frontline soldier or officer from the camp survived the Battle of Isandlwana. This situation caused much debate when, a week after the battle, it was discovered that two mounted officers of the 24th Regiment, Lieutenants Coghill and Melvill, had not only managed to escape from the camp but had reached Natal on horseback before being killed. Their departure from the battlefield, while their regiment's soldiers were still fighting for their lives, and the circumstances in which the two officers died, were to become the subject of much praise, speculation, debate and even a harsh statement from Chelmsford's successor, Sir Garnet Wolseley. Only one Victoria Cross, to Private Wassall, was initially awarded for Isandlwana – other displays of heroism went unrecorded or unwitnessed. The awards to Lieutenants Coghill and Melvill would be delayed for nearly thirty years; ironically, all three Victoria Cross recipients on that day had left the battlefield.

Because there were some survivors from Isandlwana camp, albeit only a handful, it has often been argued that the Zulus never completely surrounded Isandlwana. This premise is based on the fact that a number of survivors were able to flee through a gap in the Zulu encirclement and escape towards Natal, albeit over very rough terrain known today as the Fugitives' Trail. The Zulus did complete their encirclement and blocked the British line of retreat back to Rorke's Drift but a section of the iNgobamakhosi then detached themselves

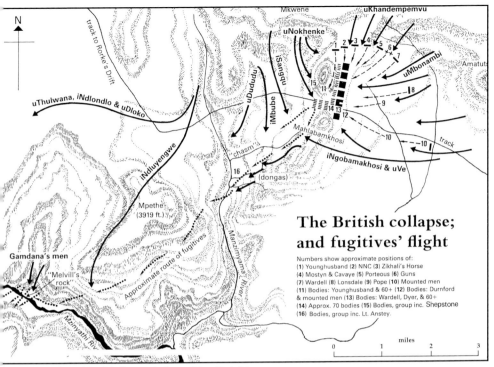

The British collapse; and fugitives' flight

Numbers show approximate positions of:
(1) Younghusband (2) NNC (3) Zikhali's Horse
(4) Mostyn & Cavaye (5) Porteous (6) Guns
(7) Wardell (8) Lonsdale (9) Pope (10) Mounted men
(11) Bodies: Younghusband & 60+ (12) Bodies: Durnford
& mounted men (13) Bodies: Wardell, Dyer, & 60+
(14) Approx. 70 bodies (15) Bodies, group inc. Shepstone
(16) Bodies, group inc. Lt. Anstey.

Reproduced by kind permission of Ian Knight.

from the closing left horn to chase fleeing NNC soldiers already trying to escape across the rough, boulder-strewn, terrain. This caused a temporary gap through which the few escaping whites were able to follow, only for most to run into the Zulus who killed them. It was through this gap that Lieutenant Curling and Major Smith rode alongside the two artillery guns, only to see them being driven out of control down the steep slope behind the camp where the guns overturned amidst the Zulus. Curling and Smith, both mounted, were able to escape the incident and rode on; Smith was killed further along the Fugitives' Trail while Curling escaped. The only whites to reach Natal did so on horseback and it can be argued that many of these survivors, with the exception of Curling, Coghill and Melvill, left Isandlwana before the main battle was under way.

> *I saw several wounded men during the retreat, all crying out for help, as they knew a terrible fate was in store for them. Smith-Dorrien, a young fellow in the 95th Regiment, I saw dismount and try to help one. His horse was killed in a minute by a shot and he had to run for his life, only escaping by a miracle.*
>
> Lieutenant Curling RA, Letter to his mother, 2 February1879

As the fleeing NNC reached the river bank the chasing Zulus caught them. Because the river was in flood, and few blacks could swim, they tried to make

61

a stand against the Zulus but were quickly overwhelmed and killed. It was through the midst of this slaughter and chaos that the last of the escapers, including Coghill, Melvill and Curling, were able to reach the river. An unknown number of other fugitives were killed in the river under the hail of Zulu gunfire or spears.

The bodies of Coghill and Melvill were initially buried under a rough cairn of stones on 3 February. This internment was conducted by the famous Padre George Smith of Rorke's Drift fame. Charles Harford described the site in detail, and a sketch appeared in the *Illustrated London News*. The next day the Queen's Colour was found by Captain Harber and dragged from the river by Charles Harford. On 14 April these bodies were reburied in coffins on the instruction of Sir Bartle Frere who had employed Coghill as an ADC. He also erected, at his personal cost, a cross that was placed on the top of the large rock where they were killed.

This site is a wild and beautiful place. It inspired the Empress Eugénie, mother of the Prince Imperial of France, who laid two wreaths on the site, on behalf of Queen Victoria, in mid June 1880. The famous novelist and traveller Bertram Mitford described the site in detail in 1882 (see *Through the Zulu Country*) and the site features in many early photographs and paintings.

It continues to attract thousands of visitors who are captivated by the setting, today in a game reserve. The coffin-shaped rock is still clearly identifiable, as is the whirlpool where Wassall saved Westwood, and the great grey cliff of rock over which Smith-Dorrien plunged still looms over the waters of the Umzinyathi River.

David Rattray at Coghill's and Melvill's memorial. *David Rattray collection*

Fugitives' Trail. *David Rattray collection*

1999 – The Royal Regiment of Wales visits the graves of Coghill and Melvill with the Regimental Queen's Colour.
David Rattray collection

Tourist swimming the Buffalo River at Fugitives' Drift. *Adrian Greaves collection*

FUGITIVES' DRIFT

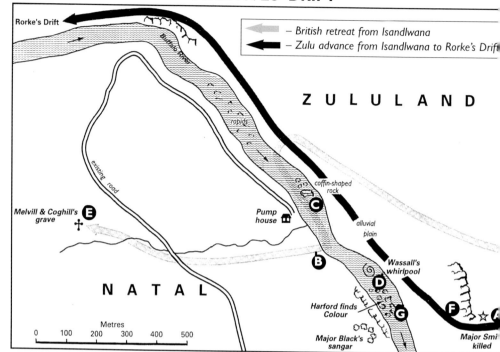

Rorke's Drift

— British retreat from Isandlwana
— Zulu advance from Isandlwana to Rorke's Drift

Z U L U L A N D

rapids

coffin-shaped
rock

Melvill & Coghill's
grave **E**

Pump
house **fff**

alluvial
plain

B

C

D

Wassall's
whirlpool

N A T A L

Harford finds
Colour

G

F ☆ **A**

Metres

0   100   200   300   400   500

Major Black's
sangar

Major Smi
killed

Points of interest

A *The cliff where the Zulus killed Major Stuart Smith RA.* The location of his grave is unknown.

B *Where Lieutenant Coghill rode down to the river,* successfully crossed with his horse and saw Lieutenant Melvill and Lieutenant Higginson in difficulties at the coffin rock with the Queen's Colour. Coghill went to their rescue but lost his horse. All three men swam for their lives to the Natal bank but lost the Colour. Higginson went to look for horses while Melvill carried Coghill to the lip of the gorge where they were killed at the site of present day monument. Higginson successfully escaped to Helpmekaar.

C *The 'coffin rock'* to which Higginson and Melvill clung before being swept off by the force of the river.

D *The whirlpool where Private Wassall rescued Private Westwood* – for which he won the Victoria Cross. (see section below)

E *The Coghill and Melvill cemetery and memorial.* Sir Bartle Frere erected the original cross. He had employed Nevill Coghill as an aide, and when he heard that their bodies had been roughly buried, he ordered that they be exhumed and buried properly and with his own funds he paid for the cross with the famous inscription 'For Queen and country, Jesu mercy.' The cross was knocked off its plinth when the site was vandalized in 1973 and in its position was erected the new black marble cross. This incident of vandalism constituted one of the reasons why the Rattray family purchased the property on which this monument lies and added it to their old farm 'West Kirby' where Fugitives' Drift Lodge is situated. The original cross was eventually found after a long search, thanks to the tireless efforts of Ken Gillings who responded to pleas to initiate a search for the old cross. It was found and carefully re-erected above the graves in September 1993 where it would be better protected from the weather. It was decided to leave the new replacement cross on the top of the main rock overlooking the graves. This site constitutes one of the most famous of all Imperial war graves, housing as it does the remains of the men who were amongst the first to win posthumous VCs; it has been visited by a string of Royal and illustrious visitors. One of the most poignant moments was the return of the Royal Regiment of Wales in January 1999, with Coghill's sword and a piece of the original Queen's Colour.

F *Where Lieutenant Smith-Dorrien arrived from Isandlwana* on horseback and helped Trooper MacDonald before he made his way across the alluvial plain, got caught up in the cliffs, his horse was killed, he jumped off the cliff into the river, grabbed another horse's tail and escaped.

G *Lieutenant Harford finds Colour in backwater* on 4 February while Major Black builds the famous sangar, still standing.

Finding the bodies of Lieutenants Coghill and Melvill

An account by Lieutenant Henry Harford 1/3rd NNC. (the beetle collector and the Sihayo stronghold incident)

[We were] following as well as we could over the stony and precipitous ground, the path by which, it was said, the fugitives had made their way. Suddenly, just off to the right of us, we saw two bodies, and on going to have a look at them, found that they were those of Lieutenant Melvill and Coghill! Both were clearly recognisable. Melvill was in red, and Coghill in blue, uniform. Both were lying on their backs about a yard from each other, Melvill at right angles to the path and Coghill parallel to it, a little above Melvill with his head uphill. Both had been assegaied, but otherwise their bodies had been left untouched.

Major Black at once said, 'Now we shall see whether they have the Colours on them,' and proceeded to unbutton Melvill's serge, while I opened Coghill's patrol jacket, but there were no Colours.

Presently Major Black said, 'I wonder if Melvill's watch is on him. He always carried it in the small waist-pocket of his breeches', and, on looking, there was his gold watch, which was subsequently sent to his widow. Nothing was found on Coghill, but his bad knee was still bandaged up. Undoubtedly, Melvill must have stuck to him and helped him along; otherwise he never could have got so far over such terrible ground.

How to find their graves

Take the **D31** road that runs south from Rorke's Drift. At the end of the **D31**, the graves are clearly marked. They lie within the Fugitives' Drift Game Reserve and visitors should be aware that the main gate is closed at sunset. If visitors want to explore the area beyond the graves and memorial, such as visiting the river or ledges, they must obtain prior permission from Fugitives' Drift Lodge. There is a small fee payable for this facility.

Participants

Imperial survivors: Captains Essex and Gardner; Lieutenants Cochrane, Curling and Smith-Dorrien plus a small number of mounted soldiers from the following units; Royal Artillery, 1st Sqd. Mounted Infantry and Column Headquarters staff.

Colonial survivors: Captains Barton, Nourse, and Stafford. Lieutenants Adendorff, Higginson, Raw, Vause, Henderson, Andrews, Davies, Erskine, Vaines and Quartermaster McPhail. A small number of individually mounted troopers from the following units also survived; Natal Mounted Police, Natal Carbineers, Newcastle Mounted Rifles, Buffalo Border Guard, 3rd Regiment NNC.

In total: 76 whites.

Casualties: Numerous – total number unknown.

Zulus: Elements of the iNgobamakhosi and Indluyengwe regiments – numbers unknown.

Casualties: Not known.

Location: The route is an extension of the Isandlwana battlefield and starts at the wagon park, the modern day car park, situated between Isandlwana and Black's Koppie. It covers a distance of 6 miles (10 km) and ends at the Coghill and Melvill Memorial at Fugitives' Drift.

How to find it. (The beginning of the Fugitives' Trail)

Route 1. **From Helpmekaar on Route 33. Good and dry weather conditions only.**

Take the dirt road sign posted to Rorke's Drift. After cautiously descending the steep pass, continue for two miles (3 km) to the junction; turn right towards Rorke's Drift. Half a mile (1 km) from the Mission Station, turn left towards Isandlwana, cross the Buffalo River at the actual Drift from where the British invaded Zululand and continue for three miles (5 km) to the junction. Isandlwana will now come into view from this road. Turn right towards the battlefield. Continue into the village of Isandlwana and proceed to the Orientation centre for your tickets before entering the Battlefield.

Routes continued

Route 2. Route 68. (The beginning of the Fugitives' Trail) All weather.
From Dundee, take route 68 towards Nqutu for 14 miles (21 km) and then take the dirt road to the right signposted to Isandlwana. At the first junction, turn left towards Rorke's Drift. Half a mile (1 km) from the Mission Station, turn left towards Isandlwana, cross the Buffalo River at the actual Drift from where the British first invaded Zululand and continue, with Isandlwana now in full view, for three miles (5 km) to the junction. Turn right towards the battlefield. Continue into the village of Isandlwana and proceed to the Orientation centre for your tickets before entering the Battlefield.

Route 3. Route 68 From Babanango to Nqutu. (The beginning of the Fugitives' Trail) All weather.
When eight miles (12 km) from Nqutu, take the signposted dirt road to Isandlwana. This road follows the route of the attacking Zulu Army and descends onto the battlefield from the Nqutu Plateau. As the road drops down on to the plain, the Conical Hill will be immediately to the front with Isandlwana to the right. Follow the road into Isandlwana village and proceed to the Orientation centre for your tickets before entering the battlefield.

Distinguishing features: At the beginning of the trail, there are a number of clearly marked cairns. After about one mile there is little evidence of the route.

Recommendations:
• The best advice for anyone seeking to undertake the trail is to arrange the walk via Fugitives' Drift Lodge who will arrange a guide, transport and any safety equipment for the river crossing. In this way, trekkers can leave their vehicles at the Lodge where their trek will end. The Lodge guides carry water in hot weather; they can also initiate any rescue procedures, should an emergency arise.
• The Fugitives' Drift river crossing can be viewed from the car park at the Coghill and Melvill Memorial. The memorial is thirty yards from the car park at the termination of the public road. The drift itself is part of the game reserve and prior permission must be obtained from Fugitives' Drift Lodge before entering the reserve.
Local Tel; 6421843.
From UK; 0027-34-6421843

The Story of Private Wassall VC

When the Zulus attacked the encampment, only those on horseback had any chance of escape. Of all the force left to defend the camp, only seventy-six whites were to survive. With the track to Rorke's Drift cut off, the only means of escape was across the rough countryside to the river border some six to seven miles (10 km) distant. The river was in flood and crossing was going to be a formidable task even without the attacking Zulus. The point of the river, known from that day as 'Fugitives' Drift', was where Private Wassall saved the life of a drowning comrade, Private Westwood, whilst under enemy fire.

After his escape from Isandlwana, Wassall was unofficially attached to the Northern Column under Colonel Wood VC. Westwood was still recovering in hospital at Helpmekaar from his near drowning when he overheard two officers discussing an unrecorded event of 'unparalleled bravery' by an unknown soldier in the river. Weakly, Westwood managed to provide the required information but it took the army several weeks to trace Wassall. In the meantime, Wassall had also fought with Colonel Buller at Hlobane, the second major British disaster of the war; Wassall uniquely survived both. In the *London Gazette* dated 17 June 1879 the War Office gave notice,

That the Queen has been graciously pleased to signify Her intention to confer the decoration of the Victoria Cross on the under-mentioned Officers and soldier of Her Majesty's Army, whose claims have been submitted for Her Majesty's approval, for their gallant conduct during the recent operations in South Africa, as recorded against their names.

One of these was Samuel Wassall of the 80th Regiment of Foot. On 11 September 1879 Samuel Wassall, along with Robert Jones of the 24th Regiment (for his part in the defence of Rorke's Drift), were presented with Victoria Cross medals by Sir Garnet Wolseley GCMG, KCB. Wassall was twenty-two years and nine months old and was the youngest serving soldier then to hold the award. His VC was the first awarded during the Zulu War. He was also granted a pension of £10 per annum for life.

Rorke's Drift, 22 January 1879

Overview

The story of Rorke's Drift should be contemplated together with that of Isandlwana. These are the most famous battlefields of the campaign. The battlefield covers a very small area, no larger than the size of three tennis courts, where eight officers and about 135 (exact number remains uncertain) British and Colonial soldiers held off an estimated attacking force of 4,000 Zulus for over twelve hours. The British soldiers of B Company 2/24th (2nd

Warwickshire) Regiment formed the guard of the Central Column's supply base and temporary hospital at Rorke's Drift.

The attacking Zulus had, earlier in the day, constituted the reserve of the attacking Zulu Army at the battle of Isandlwana, some ten miles (16 km) away, but had not taken part in the battle. It is most probable that this force of reserves harried the Isandlwana fugitives down to the river before attacking Rorke's Drift and neighbouring homesteads to redress this imbalance, to maintain their prestige and to obtain supplies of food. The site was originally a trading post and had been established by James Rorke in 1849. He died in October 1875 and the site was purchased by Swedish missionaries to be used as a Mission Station. The new missionary, Otto Witt, who converted Rorke's bungalow home into his own residence, turned Rorke's store into a school. Before the battle, the British commandeered the site, converting the school back into a store and Witt's home into a hospital. Today, the store has been rebuilt as a church and a fine museum now stands on the site of the hospital.

Grave of James Rorke at Rorke's Drift.
Adrian Greaves collection

Battle account

British forces invaded Zululand on 11 January 1879. During the morning of 22 January, reports began to reach Major Spalding, the officer commanding Rorke's Drift, that Zulus had been seen in the vicinity of Isandlwana. Spalding was aware that two companies of the 2nd 24th were overdue at the drift from Helpmekaar, some 15 mile distant, so he rode to Helpmekaar to ascertain their location. He left instructions for Lieutenant Chard, the most senior Imperial officer present, to take charge.

I see you are senior, so you will be in charge, although, of course, nothing will happen, and I shall be back again this evening, early.

Major Spalding Officer in Charge, Rorke's Drift to Lieutenant Chard RE

During the afternoon a message was brought to the drift that the Zulus were approaching the Mission Station. It was realized by Chard and Lieutenant Gonville Bromhead, commanding a company of 2/24th left as a garrison that, with some thirty injured or sick soldiers in the hospital, they could not escape.

Rorke's Drift today. *Adrian Greaves collection*

The British memorial at Rorke's Drift.
Adrian Greaves collection

The Zulu memorial at Rorke's Drift. *Adrian Greaves collection*

It is believed that these rare photographs of Lieutenant Gonville Bromhead (left) and Lieutenant John Chard (right), have never before been published. *Ron Sheeley Collection*

Assisted by Commissary Dalton, they began to prepare the position for defence by stacking heavy sacks of mealie corn and biscuit boxes around the position. Helping them were three hundred blacks under the command of Captain Stevenson. This officer fled with his NCOs and workforce as the Zulus approached and did not take part in the battle.

> *The camp at Isandlwana has been taken by the enemy and all our men in it massacred.* Shouted warning to the soldiers at Rorke's Drift.

One of the fleeing NCOs, Corporal Anderson, was shot in the back by a 24th defender; Anderson is buried in the cemetery along with the other soldiers killed in the action. The defended area included the hospital and the store; the defenders were now reduced to 139 men, including the Reverend Smith and Surgeon Reynolds with his 35 patients. The Zulus appeared in force at about 4pm and repeatedly attacked in successive waves until after dark, when they set fire to the hospital's thatched roof. During the following hours the soldiers occupying the hospital were forced, room-by-room, through the building until they reached the high window facing the British position. One by one, the wounded were lowered to the ground, under constant fire from the Zulus. Corporal Allen and Private Hitch, both already wounded, nevertheless successfully ferried the wounded to safety. The hospital was then abandoned to the Zulus.

Rorke's Drift Victoria Cross Winners

Gazetted	Name	Date awarded	Where awarded	By Whom
2 May 1879	Chard	16 Jul 1879	St Paul's, Zululand	Lt Gen. Wolseley
17 Jun 1879	Reynolds	16 Jul 1879	St Paul's, Zululand	Lt Gen. Wolseley
2 May 1879	Hook	3 Aug 1879	Rorke's Drift	Lt Gen. Wolseley
2 May 1879	Hitch	12 Aug 1879	Netley Military Hosp.	Queen Victoria
2 May 1879	Bromhead	11 Sep 1879	Utrecht	Lt Gen. Wolseley
2 May 1879	Jones, R	11 Sep 1879	Utrecht	Lt Gen. Wolseley
2 May 1879	Allen	9 Dec 1879	Windsor Castle	Queen Victoria
2 May 1879	Jones, W	13 Jan 1880	Windsor Castle	Queen Victoria
2 May 1879	Fielding	1 Mar 1880	Malta	Maj Gen. Anderson
17 Nov 1879	Dalton	16 Jan 1880	Fort Napier	Maj Gen. Clifford
29 Nov 1879	Schiess	3 Feb 1880	Pietermaritzburg	Lt Gen. Wolseley

The Zulus were swarming around us, and there was an extraordinary rattle as the bullets struck the biscuit boxes, and queer thuds as they plumped into the bags of mealies. And then there was the whiz and rip of the assegais, of which I had experience during the Campaign of 1877-78.

Private Henry Hook, Rorke's Drift survivor.

By firing the thatch the Zulus inadvertently illuminated the area for the defenders who were able to keep them at bay until dawn; by then the British had fired 20,000 Martini-Henry rounds and repelled numerous hand-to-hand assaults with the bayonet. The Zulus withdrew at dawn when they saw Chelmsford's force approaching the drift. The Battle of Rorke's Drift is famous, not only for the ferocious action taken by the defending officers and men, but for the recognition of their bravery by the award of eleven Victoria Crosses, seven of which went to the 24th Regiment, the most ever awarded to one regiment for a single action.

The General said we were a brave little garrison, and this showed what a few men could do if they had pluck. Gunner Howard, Rorke's Drift survivor.

Rorke's Drift – Sequence of Events

8am. Lieutenant Chard rode to Isandlwana to confer with the senior Royal Engineer officer Lieutenant MacDowel RE and to ascertain his orders. MacDowel had already left with Chelmsford so Chard was instructed to return to Rorke's Drift, he breakfasted at the officers' mess of the 1/24th Regiment before returning to the Drift. Meanwhile, Zulus were seen on the Nqutu plateau that overlooked the British camp, but this event caused no concern in the camp. On hearing of the vedette report that a large party of Zulus was moving NW across the Nqutu Plateau, Chard started back to Rorke's Drift, arriving at noon.

2pm. Major Spalding left for Helpmekaar to speed the relieving companies to the Mission Station. Lieutenant Chard was given temporary command of the small Rorke's Drift garrison, but took no action. He was probably convinced by Major Spalding who told him that 'nothing would happen'. Chard then went to his tent at the river to have lunch and to supervise the security of the ferry ponts. From the top of the Oskarsberg Hill behind the Mission Station distant rifle fire was heard and the first Zulus were seen crossing the Buffalo River. The reports were quickly relayed to Lieutenant Bromhead at the Mission Station.

3-3.15pm. At the Drift Lieutenants Vane and Adendorff reported the defeat at Isandlwana to Lieutenant Chard. They then carried Chard's orders to Lieutenant Bromhead to prepare the Mission Station defences before riding on to Helpmekaar. At the Mission Station, Commissary Dalton (a former British Army sergeant) organized the construction of defence walls of bags of Indian corn (mealies) and boxes of biscuits and with two wagons built into the south wall.

3.30pm. With the defences nearing completion, Chard returned to the Drift and ordered his men to retire with the water cart and tools. It was this water cart that Chard left outside the final defensive position at the Mission Station and had to lead a bayonet charge to recover it. Lieutenant Henderson with a large party of Durnford's Horse appeared and was ordered to guard the ferry crossing.

4.30pm. Back at the Mission Station, Chard ordered six men to guard the hospital. Reserve ammunition was to be made ready and bayonets fixed. A lookout was posted on the ridgepole of the store. Colour Sergeant Bourne took a skirmishing party to hold off the advancing Zulus.

5pm. Lieutenant Henderson and the Native Horse reported that the Zulus were approaching the Mission Station and then departed whereupon Captain Stevenson and his Native Contingent deserted. The effective strength of the garrison was reduced from 450 to 139 (including 35 sick). Men were taken from the line to construct a wall between the perimeter and the corner of the store. This became the famous wall of biscuit boxes that provided the second and final line of defence.

5.30pm. The Zulus appeared on the terraces of the Oskarsberg as Bourne and his men retreated back to the Mission Station. The initial attack on the south of the defences was contained and the leading Zulu ranks were pinned down by rifle fire. When the Zulus were in sufficient strength, their main attack was diverted to the west of the hospital and along the thinly held north-west wall. Zulu sniping from the Oskarsberg began.

6pm. In desperate hand-to-hand fighting, the defenders were forced to retire from the hospital into the yard.

Hospital 6.20pm to 7.15pm. Private Cole (suffering from claustrophobia) and Privates Howard, Beckett and Waters fled the hospital; Cole, Beckett and Private Adams were killed, Howard and Waters survived the night by hiding amongst dead Zulus. At 6.45pm the thatch was fired. John Williams smashed a hole through an inner wall whilst Joseph Williams and Horrigan held the

Rorke's Drift

22 January 1879 – Defending the Store House

Artist, Jason Askew, Anglo-Zulu War Historical Society.

Zulus at bay. John Williams pulled three patients through the hole before the Zulus burst in; they killed the remaining patients in the room. The two Privates Jones helped four patients to escape through the burning hospital's end window into the courtyard between the two buildings.

It will be remembered that Major Spalding, the Officer Commanding Rorke's Drift, had earlier ridden to Helpmekaar to speed up the overdue reinforcements. He was nearing Helpmekaar at about 3.30pm when he encountered the two companies of the 24th marching to Rorke's Drift. Spalding accompanied them to the steep pass and went on ahead together with a Mr Dickson of the local Buffalo Border Guard. As they descended the pass, they began seeing the first native fugitives from Rorke's Drift; puzzled, they rode on until they met the first fugitives from the Mounted Infantry. All told the same story; Isandlwana had fallen to the Zulus and Rorke's Drift was about to suffer the same fate.

Uncertain of the best course of action, Spalding rode on until he gained a low crest; from his vantage point he could see the Mission Station in flames. He and Dickson then saw a large group of Zulu skirmishers approaching; the Zulus came on to within 100 yards and then began to form into their traditional encircling attack formation, whereupon Spalding and Dickson retreated back to the marching column, now only one mile distant. Spalding was in a dilemma; should he proceed to relieve Rorke's Drift or return to Helpmekaar? On reaching the column, Spalding was informed that Zulu raiding parties had been seen approaching the pass they had just descended; in the light of this information, Spalding decided to retreat. He ordered the column to 'about turn' and the two companies, along with all their wagons, laboriously turned round and began the ascent of the pass. There can be little doubt that the defenders at Rorke's Drift, even in the failing light, had seen the approaching column, indeed, Spalding reached a position less than two miles from Rorke's Drift before he retreated; this would have placed the marching column less than three miles from Rorke's Drift. Due to its size and associated dust from the marching men, wagons and oxen, the relieving force would have been comparatively easy to see at that distance, especially by the attacking Zulus.

Some of the men said they saw the redcoats coming on the Helpmekaar road. The rumour passed quickly round – I could see nothing of the sort myself, but some men said they could. A cheer was raised, and the enemy seemed to pause, to know what it meant, but there was no answer to it, and darkness came.

Lieutenant Chard Second Report to Queen Victoria. See Appendix A.

Within the British position, Allen and Hitch, regardless of their wounds, continued to supply ammunition around the perimeter; it was now about 10.30pm and still the attacks came. Then the glow from the hospital fire began to dwindle and, as it did, the Zulus enthusiasm for close combat showed the first signs of waning. By midnight the battle had transformed from a constant Zulu attack into a series of isolated but determined attacks; this change in Zulu tactics enabled the British to anticipate more accurately the direction of each attack, each being repulsed with the same vigour that had characterized the whole British defence.

7pm until midnight. The Zulus continue to attack in intermittent waves. Private Hook was the last to leave the hospital, probably about 9 pm. Chard and Dunne, assisted by four soldiers, then began the task of converting the two large pyramids of bagged maize into an oblong redoubt. The purpose of their endeavours was to construct a final position for the wounded and, if the final wall was surrendered to the Zulus, the few survivors could occupy the redoubt. Chard supervised the work and in ten minutes their final position was ready. Access to the core of the pile was by a narrow entrance that could be sealed from the inside; the wounded were then placed inside the new position and Chard detailed marksmen to occupy the upper rampart. This gave them an elevated field of fire, which, with the dying glow of the hospital building, enabled them to pour several volleys into the massed Zulu ranks now pressing up against the final wall of boxes and mealie bags.

Meanwhile, the Zulus had begun to concentrate on the one remaining building still defended by the British, the storehouse. Corporal Attwood of the Army Service Corps had defended a window in the building throughout the action and now performed the vital task of shooting at the warriors trying to fire the thatch above him. Until the end of the battle, he held his position and kept the Zulus from firing the roof. Nevertheless, the pressure of hand-to-hand fighting continued unabated and eventually the British holding the outer wall of the cattle kraal were forced to retire, first to an intermediate wall which divided the kraal and then finally behind the wall which actually joined on to the storehouse. This was to be the final British position; there was nowhere else to go and there could be no further retreat.

Midnight until 4am. Apart from minor skirmishes, the Zulus make no more concerted attacks against the position.

4am. The Zulus retire for the first time. Fighting ceases.

6am. The Zulus reappear, the defenders 'stand to', but the Zulus then retire toward the Drift.

8am. The Mission Station is relieved by Lord Chelmsford and remnants of his Central Column. Chelmsford realizes that there were no survivors from Isandlwana and hears at first hand the accounts of the defenders. He remains at Rorke's Drift for a matter of hours before riding on to Pietermaritzberg with his staff officers.

10am. onwards The clearing up begins; the position is gradually fortified as it was believed the Zulus would return to attack the survivors. The wounded are tended to and plans are made for the collection and cremation of the 351 Zulu bodies found in and around the Mission Station.

Rorke's Drift
22 January 1879 – Defending the Hospital
Artist, Jason Askew, Anglo-Zulu War Historical Society.

British Forces Engaged in the Defence of the Mission Station at Rorke's Drift						
Unit	Officers	ORs	Sick	Killed	Wounded	Remarks
In Command						
Staff		1				
Royal Artillery		4	3			
Royal Engineers	Lt Chard	1				
2/3rd Regiment (Buffs)		1				
1/24th Regiment		11	5	3	2	1 died later
2/24th Regiment	Lt Bromhead	98	17	8	5	1 died later
Commissariat Dept.	Mr Dalton Byrne & Dunne	1		Mr Byrne	Mr Dalton	
Army Med. Dept.	Surg. Reynolds	3				
Chaplains Dept.	George Smith					Civilian
90th Regiment		1	1			
Natal Mounted Police		3	3	1		
Natal Native Contingent	Lt Adendorff	6	6	2	2	
Ferryman		1				Civ. Daniels
Total	8	131	35	15	9	

(Figures from contemporary rolls that are inconsistent and contain errors).

Participants

Imperial: Lieutenant Chard R.E. Officer in command 'B' Company 2/24th (2nd Warwickshire) Regiment commanded by Lieutenant Bromhead together with detachments from the 90th Regiment, the Commissariat, the Army Hospital Corps and the Chaplain's Department.

Colonial: Natal Mounted Police, the NNC and a civilian ferryman.

Total force: 8 Officers. 131 men.

Casualties: Killed, 17 men. Wounded, 1 officer and 8 men.

Zulu: Prince Dabulamanzi, a half-brother of King Cetshwayo, commanded them. The total Zulu force is estimated at 4,000 and consisted of four amabutho, or regiments, the uDloko, uThulwana, iNdlondlo and iNdluyengwe regiments.

Casualties: Unknown in total but some 500 bodies were left around the position perimeter, other bodies were found later and all were cremated or buried in three mass graves.

Location: The nearest towns are Dundee 30 miles (50 km) and Nqutu 16 miles (48 km). It is 16 miles from Helpmekaar and 10 miles (16 km) from Isandlwana by road. The facilities on site consist of the museum, tearoom, toilets and post office with an excellent Art and Craft Centre that has a worldwide reputation.

How to find it:

Route 1. From Dundee on Route 33.

Take the **R33** south from Dundee towards Greytown for 9 miles (14 km). Turn left at the Rorke's Drift sign onto a good gravel road and proceed for 17 miles (27 km).

Route 2. **From Dundee on Route 68. All weather.**
From Dundee, take the **R68** towards Nqutu for 14 miles (20 km) and then take the first turning right signposted to Rorke's Drift. At the first junction, turn left towards Rorke's Drift.
Good weather: Take the **R33** towards Greytown for 9 miles (14 km). Turn left onto the gravel road marked 'Rorke's Drift' and proceed for 18 miles (30 km).

Route 3. **From Helpmekaar on Route 33. Important! Good, dry weather conditions only.**
Take the dirt road sign posted to Rorke's Drift. After descending the steep pass, continue for three miles (5 km) to the junction; turn right towards Rorke's Drift. As you approach the Oskarsberg Hill, the red-roofed buildings at Rorke's Drift will become visible. Continue to Rorke's Drift. The Orientation Centre and battlefield are situated on the left as you enter the settlement. Obtain your tickets from the Orientation Centre before entering the Battlefield. **Note,** this route is very slippery in the rain.

Route 3. **From Babanango to Nqutu on Route 68.**
All weather.
When eight miles (12 km) from Nqutu, take the signposted dirt road to Isandlwana. This road follows the route of the attacking Zulu Army and descends onto the Isandlwana battlefield from the Nqutu Plateau. As the road drops down on to the plain, the visitor will be entranced by the view of Isandlwana and the conical hill. Follow the road into Isandlwana village and proceed past Isandlwana Mountain towards Rorke's Drift keeping the mountain on the left. After 6 miles (10 km), turn left towards Rorke's Drift. After crossing the Buffalo River, turn left at the junction. On approaching the Oskarsberg Hill, the red-roofed buildings at Rorke's Drift will become visible. Continue to Rorke's Drift, the Orientation Centre and battlefield are both situated on the left as you enter the settlement. Obtain your tickets from the Orientation Centre before entering the battlefield.

Distinguishing features: An impressive and emotionally inspiring small battlefield covering a tiny area that is strongly associated with the battlefield of Isandlwana. The site is dominated by the Oskarsberg Hill, named by Witt after his Swedish King; the Zulus know it as Shiyane, the 'eyebrow'. The actual Drift or river crossing is about half a mile by foot or one mile by car. The Orientation Centre sells light meals and drinks during the main part of the day, as well as maps, books and souvenirs.

RORKE'S DRIFT BATTLEFIELD

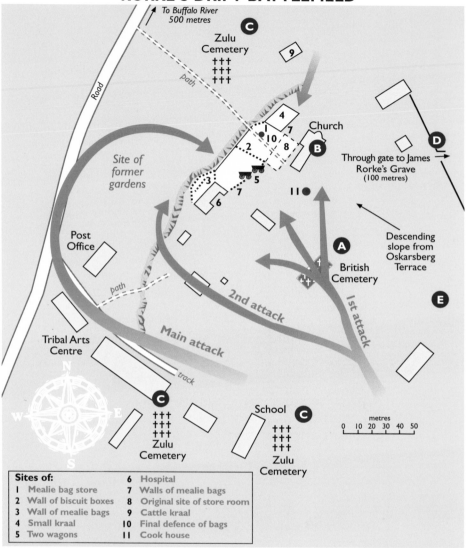

To Buffalo River 500 metres **C**

Zulu Cemetery
†††
†††
†††

path

Road

9

4

Church

1
10 7
2
8 **B**

Site of former gardens

3
5
7
6

II●

Through gate to James Rorke's Grave (100 metres) →

D

Descending slope from Oskarsberg Terrace

Post Office

path

2nd attack

A

1

British Cemetery

1st attack

E

Main attack

Tribal Arts Centre

track

C
†††
†††
†††
Zulu Cemetery

School **C**
†††
†††
†††
Zulu Cemetery

metres
0 10 20 30 40 50

N
W   E
S

Sites of:

1	Mealie bag store	6	Hospital
2	Wall of biscuit boxes	7	Walls of mealie bags
3	Wall of mealie bags	8	Original site of store room
4	Small kraal	9	Cattle kraal
5	Two wagons	10	Final defence of bags
		11	Cook house

A The British cemetery. The centre monument was crafted by Private Mellsop of C Company 2/24th; he had been a stonemason by trade before enlisting with the 24th Regiment.
B The church. (Site of the store during the battle).
C Zulu graves. There are three marked mass graves, each with a memorial stone in English, Zulu and Afrikaans. The only other Zulu memorials are at Isandlwana and the site of the Ulundi battlefield.
D James Rorke's grave. Rorke requested he should be buried under 3 ft of concrete to prevent his remains being disturbed – he then, according to local folklore, committed suicide.
E The Oskarsberg terraces, occupied by the Zulu marksmen during the battle. Following the battle, soldiers of the 24th carved their regimental number into the rocks. These engravings are still visible.

Note: re item 6. The Rorke's Drift Orientation Centre and museum. The museum was the hospital during the battle. See the excellent model with 2,500 figures on it. The museum has numerous pictures and artefacts.

The view of the Mission Station from the Oskarsberg Terraces. *Adrian Greaves collection.*

Points of Interest

① The Oskarsberg Mountain. This hill dominates the river crossing and is a commanding feature and a major landmark. One can climb it, starting at the visitors' centre at Rorke's Drift. The round trip should take about seventy minutes. The view from the top is spectacular.

② Bushmen paintings. On the east face of the Oskarsberg, in the sandstone terraces of the lower slope, there are some bushman paintings in an overhang. They appear at first to be somewhat damaged and faded, but this is because of their great age. It is quite a trek to get to them and you will need a guide to reach them.

RORKE'S DRIFT, OSKARSBERG AND THE BUFFALO RIVER

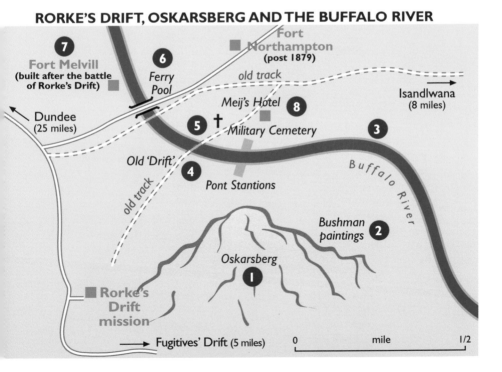

3 The Buffalo River. The Buffalo River at Rorke's Drift at the time of the Zulu War constituted the border between Natal and Zululand, and an old trading track snaked its way from Rorke's Drift to Ulundi – the route that Chelmsford intended to follow on expiry of the Ultimatum. At midnight on 10 January 1879 the Ultimatum expired. Chelmsford forded the Buffalo River at Rorke's Drift at the head of the Central Column, made up of 4,709 officers and men, 220 wagons, 82 carts, 49 horses, 67 mules and 1,507 oxen.1 His objective was the Zulu capital, Ulundi, 65 miles (108 km) away to the east.

4 The 'Old Drift'. The Old Drift is also the site of the infamous 'Sihayo incident'. In the winter of 1878, the famous Chief Sihayo KaXongo Ngobese of the Qungebe people who lived in the Batshe River area opposite Rorke's Drift had two of his adulterous wives stoned to death at the river crossing. This incident was seized upon by the British High Commissioner, Sir Bartle Frere, and woven into the pre-amble of the British Ultimatum. It was made to look like a cross-border incident.

5 Second British Military Cemetery. Until recently, the cemetery was in the centre of an untended grove of gum trees. The site has since been restored. There are some graves of soldiers, part of the garrison of Fort Melvill, who died of fever. There are also some more recent civilian graves in this cemetery. The remains of Fort Northampton, a sandbag or palisade fort built just after the Anglo-Zulu War when this region was racked with civil war, is still discernible, as is the deep well cut into the sandstone.

6 The ferry pool, just upstream from the present day low-level bridge was where the British established their ponts. This position is commanded on the Natal (western) side by a ridge, upon which the British built a sandbag and palisade fort called Fort Melvill in honour of the Lieutenant Teignmouth Melvill VC. This fort was garrisoned after the Battle of Rorke's Drift. About 400 yards downstream from the bridge the river runs over a series of rock shelves which constitute the 'old drift' – a natural causeway where people and wagons could gain purchase when crossing – hence the importance of the site. Downstream from the drift on the bend in the river, two old pont stanchions marked with the date '1863 Camel steel' still stand (used in *Zulu Dawn*), this site was probably used after the Zulu War.

7 Fort Melvill. The Rorke's Drift garrison was moved to a fresh location in April 1879 when hygienic conditions at the Mission Station deteriorated, causing mass sickness.

8 Meij's Hotel. (Sometimes referred to as May's Hotel). Built as a private venture towards the end of 1880. When it was completed the British placed it 'Out of Bounds' and the enterprise failed.

1 Figures from *The Narrative of Field Operations*, The War Office, 1879.

Note that the road you will take from Rorke's Drift to Isandlwana is only approximately the route that Chelmsford took. The old track is still visible from the air, and much care was taken when constructing the new road to minimize damage to the old track. It is significant that the old wagon track used to run from the Manzimyama River onto the saddle of Isandlwana. The new road runs from the Manzimyama River to the north of Isandlwana.

On 24 January Chelmsford's Central Column survivors returned to Rorke's Drift which resulted in the size of the garrison increasing to nearly 1,000 officers and men, with a similar number at Helpmekaar. Both positions were immediately fortified against a Zulu attack, but, due to the men being confined into small areas for safety; the resulting pollution and constant heavy rain resulted in widespread sickness. Conditions at Rorke's Drift became so serious that in March the whole position was moved to an adjacent hilltop overlooking the river and named Fort Melvill. Once it was realized that the threat of a Zulu attack was unlikely, both garrisons were closed down and the troops moved to Dundee in preparation for the second invasion.

Recommendations
• Employ a reputable guide to obtain maximum benefit.
• Allow a full day to see everything at Rorke's Drift and the graves of Lieutenants Coghill and Melvill at Fugitives' Drift only five miles (8 km) away, but do remember that Fugitives' Drift is on a game reserve.
• If you want to wander around the ledges or along the river please get permission from Fugitives' Drift Lodge before entering the reserve.
• If walking directly to the Buffalo River crossing, good walking shoes are essential.
• Spray legs and ankles against ticks if walking around in long grass.

Witt's home at Rorke's Drift – rebuilt after the battle. *Killie Campbell Library, Durban*

THE NORTHERN COLUMN
No. 4 Column:
Brevet Colonel Sir Evelyn Wood VC

Lord Chelmsford's plan

While Lord Chelmsford's Central Column was advancing towards Ulundi from Rorke's Drift, Wood was instructed to advance as part of a pincer movement and, at the same time, engage Zulus forces in order to prevent them moving south to strengthen King Cetshwayo's main army. Having crossed into Zululand, Wood was following these orders and was actually skirmishing with the abaQulusi Zulus near Hlobane when he received news of Chelmsford's defeat at Isandlwana. He immediately broke off the action and, probably realizing the serious implications of Chelmsford's defeat, withdrew his Northern Column to a strongly fortifiable position at a hill known as Khambula.

The Northern Column was commanded by Brevet Colonel Sir Evelyn Wood VC and by 20 January his force had reached the White Mfolozi River in northern Zululand. The local Zulu chief, Tinta, tendered his submission and was conducted under a strong escort into camp, together with his people and his herds. On the same day a party under Brevet Lieutenant Colonel Buller started to reconnoitre the nearby Zunguin range, and by the 22nd, the same day as the battles of Isandlwana and Rorke's Drift, Buller's force effectively cleared the area, dispersing a force of about 1,000 Zulus who opposed them and capturing a large number of Zulu cattle. That night, Buller's force heard Chelmsford's guns firing eighty miles to the south as Chelmsford retook the camp at Isandlwana.

Immediately after the relief of the garrison at Rorke's Drift, Lord Chelmsford took measures to protect the Colony of Natal and to prevent panic from spreading. The invasion of Zululand was temporarily suspended pending the arrival of reinforcements from England, and a general retrograde movement of troops from Zululand was carried out. Colonel Wood, to whom news of the events of the 22nd had been promptly conveyed by Captain Alan Gardner, fell back from the Mfolozi to the hill at Khambula, twenty miles (32 km) east of Utrecht. In this position he confined his attention to harrying the Zulus in a series of brilliantly executed reconnaissances, carried out under Buller. Such troops as could be spared from Cape Town and King William's Town were ordered to the front, and the opportune arrival in Natal of three companies of the 88th Regiment enabled two companies stationed between Durban and the Lower Tugela to be moved forward. Durban, Stanger, Pietermaritzburg and Greytown were all placed on the defensive, while the two camps of the surviving Central Column at Helpmekaar and Rorke's Drift were strongly entrenched.

On the 1 February a force from Wood's Northern Column, under Buller, attacked and destroyed an important Zulu homestead, a rallying-point of the Zulus, situated about thirty miles (50 km) east of the camp, and hitherto regarded as impregnable. Shortly afterwards Mbilini and Manyanyoba, two chiefs of the Ntombe Valley district, led marauding parties of Zulus into the neighbourhood of Luneburg and perpetrated a series of attacks on local tribesmen. On 13 February Colonel Wood despatched a force under Colonel Buller to take retaliatory measures.

On reaching Manyanyoba's stronghold Buller divided his force, sending a portion of it along a number of ridges, among which were the hiding places of the Zulus; the remainder attacked them in force from below. Five of the strongholds were successfully stormed, thirty-four Zulus being slain and a large number of cattle captured. Colonel Buller returned to Luneburg the same evening, with the intention of making a second attack on the following day. However, on being informed that Colonel Rowlands was moving a strong force in the same direction with a similar object, he abandoned his mission.

Colonel Rowlands VC, commander of the reserve No 5 Column, having vainly endeavoured to induce the Swazis to co-operate with him, had marched with a portion of his column from Luneburg on 13 February and then moved on to Derby. He was followed by the remainder of his column, under Major Tucker, which reached its destination on the 19th. On the following day a party led by Captain Harvey, Tucker's staff officer, marched across the Pongola River into Zululand and, after a brisk engagement, succeeded in dislodging a force of Zulus who had interrupted communications between Luneburg and the Khambula camp. The route between Luneburg and Derby remained dangerous and on 12 March a large supply column crossing the Ntombe River was successfully attacked and plundered by the Zulus.

A few days later Chelmsford ordered the breaking up of Colonel Rowland's Reserve Column; the mounted men joined Colonel Wood to assist with reconnoitring duties. Colonel Rowlands, with Captain Harvey and the remainder of his Staff, were ordered to proceed with all speed to Pretoria, the capital of the Transvaal. This was to strengthen its garrison, as the attitude of the Transvaal Boers had become extremely antagonistic towards the British.

During March of 1879 Chelmsford was well advanced with his plans for a second invasion of Zululand, but first it was essential to remove the threat of the belligerent abaQulusi Zulus who occupied territory to the north of Chelmsford's route. While Wood was pondering how to tackle the abaQulusi, he received an order from Chelmsford to seize the Hlobane stronghold to both neutralize the abaQulusi and draw Zulu forces away from southern Zululand where Chelmsford's relief column was attempting to lift the Zulu siege on Eshowe. Wood decided to attack Hlobane on the evening of 27 March with two columns of mounted troops, led by Colonels Buller and Russell.

Against all expectations, the action at Hlobane was a military disaster for Buller who lost fifteen officers and nearly 200 of his men when they unexpectedly encountered the main Zulu Army. Buller and the survivors were forced to retreat back to Khambula. The following day the victorious Zulus anticipated a similar victory when they attacked the nearby British fortified position of Khambula, only to suffer a crushing defeat.

Ntombe River (Meyer's Drift), 12 March 1879

Overview

This battlefield marks the location of the second Zulu victory over the British. Colonel Wood's Northern Column was supplied by regular ox-drawn wagon trains to and from Lydenberg and Derby in the Transvaal, a distance of 130 miles (210 km). The route crossed the Ntombe River some four and a half miles (7 km) from the hamlet of Luneburg where Major Tucker was in command of five companies of the 80th Regiment. The road ran close to the Zulu border, an area controlled by a pro-Zulu chief of Swazi origin called Mbilini ka Mswati. On 11 March one such supply column coming from Derby in the north was loaded with ammunition, rifles and general stores under the command of Captain Moriarty when it reached the Ntombe River in atrocious weather. In driving rain, only two of the wagons reached the south bank before the river level rose to an impossible height, leaving sixteen wagons stranded on the north bank. These sixteen wagons were formed into a defensive inverted 'V' pattern immediately opposite the two wagons that had reached the far bank. Four Bell tents were erected on the north bank, two on the south bank.

During the evening of 11 March Moriarty was allegedly informed by one of his sergeants that the Swazi chief, Mbilini ka Mswati, had been seen in the camp eating with the convoy's black soldiers. Moriarty apparently dismissed the report as improbable.

Battle account

At about 4am the rain stopped and a heavy mist settled along the river and across the camp. A few minutes later a sentry thought he saw some Zulus and fired a shot; Lieutenant Harward was in command on the far bank and after an initial 'stand to' he dismissed his men and all returned to their beds, as did Moriarty's men.

Meanwhile, the Zulu force crept to within fifty yards of the British position and then fired several massed volleys into the British tents before they charged the sleeping soldiers. Captain Moriarty managed to shoot three Zulus with his revolver before shouting out, 'Fire away boys I'm done'. With that he and most of his men died, a few survivors threw themselves into the river and several managed to reach the south bank, now manned by Lieutenant Harward and his men who covered their escape. The Zulus also began to cross the river and Harward saw his command begin to disintegrate; he had the only horse, so, leaving Sergeant Booth in command, he set off to Luneburg to get help. Sergeant Booth, assisted by Corporal Burgess, rallied his small force and led a tactical withdrawal towards Luneburg. On Harward's arrival at Luneburg, Major Tucker rallied every available mounted man and set off to rescue the survivors.

When the Zulus attacking Booth and his men saw the approaching mounted troops, they broke off their attack and fled the scene. Tucker and his men then moved to the devastated camp where they discovered sixty-four dead soldiers and fifteen dead black wagon drivers. Twenty soldiers were unaccounted for and their bodies were never found. Major Tucker buried the dead and recovered the wagons, now minus the rifles and ammunition, to Luneburg. Lieutenant Harward was later court-martialled for having 'misbehaved before the enemy'. At his trial, he was found 'not guilty' but when the finding reached Sir Garnet Wolseley, he remarked:

> that a regimental officer who is the only officer present with a party of soldiers actually and seriously engaged with the enemy, cannot, under any pretext whatever, be justified in deserting them, and by so doing, abandoning them to their fate. The more helpless the position in which an officer finds his men, the more it is his bounden duty to stay and share their fortune, whether for good or ill.
>
> Sir Garnet Wolseley

The Duke of Cambridge, the Commander in Chief of the Army, instructed Wolseley's comment to be read to every regiment throughout the British Empire. Harward's position was unbearable and he resigned his commission on 11 May 1880. In most instances, Harward's name has been expunged from his regiment's records.

Sergeant Booth was awarded the Victoria Cross for rallying and holding the survivors, some stark naked, in a tight group; they were still fighting and retreating when Major Tucker's rescue force arrived on the scene.

Participants
Five companies of the 80th Regiment at Luneburg under the command of Major Tucker. At the scene of the defeat, there were 103 non-commissioned men under the command of Captain Moriarty.

Casualties: 1 officer, 1 doctor, 64 soldiers and 15 black levies killed; the 20 missing soldiers were presumed drowned in the river.

Zulus: The Zulu force consisted of some 800 warriors (accounts vary) and was commanded by Prince Mbilini ka Mswati.

Zulu Casualties: 25 Zulu bodies were found at the river crossing.

THE BATTLEFIELD OF NTOMBE DRIFT

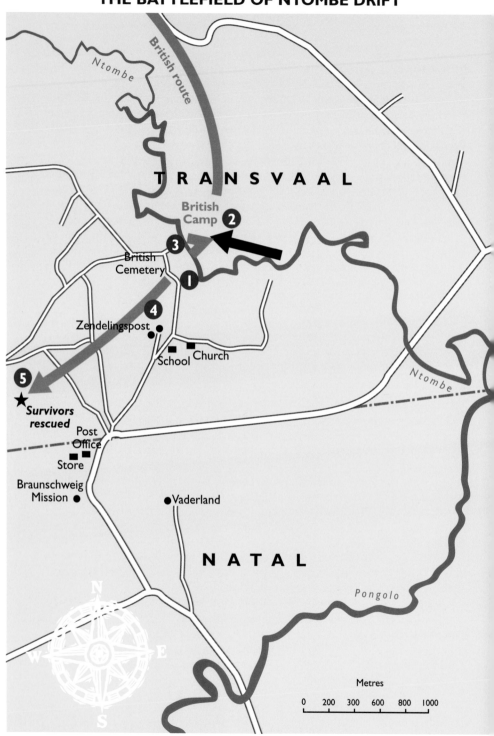

Points of interest

① The British cemetery dedicated to the 80th Staffordshire Regiment. The cemetery was severely damaged in 2000 by vandals.

② The river bank where Moriarty and most of his men camped – and were killed by the Zulus.

③ The river bank commanded by Lieutenant Harward.

④ Route taken by survivors under command of Sergeant Booth.

⑤ Direction of the nearby small German settlement at Luneburg and the cemetery where Captain Moriarty and Surgeon Cubbin are buried. As officers, they were not buried with their men. The church in Luneburg is also well worth visiting. The residents of Luneburg always make visitors welcome.

British memorial at Ntombe River.
Adrian Greaves collection

British Cemetery at Ntombe Drift.
Adrian Greaves collection

CONTEMPORARY MAP OF NTOMBE DRIFT

INTOMBE RIVER DRIFT

[*Not drawn to scale.*]

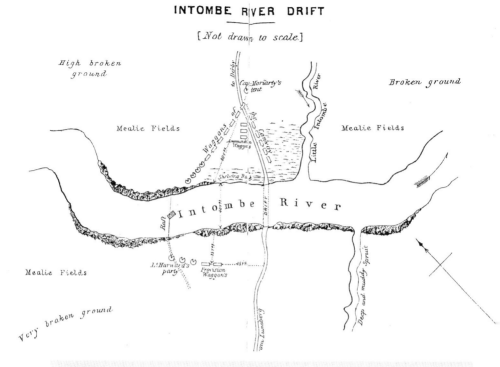

Location: The nearest town is Paulpietersburg, which has all the facilities of a small town.

How to find it: *From Vryheid* – Take the **R33** north from Vryheid to Commondale and then take the left turn due west towards Luneburg. From Commondale, stay on the road for 16 miles (25 km) and then take the left turn to Luneburg itself. After one mile there is a battlefield marker post to the left indicating the Ntombe battlefield. Follow the dirt road for half a mile and approach the modern tall-spired church situated on a small rise. Go past the church and the battlefield cemetery will be to the front. The actual battlefield is situated on both sides of the river just two hundred yards beyond the cemetery. In dry conditions the river can be crossed on foot to where the main British force was attacked. Lieutenant Harward defended the nearside of the river before he left his men to get help.

Distinguishing features: The services of a guide should be sought as this battlefield lies well off the road and cannot be seen from the **R33**. Follow the signs from the road and then look for the very stark-looking church.

Recommendations
• Park on the high ground beyond the church and walk to the cemetery. The drift is further down the slope at the river, which is partially hidden by trees.

Hlobane, 28 March 1879

Lord Chelmsford's plan

After the Zulu victory at Isandlwana, Wood subsequently received massive reinforcements consisting of mounted infantry, Natal Native Horse, Weatherley's Horse, some German settlers, some Boers including the famous leader Piet Uys, together with 5 companies of the 80th Regiment. Wood's main function was to draw off Zulus from the south where Pearson was besieged so that Chelmsford could orchestrate the relief of Eshowe. The position at Khambula was heavily fortified and by March 1879 Chelmsford was well advanced with his plans for the relief of the Eshowe garrison besieged by the Zulus. It was also essential that the belligerent abaQulusi to the north should be neutralized. Chelmsford could not risk having such a powerful force within striking distance of this potentially viable invasion route for the second invasion, so, once again, Wood was instructed to engage the abaQulusi Zulu stronghold at Hlobane. Wood decided to attack on the evening of 27 March with two columns of mounted troops, led by Lieutenant Colonel Buller and Lieutenant Colonel Russell respectively.

Overview

This battlefield marks the location of the third Zulu victory over the British, after Isandlwana and Ntombe. In early January of 1879 three columns were poised ready for the invasion of Zululand. As Chelmsford proposed to accompany the Central Column, which was also the largest, King Cetshwayo focused his main force against this column.

In order to distract the large Zulu force waiting for his Central Column, Chelmsford instructed Wood to harass the local Zulu tribes, especially the aggressive and fiercely loyal abaQulusi tribe. Chelmsford wanted them 'tied up' to prevent them coming to attack the Central Column. Whilst patrolling on 17 January, Lieutenant Colonel Buller was investigating the Zulu stronghold of Hlobane Mountain when 1,000 Zulus attacked him. He retired to the main British position near Khambula. British intelligence reports indicated that Hlobane was being used to hide the abaQulusi cattle and on 21 January Wood and Buller observed large numbers of Zulus drilling on Hlobane. The British engaged the Zulus on the 23rd just as the news of the British defeat at Isandlwana reached Wood. Realizing his predicament, Wood broke off the engagement and returned to Khambula where the position was strongly fortified. After Isandlwana, Wood was instructed to 'demonstrate' to draw off the Zulus. Wood and Buller wanted an excuse to clear the abaQulusi stronghold of Hlobane and this instruction provided them with the ideal opportunity.

THE BATTLE OF HLOBANE

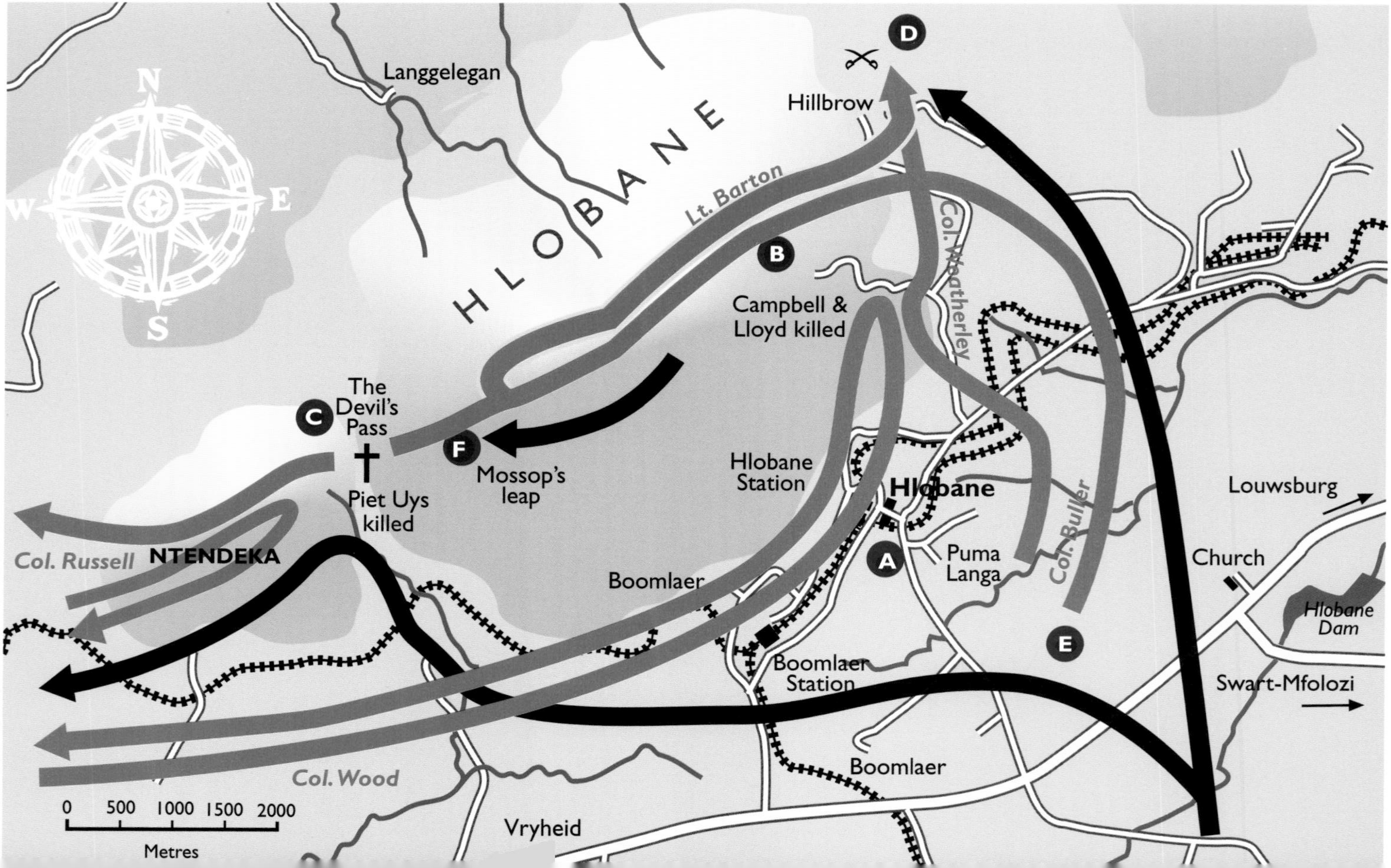

Points of interest

A Hlobane village – formally a coal-mining village. Ideal for long-range photographs of the mountain itself.

B Site of Campbell and Lloyd's graves and point reached where Colonel Wood and escort came under fire. This can be reached using a 4WD. Do not attempt the route in a private car due to rocks and deep ruts. The graves can be reached on foot but the track is difficult to find without an experienced guide. The graves, set in concrete by the mining company (to prevent vandalism!), are enclosed within the dry stone walls.

C Devil's Pass and original site of Piet Uys memorial (now seriously vandalized) that marked the point of his death. Only accessible from the top of Hlobane, or by undertaking a 2-mile (3.2 km) trek across farmland and very rough country from the main road. In both instances, the service of an experienced guide is essential and permission must be obtained from the mine security office before going up the mountain.

D Site of Weatherley's Horse massacre. This site is accessible by car. Park your vehicle at the top of the pass. The site where Weatherley and his men were killed lies just beyond the crest of the pass before the downwards slope reaches the sheer cliffs about 200 yards from the crest. There is, as yet, no memorial to Weatherley and his men.

E British route to the top of Hlobane.

F Point where Trooper Mossop jumped off the cliff top with his Basuto pony, Warrior.

View from R69 of Hlobane and the Devil's Pass. *Adrian Greaves collection.*

Battle account

The Northern Column under command of Colonel Wood was by now properly laagered at Khambula, 20 miles (32 km) from Hlobane, stronghold of the abaQulusi Zulus. The British were fully aware that a rich prize of over 4,000 cattle grazed the flat mountaintop. At Chelmsford's request, Wood dispatched Buller to attack Hlobane on 28 March. The force, under Buller, consisted of two groups of Colonial horsemen and black auxiliaries. Each would attack the mountain, Buller's from the east and Lieutenant Colonel Cecil Russell's from the west.

Russell's force was made up of approximately 200 mounted troops and 440 black auxiliaries, including 200 Zulu warriors who had defected to the British, along with their leader Prince Hamu, a half-brother of King Cetshwayo.

Buller's force consisted of 400 mounted men, all local volunteer horsemen except for a few Imperial officers, and 280 black auxiliaries. Included in the horsemen were the Border Horse commanded by an experienced ex-cavalry office, Lieutenant Colonel Frederic Weatherley, who had fought in both the Crimean War and the Indian Mutiny.

The attack on Hlobane was ill conceived; it had not been subjected to any form of reconnaissance and the routes up and down the mountain were unknown to the British. The flat top of Hlobane is three miles (5 km) long and one and a half miles (2 km) wide; it is generally 1,000 feet above the surrounding plain and, apart from two or three precipitous pathways, the flat-topped mountain is virtually inaccessible. No doubt the possible acquisition of so much booty was an added bonus to the main object of defeating the abaQulusi.

The intention of the two-pronged attack was to take the abaQulusi by surprise. Buller lit campfires on the plain to give the abaQulusi the impression that the real target of his column was the Zulu Army advancing from Ulundi and that he was bypassing Hlobane to the south. In the early hours he and his men began to move towards Hlobane leaving their campfires burning to deceive the Zulus. In reality, Buller had no idea of the close proximity of the approaching Zulu Army, camped only five miles (8 km) away. In the confusion and darkness, Weatherley and his Border Horse missed the departing column and spent most of the night trying to find Buller.

In fact, Weatherley's scouts discovered the approaching Zulu Army and Weatherley reported to Wood when they met early the following morning. Wood dismissed the report out of hand.

Nonsense, I have had my men out yesterday, there is no Zulu impi about.

Colonel Wood 28 March, prior to the Zulu attack.

The abaQulusi had seen Russell's column heading for the western end of the mountain and correctly anticipated that their stronghold was to be attacked from both ends. They prepared for the attack with confidence, knowing that the approaching Zulu Army, which Lord Chelmsford had assumed would be opposing him 100 miles (160 km) away at Eshowe, was camped only five miles (8 km) away from Hlobane. Buller's attack against Hlobane, undertaken in a violent thunderstorm under cover of darkness, was made difficult by breastworks that had been constructed by the Zulus to hinder such an attack. Buller's advancing force was fired upon and some casualties were incurred; boulders were also rolled down on the advancing British force struggling up a steep cattle track. Once successfully on top, Buller left 'A' Company at the top of the path as a rearguard and detached Lieutenant Barton to bury the dead who had been killed on the ascent. The abaQulusi had disappeared into a number of caves, enabling the British to loot their cattle as they headed to the western end of the plateau to meet up with Russell. Unbeknown to Buller, Russell had arrived at the bottom of the precipitous pass, later known as 'Devil's Pass'. Russell was appalled by the steep ground and deemed the pass impassable. The abaQulusi warriors then saw the main Zulu Army approaching Hlobane; they left their caves and again attacked Buller's men. They quickly recovered their cattle and routed 'A' Company, harrying them towards Buller's main force against the lip of the Devil's Pass. It was several minutes before Buller became aware of the even greater threat of the main Zulu Army moving to encircle his entire force.

With the Zulus bearing down on them, both columns then panicked. Russell received an ambiguous message from Wood incorrectly instructing him to move to another location some five miles from the scene, so he and his men departed as fast as they could ride, controversially abandoning Buller and his men to the advancing Zulus.

Equally unaware of the fast approaching Zulu Army, Colonel Wood, together with his personal staff officers and small escort, had ridden out from Khambula to watch Buller's ascent of the eastern end of Hlobane. Instead they met up with Weatherley and his Border Horse, who were clearly lost, under the southern face of the mountain. According to Wood, hardly had the two parties met when they were fired upon by Zulus hiding in a lofty cave, causing the Border Horse, who were leading, to take cover. Within moments, a Zulu marksman killed Mr Llewellyn Lloyd, Wood's Political Officer. Lloyd's father was a retired British general and a member of the Natal Legislative Assembly.

Lloyd's body was then recovered by Captain Ronald Campbell, Wood's staff officer, and carried a short distance to a stone cattle kraal where Wood's escort and the Border Horse were sheltering. Wood then told Campbell to order the Border Horse forward, but Campbell found difficulty in inducing Weatherley's men to advance, as they alleged the position was unassailable. Wood later

Site of Weatherley's Horse massacre (See **D**, p.95). *Adrian Greaves collection*

claimed that three of his staff then attacked the snipers, leaving most of the Border Horse 200 yards behind. Campbell then went forward with a few of Wood's escort, but in spite of his impetuous bravery, he was shot dead as he reached the snipers' cave. Captain the Hon Ronald Campbell, Coldstream Guards, was only thirty years old and the second son of the Earl of Cawdor. Wood and his remaining escort rode off to Khambula, narrowly escaping the advancing Zulu Army. Meanwhile, Barton and his men who had been detailed as a burial party, and Weatherley's force that was still trying to join Buller's force, were caught by the approaching Zulus. The Zulus killed Weatherley, his son who he was trying to save, and sixty-six men while Barton managed to

Top of Devil's Pass on Hlobane Mountain (See **F**, p.95). *Adrian Greaves collection*

Route to Devil's Pass on Hlobane Mountain. *Adrian Greaves collection*

make his way off the precipitous plateau and, while riding away, came across Lieutenant Poole of the Border Horse, now on foot. Barton took Poole on his horse and set off, trailed by a party of Zulus. They were eventually caught on the bank of the Manzana River, eight miles from the scene of their escape, and killed. The following year Wood was escorted to the scene by a Zulu who claimed to have killed Barton. Barton's body was buried on the riverbank.

Still at the top of the pass, Buller realized his predicament and gave orders for the remaining Zulu cattle to be abandoned. Ignoring the steepness of the pass, he ordered his men over the edge. Many men and horses fell to their deaths while descending the pass, yet worse was about to happen; Zulus from the main force now reached the pass and began firing into the descending soldiers or darting among them, stabbing them with assegais. As the survivors reached the bottom of the pass, the Zulus began to close in on them.

One trooper of the Frontier Light Horse, sixteen-year-old George Mossop, found himself trapped by Zulus at the edge of a cliff; rather than be assegaied, he jumped off the cliff with his horse, Warrior, landing amid trees and boulders. Both Mossop and his horse survived the fall and made it back to Khambula, although the horse died the following day of its injuries. Buller and several of his officers did what they could to hold off the attacking Zulus; they even rode back into them to rescue men whose horses had been killed. In the end those who survived the Devil's Pass and still had horses were forced to flee for their lives back to Khambula, a distance of 20 miles (32 km).

Zulus, crawling over the huge rocks on either side, were jabbing at the men and horses. Some of the men were shooting, and some were using clubbed rifles and fighting their way down. Owing to the rocks on either side the Zulus could not charge. The intervening space was almost filled with dead horses and dead men, white and black. Trooper Mossop Running the Gauntlet

Participants
Buller's force: Amounted to 675 officers and men and represented the following units;
Imperial: The Royal Artillery Rocket Battery.
Colonial: The 2nd Bn. Wood's Irregulars, Frontier Light Horse, Border Horse, Transvaal Rangers together with Dutch burgers under Piet Uys.
Casualties: 15 officers and 79 men plus some 140 blacks troops.

Russell's force: Amounted to 640 officers and men including;
Imperial: The Royal Artillery, Mounted Infantry.
Colonial: Natal Native Horse, Kaffrarian Rifles, 1st Bn. Wood's Irregulars and a detachment of Prince Hamu's disaffected Zulus.
Zulu Casualties: Not known

Awards: Colonel Buller and Major Knox-Leet were awarded the Victoria Cross in 1879. Two further VCs were awarded three years later to Lieutenant Lysons and Private Fowler. Corporal Vinnicombe was immediately awarded the DCM. Three years later awards of the DCM were made to Privates Walkinshaw and Power, and Trooper Browne. It was previously thought that Lieutenant Browne, on loan from the 1/24th Regiment, had received a VC for bravery at Hlobane, but it is now known that this VC was awarded for his bravery at Khambula the following day. The debate arose because inscribed on the VC is Khambula's date juxtaposed with 'Inhlobana'.

Location: Hlobane battlefield is 3 miles north of the **R69** next to the village of Hlobane, fifteen miles (24 km) from Vryheid. There are no facilities at Hlobane village.

How to find it: *From the town of Vryheid.* Take the **R69** from Vryheid travelling eastwards for a distance of eleven miles (18 km) in the direction of Louwsburg. After leaving Vryheid, the prominent hill of Zungwini will initially dominate the view to the left (north). Continue along the **R69** for about another four miles (13 km) when Hlobane itself and the prominent Devil's Pass will come into view on the left. The battlefield is situated on the left-hand side of the road, approximately three miles (5 km) from the road. Take the road to the left signposted to Hlobane. The best view of the mountain can be obtained from this road, which runs through the old coal-mining village and colliery of Hlobane. The road is quiet and there are good photographic opportunities here. To reach the site where Weatherley and his men died follow the Battlefield marker post to the saddle about two miles (3 km) from the village; once on top of the saddle there are spectacular views to the north. Do not proceed further without a guide – the track is a disused mining track and a cul-de-sac of no significance to the battlefield.

This is a battlefield that is one of the most magnificent of all Zulu battlefields, but it needs a whole day and a well-experienced guide. The fit visitor should be encouraged to climb the eastern end, visit the site of Campbell and Lloyd's grave, see the site of Buller's ascent and then walk across to the Devil's Pass. Beware of thunderstorms.

Distinguishing features: After driving along the **R69** for fifteen miles (24 km), the mountain of Hlobane will dominate the road from the left-hand side. There is a lay-by on the right hand side of the **R69** road, which is ideal for taking long-range photographs, but do take care of fast-moving traffic. Road signs will indicate that Hlobane village is ahead and to the left. Take this left turn.

Recommendations

• Hlobane is a notoriously difficult battlefield to visit and an experienced guide, who will obtain the necessary permissions, is absolutely essential for those wishing to reach the flat mountaintop or visit the Devil's Pass.
• Once on top, it is difficult to remain orientated, as there are no obvious landmarks; this makes it virtually impossible to find the way down unless a prominent marker is left clearly displayed near the only exit pathway. Remember that the whole lip of Hlobane Mountain consists of sheer cliffs and there is only one safe way down. The mountain is frequently affected by fog or mist that can cover Hlobane in a matter of minutes. There are also numerous hidden holes across the top, which drop down into caves and underground caverns.
• Even with a guide, take sufficient water, refreshments and clothing for every weather condition.
• Good strong walking boots are also essential due to the very rocky surface on top of Hlobane.

Private Mossop's
escape from Hlobane

Artist, Jason Askew, Anglo-Zulu War Historical Society.

Caves at Hlobane where Zulus
fired on Colonel Wood.
Adrian Greaves collection

Graves of Campbell
and Lloyd at Hlobane.
Adrian Greaves collection

Khambula, 29 March 1879

Overview
This site marks the location of one of the most important British battles of the whole Zulu War: its outcome marked the turning point of the war and led Chelmsford to believe that he could defeat the Zulus; likewise it was the battle that convinced King Cetshwayo that he had lost the war.

Battle account
The ill-conceived attack on Hlobane resulted in a major British defeat. The British survivors were forced to flee for their lives back to Khambula, which was the main permanent British position in the north. Those who had lost their horses in the battle were all overwhelmed and killed. The Zulu force that inflicted the defeat at Hlobane was, by sheer coincidence, *en route* to attack the British fortified hilltop at Khambula, 20 miles (32 km) to the west.

Following the battle at Rorke's Drift, King Cetshwayo knew the dangers of attacking fortified camps and gave his commanders strict instructions to avoid such positions. Instead, they were ordered to strike at the British supply lines and draw the troops out into the open. After their victory the previous day at Hlobane, the Zulus were understandably confident of further victory and, after resting overnight in the area of the present day town of Vryheid, they set off towards Khambula some 10 miles (16 km) to the north. When in sight of Khambula, the Zulus paused to take stock of the situation; the younger warriors convinced the senior indunas that they should attack the British while they were still recovering from their mauling the previous day at Hlobane. Wood feared the Zulus would bypass his position and attack Utrecht, but the Zulus had already decided to attack Khambula; the Zulu force divided into two main columns that rapidly spread out in an attacking formation several miles wide.

Wood remained calm and prepared his force for the Zulu onslaught. After his troops had received a substantial lunch at 12 noon, the tents were struck to give everyone a clear field of fire across the battlefield.

The Zulu plan was to attack the small British hill redoubt on two fronts, the classic 'horns of the bull' tactic, with the main body then attacking between the two flanks. The left horn approached the British position along the course of a stream and, according to local belief, became bogged down in soft marshland. The right horn meanwhile, shouting 'we are the boys from Isandlwana' arrived in its pre-attack position without being able to see that the left horn was still 2 miles (3.2 km) distant. Buller recognized the opportunity and led his mounted men out of the British lines and to within two hundred yards of the Zulu right horn. His men fired several volleys into the packed Zulu ranks, which was sufficient to provoke the Zulus to charge. Buller and his men then raced back to the camp as the artillery opened fire over their heads and into the charging Zulus. Several of Buller's men from the Frontier Light Horse were overtaken by the Zulus and it was at this point that Lieutenant Browne won his Victoria Cross for bravery. The Zulus were not able to advance against controlled rifle and artillery fire and took enormous casualties, which quickly forced them to retreat.

I never saw anything like it, nothing could frighten them, and when any of their numbers were shot down, others took their place.

Unidentified British soldier, AZWHS Journal No.9.

The Zulu left horn then massed to attack, but, with the right horn now defeated, the British were able to concentrate their fire against the assembled warriors. The centre body of Zulus could not approach the British due to their firepower although some Zulu marksmen occupied a knoll to the east of Wood's position from which they proceeded to enfilade his position. The left horn did reach the cattle kraal but were beaten back by Major Hackett and a company of the 1st/13th Regiment with fixed bayonets. These were tense moments for the British. A shot from a Zulu marksman hit Major Hackett in the head blinding him; he nevertheless survived into old age.

By 5pm the battle was over and the Zulus began their retreat. Buller and his riders then rode out from the camp and turned the Zulu retreat into a rout; they killed as many of the Zulus as they could find until darkness fell.

I confess that I do not think that a braver lot of men than our enemies in point of disregard for life, and for their bravery under fire, could be found anywhere. We were all employed burying the dead yesterday, and we had not finished by dark, pits being made three-quarters of a mile from camp, and the dead taken in carts. A more horrible sight than the enemy's dead, where they felt the effects of shellfire, I never saw. Bodies lying cut in halves, heads taken off, and other features in connection with the dead made a sight more ghastly than I ever thought of.   Sergeant Jervis, 31 March.

Participants
Colonel Wood's force totalled 2,086 officers and men and represented the following units;
Imperial: The Royal Artillery, Royal Engineers, 1/13th (Somerset) Light Infantry, the 90th (Perthshire Volunteers) Light Infantry and Mounted Infantry.
Colonial: Baker's Horse, Border Horse, Frontier Light Horse, Kaffrarian Rifles, Mounted Basutos, Raaf's Transvaal Rangers and Woods Irregulars.
Casualties: 3 officers and 26 men killed and 5 officers and 50 men wounded.
Zulus: The Zulu force consisted of some 20,000 warriors and was commanded by two senior indunas, Ntshingwayo and Mnyamana Buthelezi. The right horn consisted of the iNgobamakhosi, the left horn, the uMcijo; the centre force, the uDloko, uDududu, imBube, uThulwana and the inDlondlo. Most of these units had fought at Isandlwana. Many units of the local abaQulusi had joined the Zulu force.
Zulu Casualties: At least 1,200 Zulus were killed around the battlefield. Many more died from their injuries post battle.

Location: The nearest town is Vryheid, ten miles (16 km) away, which has all the usual facilities of a large town.

How to find it: *From the town of Vryheid.* Take the **R33** northwards for ten miles (16 km) towards Paulpietersburg. The road runs through a blue gum tree forest and the first indication of the battlefield will be the battlefield marker post on the left-hand side indicating the route to the left. Follow the sign along the dirt road for about one mile (1.6 km) to a junction when another battlefield sign will indicate the dirt road to the left. After about another two miles (3.2 km) the hill redoubt will become obvious to the front. About five hundred yards from the position, the track passes through an old gateway and in January 2002, there was a village football field with goalposts to the right of the track.

KHAMBULA BATTLEFIELD

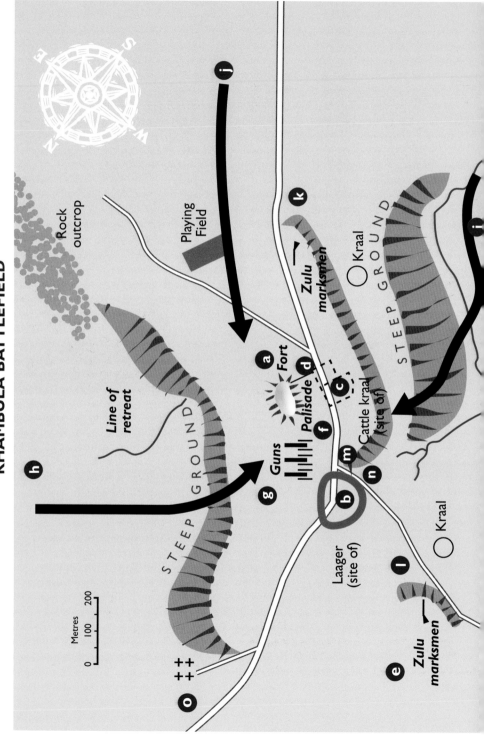

Distinguishing features: This battlefield lies well off the main road and cannot be seen from the **R33.** On arrival at the hill redoubt, climb the short distance to the crest; at this point all the features of the battlefield can clearly be seen, as can the British cemetery, which lies 800 yards further along the pot-holed track to the west. Once at the site of the hill redoubt, all points of the battlefield can be reached on foot. It is sometimes possible to take a car to the cemetery, but this is not advisable in wet conditions.

Points of interest

a Site of headquarters and hill redoubt. This position dominates the battlefield.

b Site of main camp and laager. The trench of the wooden palisade between the redoubt and cattle kraal is still visible.

c Cattle kraal – this was temporarily seized by the Zulus during the battle.

d Palisade. This facilitated troop movements between the redoubt and main camp area when under fire.

e Site of earlier British camp, (moved due to fouling).

f Site of the six 7-pounder Royal Artillery guns.

g Position of Buller's horsemen who precipitated the Zulu attack.

h Position the Zulu right horn retired to.

i Where Zulu left horn was delayed, below the British campsite, bogged down in marshland.

j Route of Zulu central body.

k Position of Ntshingwayo who directed the attack and Zulu snipers.

l Position of Zulu snipers from left horn; all were killed following several aimed British volleys.

m Site of British bakery and farriers.

n Site of Hackett's bayonet charge.

o British cemetery. Note that the date on the memorial is incorrect – the stonemason's error.

Khambula. *Adrian Greaves collection*

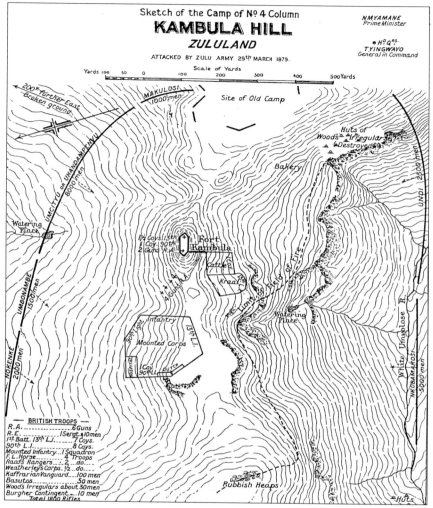

Sketch of the Camp of No 4 Column

KAMBULA HILL
ZULULAND

ATTACKED BY ZULU ARMY 29th MARCH 1879.

NMYAMANE
Prime Minister

● *H Q ns.*
TYINGWAYO
General in Command

Recommendations:

• Khambula is an important battlefield in the historical sense, but it is an infrequently visited site as it lies off the beaten track.

• It is a difficult place to visit in the rainy season and in wet conditions visitors would be advised to take a reputable guide; most guides use 4WD vehicles that can deal with waterlogged tracks. In dry conditions, the tracks are easily passable to all vehicles.

• This battlefield is generally considered to be well worth the effort of getting there. Khambula is a truly splendid battlefield. It is easy to relate what happened onto the topography.

108

THE COASTAL COLUMN

If the Zulu victory at Isandlwana and the heroics of Rorke's Drift had not occurred, then the exploits of the Coastal Column might well have ranked with the later sieges and reliefs of Chitral and Mafeking. Instead, the invasion of Zululand by the Coastal Column was totally overshadowed by the fate of the Centre Column and, until recently, all but neglected by historians.

Lord Chelmsford's plan

Chelmsford originally planned to invade Zululand with five columns. He later modified his plan due to logistical problems and invaded with three. He chose to accompany the largest Central Column from Rorke's Drift, with Colonel Wood's Northern Column on his left flank and Colonel Pearson's Coastal Column at the Lower Drift of the Tugela River on his right. He tasked Pearson with the role of marching over 37 miles (59 km) of rough twisting track from the Lower Drift on the Tugela River to occupy the mission station at Eshowe in order to protect the buildings. Here the column's supply wagons were to be unloaded and return to pick up more stores, while defences were built to convert Eshowe into a fortified advanced supply depot. From here it was intended to advance on the Zulu capital, Ulundi, in a converging movement with the other two columns.

The man Chelmsford chose to lead the Coastal Column was forty-five year-old Colonel Charles Knight Pearson, of the 3rd Regiment (The Buffs). He was regarded as an experienced and steady officer whose regiment had served in South Africa for three years. During the planning stage of the invasion, he had resigned from the regiment in order to serve on Chelmsford's staff. Given the command of the Coastal Column, he was re-united with his old regiment who, together with the less experienced 99th Regiment, made up the Coastal Column's infantry force.

The Royal Artillery and the Naval Landing Brigade supplied two 7-pounder guns and a rocket battery each. The 136-strong Bluejackets from HMS *Active* and HMS *Tenedos* also provided two rocket tubes and the American Gatling gun, about to be used in action by the British for the first time. At this time the Gatling gun was used only by the Navy and mounted on board ships to give covering fire to landing parties. In 1873 it had been present during the Ashanti War, but not used in action.

In tactical terms, a coastal column in support of the main Centre Column was a sound enough strategy but one that overlooked some important factors; the unseasonably bad weather, rugged terrain, prevalent sickness and the constant threat of an enemy whose tactical abilities and bravery were badly underestimated. The early Zulu victory at Isandlwana effectively halted the whole invasion and made the Coastal Column's position virtually untenable. Because of slow communications, Pearson only learnt of the full scale of the British defeat at Isandlwana on 2 February, by which time his advance force of some 1,800 men had reached Eshowe, only to be surrounded by the Zulus. In the aftermath of Isandlwana, Chelmsford made the relief of Eshowe his number one priority. By focusing British attention on extricating Pearson's column, he was eventually able to ameliorate the storm that broke over him and the relief column's ultimate success undoubtedly helped to restore his confidence.

With the column was a force of about 2,000 black men of the NNC who were not expected to fight as infantry but to scout and pursue a beaten foe. The Royal Engineers supplied 85 sappers, and the 312-strong squadron of horsemen were made up from the Mounted Infantry as well as the more colourfully named local units from the Natal Hussars, Victoria Mounted Rifles, Alexander Mounted Rifles and the Durban Mounted Rifles. The total number of fighting men was over 4,000. In addition, 620 civilians were employed to drive the 384 ox wagons. All in all it was a formidable force, but it constituted a logistical nightmare.

An intermediate but strong fortification was built on a bluff on the Natal bank of the Tugela River overlooking the Lower Drift and named in honour of Colonel Pearson. Its commanding position must have appeared formidable to the Zulus as they looked across the 300 yards of the Tugela River that separated the two countries. Having assembled his forces, Pearson's first task was to move them across the Tugela, treacherously swollen by heavy rain, and establish a base on the opposite bank. This laborious task was accomplished in five days by the use of a large pont constructed by the carpenters from HMS *Active*. A member of that ship's crew also had the sad distinction of becoming the first casualty of the Zulu War when he fell into the fast-flowing river and was drowned.

Once across the Tugela River and in enemy country, Pearson constructed a fortified camp that was named Fort Tenedos. So far the few Zulus seen had kept their distance, content to observe and report back to King Cetshwayo. Leaving a garrison of sailors, two companies of the 99th and some NNC to guard the fort, Pearson set off for Eshowe in two columns. Because of the heavy rains, the track was soon turned into a quagmire and the many dongas and rivers were swollen with rushing water. Progress was slow but steady. The most difficult part was getting the heavily laden wagons across the flooded watercourses, which necessitated the Native Pioneers digging away the steep banks to create a crossing point. Soaked to the skin and exhausted from each day's slog, the men endured miserable nights in their leaky tents. The inexperienced and nervous recruits of the 99th further tried their comrades' patience with several false alarms when on night guard. Notwithstanding Chelmsford's orders, no attempt was ever made to laager the wagons and, with the two columns stretched out for several miles along the track, they were highly vulnerable to Zulu attack. In fact, a Zulu force of about 3,500 warriors had already been detached from Cetshwayo's main impi and was marching to intercept Pearson's struggling column. As they headed south, the approaching Zulus were joined by increasing numbers of warriors until they totalled more than 6,000.

The next obstacle for the British was to cross the Nyezane River. On 22 January Pearson sent his mounted scouts ahead, who reported that a flat plateau on the far bank would make a suitable place to halt for breakfast. Despite having reservations about halting in an area surrounded by thick undergrowth, Pearson decided to halt for a couple of hours to allow the men to breakfast before ordering the first wagons across the river. It was here that the battle of Nyezane took place. The Zulus failed to synchronize their attack and were driven off with heavy losses.

The Battle of Nyezane had taken place just a few hours before Isandlwana, which lay one hundred miles (160 km) to the north-west, but the victory was all but forgotten in the wake of that disaster. Pearson paused only to bury his own dead in a single grave before ordering the march to resume. He did not want to give the Zulus the impression that they had checked his advance in any way; he also wanted to be clear of the very rough bush country. The day became insufferably hot and, after a further tough four-mile march, Pearson called an early halt for the night.

Rising at 3am on the morning of the 23rd, the column moved off with the dawn and advanced the 5 miles (8 km) to Eshowe, which they reached at 10 a.m. Here they were pleasantly surprised to find the Mission Station in good condition and complete with a garden filled with orange trees. The buildings consisted of a steepled church with a corrugated iron roof and three other adobe-built structures. The mission covered an area of 120 yards by 80 yards, sloping west to east and there was a good supply of water from two nearby streams. In addition there were three more buildings standing a short distance away. Although the site seemed to be an excellent choice, the senior Engineer, Captain Warren Wynne, had reservations. Despite being on high ground, the Mission Station was overlooked by higher ground within firing range. Furthermore, a deep ravine filled with undergrowth came right up to the perimeter and could conceal an enemy advance. As soon as camp was made, work started on making the area defensible.

Undergrowth was cleared to give clear fields of fire and entrenching began. Stores were unloaded and placed in the outlying buildings. On 25 January 48 of the empty wagons were escorted back to Fort Pearson to collect more stores. They passed another convoy en route to Eshowe and heard the first rumours that all was not well with the Central (No 3) Column and that Colonel Durnford and his NNC had been annihilated.

It was not until the 28th that Pearson received a message, brought by runner, from Lord Chelmsford. Inexplicably, it did not mention the catastrophe at Isandlwana, but stated that Chelmsford had pulled back to Natal and that Pearson was to prepare for the whole Zulu Army to descend on him. Chelmsford gave Pearson the option of retreating back to Fort Tenedos. In the absence of firm information, Pearson logically concluded that Durnford's No 2 Column had been defeated and took the unusual step of calling all officers to a council of war to decide whether to retreat or stay. Having endured a gruelling journey to occupy and fortify Eshowe, Pearson was reluctant to withdraw. His Royal Engineer officer, Captain Wynne, strongly advocated defending the position, fearing that a strung-out retreating column would present the Zulus with an easy target. If the might of the Zulu Army was heading his way, any retreating column would risk being overwhelmed. Having listened to the opinions and suggestions of Wynne and the other officers, Pearson decided to remain at Eshowe. King Cetshwayo was so infuriated that Pearson's column had settled at Eshowe that he ordered the Zulu regiments in the area to surround the British position and prevent their withdrawal.

The Relief of Eshowe

Lord Chelmsford's plan

During early March of 1879 Lord Chelmsford built up a strong enough force to attempt the relief of Pearson's column. Beside the 3rd Regiment and 99th left at the Lower Drift by Pearson, the infantry comprised the newly arrived 57th, 91st Highlanders and 60th Rifles. He also had 400 men from HMS Shah *and 200 from HMS* Boadicea *with two Gatling guns. The NNC and Major Barrow's mounted troops made up the balance of the relieving column. The total strength was 3,390 white and 2,280 black troops. It was Chelmsford's intention that Major General Henry Hope Crealock, brother of his military secretary, Lieutenant Colonel John North Crealock, would command the column. As Crealock did not reach Natal in time, Chelmsford took personal command on 23 March. Chelmsford wrote to Evelyn Wood in the north and asked him to make some demonstration to divert Zulu forces away from the south to take pressure off Pearson's besieged garrison. The result was the Zulu victory at Hlobane on 28 March and the British victory at Khambula the next day.*

The column to relieve Eshowe was ferried across the Tugela River and began its advance using a route further to the east than the one Pearson had taken. Chelmsford's re-found caution made him choose more open country where he could laager his wagons and entrench each night. He further ordered that the ammunition boxes were to be readily available on the wagons and that the lid screws should be removed. Once he had reached Eshowe, Chelmsford intended to relieve the garrison and replace it with fresh troops and supplies. The progress of the column was slowed by torrential rain that beset them almost every evening, swelling the rivers and streams and turning the track into a morass. As Chelmsford wished to reduce the number of wagons, he ordered that all tents were to be left behind, so officers and men had to sleep on the muddy ground totally unprotected from the regular downpours. Due to the adverse weather, their early attempts at laagering were chaotic and experienced men like John Dunn despaired of the British ever beating Cetshwayo. By the third evening, a simpler system had been devised so that the laager would be a square of 130 yards each side, made up of thirty wagons butted together and all the livestock placed within. The troops dug a shelter trench fifteen yards in front of the laager's sides and sited the artillery and Gatling guns at each corner.

It was as well they managed to get themselves into order for, as anticipated, the Zulus were about to launch an attack in force. The two forces met early on the morning 2 April near a kraal named Gingindlovu where the British had established their overnight defensive laager on a small rise.

Meanwhile, in Eshowe those with telescopes and binoculars had keenly followed the battle. Pearson ordered congratulations to be flashed to Chelmsford and the garrison waited impatiently to be relieved. Chelmsford's men finally reached Eshowe after a tough fifteen-mile march. After the initial euphoria of seeing new faces and catching up with news, the defenders were somewhat deflated by Chelmsford's decision to abandon the fort instead of leaving a fresh garrison, a decision which upset many of the defenders who felt their efforts had been in vain.

Pearson was ordered to take his command from Eshowe on 4 April, while Chelmsford accompanied Barrow's mounted troops to attack the nearby homestead of Cetshwayo's brother, Prince Dabulamanzi. They failed to surprise the Zulu chief who had retreated to some nearby heights from where he watched his homestead put to the torch. Collecting the rest of his men, Chelmsford abandoned Eshowe and marched after Pearson's column. As soon as it was deemed safe, the ever-watchful Zulus entered the deserted mission and burnt it to the ground. Catching up with Pearson, Chelmsford ordered him to head back by the most direct route to the Lower Drift, which he subsequently reached on 7 April. Chelmsford then marched his column back to his old laager at Gingindlovu, where the stench from the many Zulu dead drove him to move to a fresh site nearby. There was still the threat that the Zulus would attack again and the troops remained on the alert. Despite their victory, the new troops had seen that the Zulus were a formidable force and were greatly unnerved by them.

It was in this climate of anticipation that a tragedy occurred the night

Contemporary sketch by Lieutenant Lloyd,
24th Regiment. On Active Service, *Lloyd*

Our best drinking water!

before they reached the old laager. While on piquet duty in the early hours of the morning, panic seized some of the young recruits of the 60th when they mistook John Dunn's black scouts for Zulus. When the pandemonium had died down two NNC scouts lay dead and eight wounded, with a further five white soldiers wounded. This was the worst incident of soldiers shooting at their own side in a war that was littered with similar accidents.

Chelmsford's column reached the border soon after Pearson had arrived. He had left a strong force behind at the entrenched campsite just a mile south of the Gingindlovu battlefield, which he felt could be supplied comfortably from Fort Tenedos.

Chelmsford was fulsome in his praise for the tenacious Colonel Pearson and his men, and well pleased with the outcome of the two battles that had dealt the Zulus a severe blow. The human cost of holding Eshowe was evidenced by 28 crosses in the cemetery below the mission and hundreds of sick. Some 200 of these men were so ill they were ferried to the hospital at Fort Pearson. One of whom was Captain Wynne whose energy and skill had turned the mission into an impregnable fortress. Sadly he succumbed to typhoid and died on his birthday, 19 April. Colonel Pearson, himself suffering the effects of typhoid, was appointed a brigade commander for the new invasion. But he never fully recovered from his ordeal; unable to take up this post, he was eventually invalided home in June.

The replacement 2nd Division commander for the re-invasion, Major General Henry Hope Crealock, took charge on 18 April and set about building up the column's strength and supplies. Chelmsford's new plan was to invade with just two columns. He would accompany the larger Second Division, augmented by Colonel Evelyn Wood's Flying Column, for their advance from the north. General Crealock's mandate was similar to that earlier given to Colonel Pearson except that he was to establish strongly fortified staging posts along his advance and to use these as a springboard to destroy two large Zulu homesteads before supporting the First Division's advance on Ulundi. Having established two forts named Crealock and Chelmsford, he ran into the same problem that dogged the British throughout the campaign, namely lack of wagons and oxen. The new posts had to be laboriously supplied but only at the expense of overworking the already exhausted draft animals, many of which died. The putrefying carcasses left at the side of the busy track and in nearby watercourses made conditions very unpleasant and men began to fall sick in increasing numbers.

In order to hurry supplies forward, a pontoon bridge was constructed across the Tugela River and a suitable beach for landing supplies was established 30 miles (50 km) up the coast at Port Durnford. A third post, Fort

PLAN OF FORT AT ETSHOWE: ZULULAND.

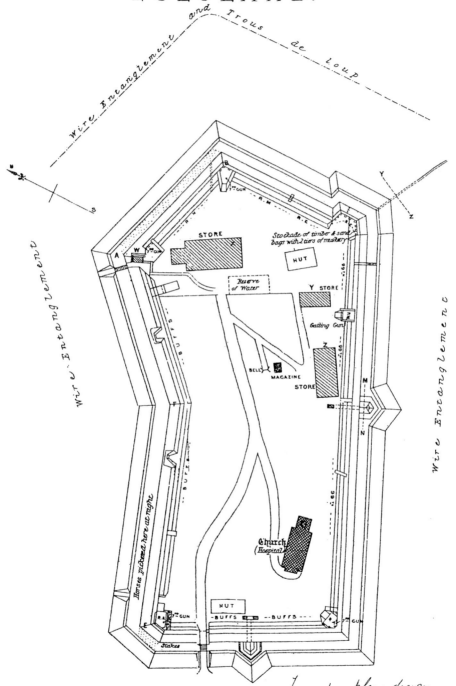

Traced from plans drawn by Lieuts Main & Willock R.E.

Napoleon, was constructed as Crealock slowly advanced further inland. Because of his logistical problems, Crealock's progress had been painfully slow and he had little influence on the main events happening further north. Even though he destroyed the two large military homesteads and accepted the surrender of many of the enemy, he was inevitably castigated for being slow and ineffective. General Wolseley, who had arrived just too late to prevent Chelmsford from finally defeating the Zulus at Ulundi, dismissed Crealock's efforts by suggesting that 'the First Division might as well have been marching along the Woking and Aldershot road'.

Of all the different terrain that was fought over in Zululand, the coastal area was the most difficult. Although casualties from fighting were light, the sick list was extensive. No awards for bravery were made or personal reputations enhanced and the participants had to be content with the campaign medal as the sole reward for their exceptional endurance. Colonel Pearson, though, was an exception. For leading the Coastal Column during the initial phase of the war he was made Companion of the Bath.

The Ultimatum Tree
Fort Pearson, Fort Tenedos, Euphorbia Hill and British Cemeteries

Overview
Full details of the Ultimatum can be found in Part 1 of this guide.

On 11 December 1878 Zulu chiefs were summoned to the site of a shady fig tree on the Natal bank of the Tugela River to learn the result of the Boundary Commission's deliberations concerning border disputes. John Wesley Shepstone represented the British officials, while Cetshwayo sent three of his senior indunas together with eleven chieftains to listen to the findings.

Most Zulus in this period were illiterate, but they were nevertheless accomplished at memorizing even lengthy speeches. In the morning John Shepstone read out the findings of the Boundary Commission; Mr Fynney, the Border Agent, translated these to the Zulu chiefs. The outcome was generally in the Zulus' favour and they were relieved at the terms. The meeting then adjourned for lunch and reassembled in the afternoon when the hitherto secret Ultimatum was read and translated, sentence by sentence, again by Mr Fynney. The astonished Zulus then set off to report the terms of the Ultimatum to their king. A white resident, John Dunn, soon learned of the Ultimatum and sent his own messenger to King Cetshwayo with advance warning.

In anticipation that the Zulus would not comply with the Ultimatum, the British invasion force was already advancing towards the borders of Zululand.

The Ultimatum Tree today, looking across the Tugela River to Fort Tenedos. *Adrian Greaves collection.*

Location: On the south bank of the Tugela River, the 1879 border of Natal with Zululand.

How to find it: *From Durban.* Take the **R102** or the **N2** northwards from Durban; turn off the motorway at the Zinkwazi Beach exit. Follow the signs to Tugela and the **R102**. On reaching the **R102** turn right. After 5 miles (8 km), take the right-hand turning signposted to the Ultimatum Tree and Fort Pearson. Follow the dirt road for 3 miles (5 km); Fort Euphorbia and Fort Pearson are on the obvious small hill to the left next to the river. Take the obvious left fork and drive to the top of the hill where there is adequate parking and a pleasant picnic spot next to the cemetery overlooking the Tugela River. Fort Pearson is 100 yards further along the track; it is located by the orientation hut in the centre of the fort. From the site of Fort Pearson, the Ultimatum Tree can easily be reached on foot by walking across the pedestrian bridge spanning the motorway – distance about 300 yards. Alternatively, one can drive to the car park at the site, which has been declared a National Monument and lies in the shade of the new motorway.

Distinguishing features: The Tugela River and the **N2** motorway, which is immediately next to the site. Although the new **N2** motorway straddles the site, there is no immediate access from the motorway to the location.

Points of interest
➤ The Ultimatum Tree. This tree still survives in the form of the original stump and strongly growing shoots; the site has been declared a National Monument.

➤ Fort Pearson and orientation hut. The lines of defence and trenches are still clearly visible.

➤ Fort Euphorbia, initially manned by the troops of HMS *Tenedos*. At its summit can be found the original British Cemetery with Captain Wynne's grave. (He was the constructor of Fort Eshowe and Fort Tenedos.)

➤ Second British cemetery where those who died of fever between the 1st and 2nd invasions are buried.

➤ Fort Tenedos, on the Zulu bank of the river. It was named after HMS Tenedos and was also built by Captain Wynne RE for easier distribution of stores to the front line. The fort can be reached from the **R102**. Its outline can best be seen from Fort Pearson or Euphorbia Hill.

➤ Site of the river crossing used to ferry the Zulu chiefs to the reading of the Ultimatum, and to ferry troops across using floating ponts. It is also the site of the first casualty of the war; Private Martin fell in the river and was drowned.

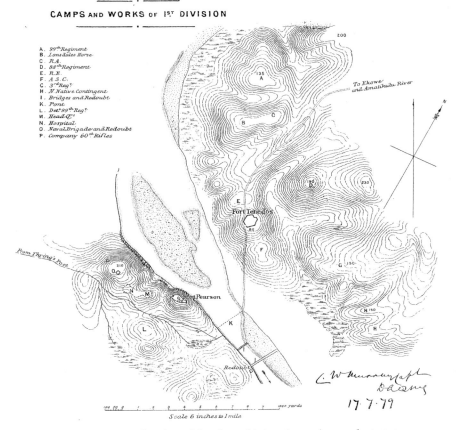

TUCELA RIVER

CAMPS AND WORKS OF 1ST DIVISION

A . 99th Regiment
B . Lonsdales Horse
C . R.A.
D . 88th Regiment
E . R.E.
F . A.S.C.
C . 3rd Reg.t
H . N Native Contingent
I . Bridges and Redoubt
K . Pont
L . Det.t 99th Reg.t
M . Head Q.rs
N . Hospital
O . Naval Brigade and Redoubt
P . Company 60th Rifles

To Ekowe
and Amatikulu River

From Thring's Post

Fort Tenedos

Fort Pearson

Redoubt

Scale 6 inches to 1 mile

17·7·79

A contemporary drawing with points of interest superimposed. *Blue Books.*

Nyezane, 22 January 1879

Overview

This battlefield, named after the nearby river, marks the location where the Coastal (No1) Column, commanded by Colonel Pearson, met with the Zulus as it advanced on Eshowe. Pearson's column was part of the first British invasion of Zululand, which had begun on 11 January. Eshowe had been a Mission Station and it was intended to be the Column's main staging and supply post; it occupied high ground and contained several buildings that Pearson wished to utilize for stores. After his column had rested on the night of 21 January, they ponderously set off to climb the plateau between two low hills; the plateau is dominated by Wombane Hill to the front and right of the track, which was being followed by the British. All column commanders had been given specific orders for deployment in the face of attacking Zulu forces and at 8.30am sufficient Zulus were seen on Wombane Hill to induce a full defensive deployment of British troops. This battle is significant for its timing as it took place at about the same time and on the same day that the Zulus attacked the British at Isandlwana.

Battle account

At 7am on 22 January 1879 the British set off from their overnight campsite; they began to cross the Nyezane River at the same time as Zulu scouts were seen observing them from the nearby Wombane Hill. It quickly became evident to Pearson that the scouts were not alone when a larger force of Zulus was seen approaching the hill from the distant plateau. Pearson deployed a company of the NNC to take the hill, but the NNC were quickly routed when they blundered into the Zulu vanguard. The NNC officers did not understand their own black troops' language and confusion ensued. The Zulus then advanced towards the column leaving the British officers in no doubt they were under a serious attack. Pearson deployed two companies of the 3rd Regiment (The Buffs) and part of the Naval Brigade, along with two guns and a rocket tube from the Royal Artillery. Midshipman Coker, who had been in camp servicing the Gatling gun, rapidly completed his work and ran with the Gatling to a commanding knoll where he opened fire with devastating results. Sustained fire from the column halted the Zulu advance and Pearson ordered a combined force of NNC, the Buffs and the Naval Brigade to clear Wombane Hill. As the Naval brigade advanced waving their cutlasses, the Zulus fled. By 9.35 a.m. the battle was over; the British buried their dead and the column continued unmolested towards Eshowe.

Participants
Imperial: The Coastal (No. 1) Column, commanded by Colonel Pearson, included detachments of Royal Artillery, Royal Engineers, 2nd Battalion 3rd Regiment (The Buffs), 99th Regiment (Duke of Edinburgh's), The Naval Brigade from HMS *Active* and 2 Sqd. Mounted Infantry.
Colonial: Natal Hussars, Stanger Mounted Rifles, Victoria Mounted Rifles and the 1st and 2nd Battalions of the 2nd Regiment NNC plus No 2 Company Natal Native Pioneers.
Casualties: 2 officers of the NNC and 8 men were killed, with 1 officer and 15 men wounded.
Zulus: The total Zulu force was estimated at 6,000 warriors and consisted of 5 amabutho under the command of Chief Godide.
Casualties: Not less than 450 dead Zulus were found around the battlefield.

Location: The nearest town is Eshowe, which has all the usual amenities of an average-sized town.

How to find it: *Route 1*. From Durban. Take the **R102** or **N2** motorway north from Durban. If travelling by motorway, take the first exit to Eshowe and Gingindlovu, which brings one onto the **R102**. Follow the signs to Eshowe and Gingindlovu. On approaching the town of Gingindlovu, remain on the **R102** that bypasses the town centre. Within a few hundred yards, take the left fork to Eshowe, the **R66**. After passing the Gingindlovu battlefield on the left side of the road, remain on the **R66**. After crossing the (small) river of Nyezane, Wombane Hill will begin to dominate the road from the right-hand side. There is a battlefield marker on the left-hand side of the road that indicates the site of the Memorial to those killed in the battle. The memorial is about 250 yards down the track to the right; follow the pathway for a few yards to the memorial. It is best to park off the road to explore this battlefield.

Route 2. **From Eshowe. Route 68.** Follow the **R68** southwards towards Gingindlovu for 2 miles (3.2 km). The road will then begin to drop down towards the plain and Wombane Hill will appear and dominate the left-hand view. Look out for a battlefield marker on the right-hand side of the road and pull off on to the dirt road. The battlefield marker on the right-hand side of the road indicates the site of the Memorial to those killed in the battle. The memorial is about 250 yards down this track on the right-hand side; follow the pathway for a few yards to the memorial. It is best to park off the road to explore this battlefield.

Distinguishing features: The only obvious feature of the battlefield is Wombane Hill in conjunction with the battlefield sign on the main road.

THE BATTLE OF NYEZANE

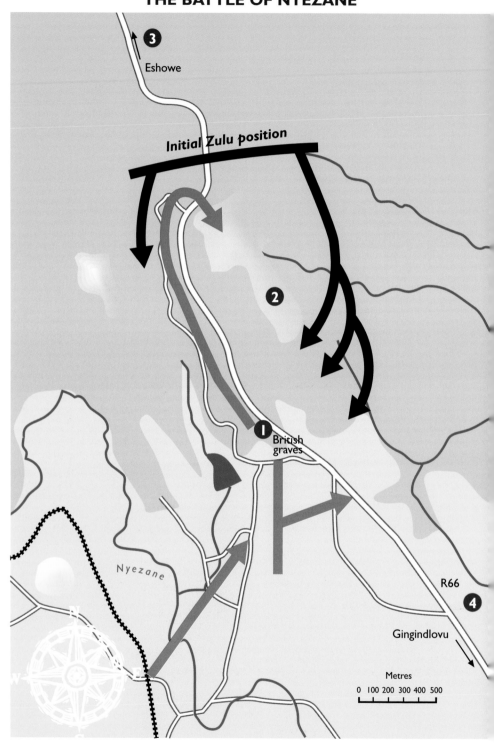

Eshowe

Initial Zulu position

British
graves

Nyezane

R66

Gingindlovu

Metres
0 100 200 300 400 500

Points of interest
1. The memorial and graves of the British dead.
2. Wombane Hill.
3. Fort Eshowe is 2 miles (3.2 km) to the north along the **R68**.
4. The battlefield of Gingindlovu is 10 miles (16 km) to the south along the **R68**.

Recommendations
• A competent guide is essential if exploring this battlefield. It covers a wide area and there are no remaining features to be seen of the battle itself. • The battlefield from the Nyezane River to the British 'form up' point is usually covered in sugar cane. From the **R68** road across to Wombane Hill the route to the base of the hill is through very rough scrub before the long sharp climb to the top of Wombane Hill can be undertaken.
• Nyezane is a battlefield for the very fit enthusiast only unless the visitor is content to view the scene from the graves or the roadside.

The Siege of Fort Eshowe
2 February-29 March 1879

Overview
After Colonel Pearson had defeated the Zulus at Nyezane, he quickly moved on to Eshowe as intended and began to fortify that position.

In tactical terms, a Coastal Column in support of the main Centre Column was an obvious strategy but the British underestimated the difficulties in the terrain and the skill and bravery of the Zulus. Furthermore, the unseasonable heavy rain, prevalent sickness and the early British defeat at Isandlwana effectively brought the whole invasion to a standstill and rendered the Coastal Column's position untenable. Due to a breakdown in communications, Pearson only learnt of the full scale of the British defeat at Isandlwana on 2 February by which time his advance force of some 1,800 men had reached Eshowe.

Pearson decided to reduce the number of men in the camp and ordered Major Barrow to take his mounted men and the NNC back to Fort Tenedos. He also sent a note to Chelmsford explaining his position and requested a full tactical appraisal of events along the border. The strength of the garrison was reduced to 1,460 combatants and about 335 civilians. Because of a lack of space, it was decided to drive away about 1,000 oxen of which about a half returned to Natal with their drivers. A cattle laager was then constructed for the remaining cattle west of the entrenchment, which, in the days to come, became a noisome health hazard for the garrison. The Zulus then surrounded Eshowe.

After working in the oppressive heat of the day, the men had to sleep as best

1879, PLAN OF AREA – TAKEN FROM BLUE BOOK

SKETCH OF ROAD FROM FORT TENEDOS TO EKOWE .

they could under the wagons, there being no room to erect their tents within the encampment. False alarms often interrupted their sleep and demoralized them. Large bodies of Zulus were regularly seen, but none approached Eshowe. The hot weather broke and heavy rain added to the soldiers' miseries. With no tents, everyone was constantly soaked and, as a result, sickness broke out. Although the garrison had sufficient food and plenty of ammunition, it lacked adequate medical supplies; it was only a matter of days before the first man died of fever.

The heavy rains caused the area within the entrenchment to become a sea of deep mud that added to the garrison's discomfort. News brought by runners on 2 February plunged everyone into a state of shocked depression. At last they learned the truth of the fate of the Centre Column and it is indicative of the problem of communications that it took twelve days to acquaint Pearson with news of the disaster at Isandlwana. One wonders, if he had known days earlier, whether he would have ordered a withdrawal back to the Lower Drift. Instead, nearly 1,800 men were effectively under siege with no immediate prospect of receiving supplies or reinforcements and, in the light of this news, Pearson ordered the commissariat to put the garrison on three-quarter rations.

Meanwhile work continued on the defences and by the second week of February Captain Wynne had turned the hastily built entrenchment into a formidable-looking fortress. The whole area was now surrounded by a deep wide ditch and was further protected by a six-foot-high defensive wall. Firing platforms for the cannon and Gatling guns were constructed at the angles of the ramparts and drawbridges were built at the two gates.

Conscious of the danger of sickness breaking out in such an overcrowded area, Pearson gave great attention to preventing their fresh water from becoming polluted and to siting and rotating the latrine area downhill away from the camp. Despite these precautions, the stench within the camp and from the nearby cattle laager became increasingly offensive, attracting clouds of flies that infested the garrison's food supplies. The general health of the men rapidly deteriorated, with the majority of soldiers suffering from serious stomach disorders. By the end of February seven men had died, including one suicide by drowning. Unsanitary conditions, exposure and a lack of appropriate medicines caused a steady decline in the health and morale of the defenders. Apart from an occasional skirmish with the outlying vedettes, the Zulus kept their distance but constantly made their

The Fort of Ekowe, relieved by Colonel Chelmsford's Column, 3 April. *Illustrated London News*

presence known. An estimated 5,000 Zulus were in the immediate vicinity, but, having learned from their experience at Rorke's Drift, were not inclined to attack such a well-defended position. Instead, they maintained a loose mobile ring of some 500 warriors to watch and harry the defenders in the hope that starvation would force them into the open where they would be vulnerable to attack.

Frequent heavy storms worsened the situation, while strong winds battered the fort. During one storm at the end of the month the Naval Brigade's position was all but washed away by a flash flood, which also seriously damaged the parapet. The livestock had exhausted all the grass near the fort and now had to be sent further afield to graze. This necessitated strong escorts drawn from the Buffs, the 99th and the Bluejackets, who disliked this tedious detail. The monotony was often broken by distant Zulus taunting and shouting insults at them.

As supplies diminished, the meagre rations, consisting of hard biscuits, mealies and stringy meat were further reduced. This depressing state of affairs was relieved somewhat by Colonel Pearson ordering the auction of rations left behind by the mounted volunteers. It is a measure of how desperate the besieged troops had become for a change from the monotonous food that certain defenders were prepared to pay highly inflated prices for items like a jar of pickles or a tin of cocoa. Pearson estimated that £7 worth of goods fetched in excess of £100! Looking further to raise flagging spirits, Colonel Pearson led a 500-strong night raid on 1 March to a Zulu kraal a few miles distant. Just before dawn, as they manoeuvred into position, a lone Zulu then raised the alarm. Nevertheless, the faltering attack commenced. Although 62 huts were burned and the artillery inflicted some casualties, Pearson's men had to make a fighting retreat for several hours before they reached the fort.

The next day brought a more lasting boost to morale. One of the mounted vedettes noticed a distant bright flashing light coming from the direction of the Lower Drift. It took a while to realize that it was an improvised heliograph sending out a signal to establish communications with Eshowe. At last Pearson and the garrison were informed that the Zulus had not overrun Natal and that help could soon be on the way. Although the heliograph was available, no signalling equipment had been used to date in this war. By using a mirror borrowed from a local settler, the men on the Fort Pearson promontory were able to establish contact. In response, the Eshowe garrison tried a variety of unsuccessful signalling methods ranging from a large moveable screen that sent Morse code messages to making a hot air balloon that was expected to drift all the way to the border. In the end, they were able to fashion their own heliograph, which was successful. It took four frustrating

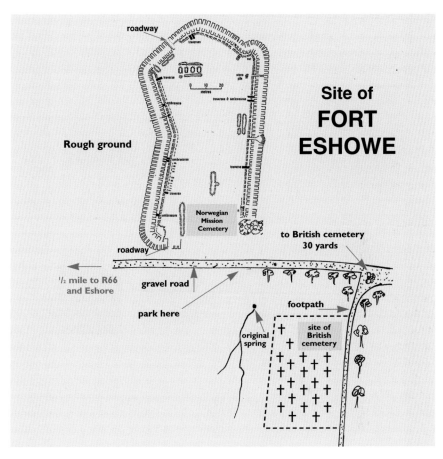

Site of
FORT
ESHOWE

days to get a cloud-interrupted message through to Pearson that his wife had given birth to a son. It also advised him that a 1,000-strong column would be setting off on 13 March to relieve him.

Participants
The total number of fighting men was initially over 5,000; this was reduced to less than half. Surplus troops and civilians were returned to Fort Pearson before the Zulus surrounded Eshowe.
Imperial: The Coastal (No. 1 Column) commanded by Colonel Pearson, which included; Royal Artillery, Royal Engineers, 3rd Regiment (The Buffs), 99th Regiment (Duke of Edinburgh's), The Naval Brigade from HMS *Active* and 2nd Sqd. Mounted Infantry.

Colonial: Natal Hussars, Stanger Mounted Rifles, Victoria Mounted Rifles and the 1st and 2nd Battalions NNC. In addition, 620 civilians were employed to drive the 384 ox wagons.
Zulus: Local Zulu amabutho under the command of Prince Dabulamanzi.

How to find it: From Durban. Proceed along the **N2** north from Durban. Cross the Tugela River, take the **R102** to Eshowe. On the approach to Eshowe, do not take the left turn into the town, but continue a short distance on the **R66** until reaching an obvious crossroads next to a petrol station. Take the right-hand turn, which immediately becomes a dirt road. Follow this road for about three-quarters of a mile. The actual fort is situated behind the Norwegian cemetery, which is clearly signposted. The British cemetery is 100 yards further along the road and hidden by trees; take the first footpath to the right. After about 25 yards the cemetery can be seen to the right of the path. At the time of writing the site was in a state of disrepair and overgrown.

Distinguishing features: Sadly, both the fort and cemetery are often in a state of disrepair. The sole distinguishing feature of the site is the signpost on the dirt road to the Norwegian cemetery, which is a civilian burial ground, and the overgrown remains of the ramparts and trenches.

Points of interest
➤ Site of Fort Eshowe.
➤ British cemetery.
➤ Direction to Fort Nongqayi. This is situated in the nearby town of Eshowe and relates to the Zulu Uprising of 1906. It has a fine museum with many interesting Zulu War exhibits. The fort has a pleasant car park with picnic and refreshment facilities.

Recommendations
• Time permitting, visit the town of Eshowe and the museum at Fort Nongqayi.

Gingindlovu, 2 April 1879

Overview
This battlefield marks the location where Chelmsford met with the Zulus as he advanced to relieve the besieged post at Eshowe. The garrison at Eshowe had been surrounded since the first invasion in January and it was essential for Chelmsford to lift the Zulu siege.

Lord Chelmsford's plan

Apart from the embarrassment of having so many of his first invasion force trapped at Eshowe, they were running out of supplies and Chelmsford urgently needed its 2,500 men and 384 wagons for his second invasion of Zululand. In order to relieve Eshowe, Chelmsford mounted and commanded a force of 5,700 troops, including 2,300 black auxiliaries. He referred to the force as the 'Eshowe Relief Column'.

The battlefield site was originally on open land, slightly elevated above the surrounding countryside with excellent views across the Nyezane valley towards the hills at Eshowe, some ten miles (16 km) to the north. Today the site is part of a large sugar cane farm and little can be seen of the site itself. The British cemetery, which was built adjacent to the battlefield, is usually well maintained. It is from the cemetery that the best overview can be obtained, both of the battlefield and towards Eshowe. There is a fine marble monument to those who lost their lives during the battle. It is located between the main road and the dirt road leading to the cemetery.

Battle account

During the night of 1 April the force went into a well-defended square-shaped defensive position as large numbers of Zulus had been seen approaching. At just after 6am the Zulu left horn, consisting of two columns of warriors, attacked the camp at its most north-easterly point and then fell heavily on the British across the north face. As this attack was being repulsed, the Zulu right horn then attacked the west face and rear of the British position. Due to the heavy rifle volley-fire together with the destruction caused by the Gatling gun, the attack was repulsed; the waiting Zulu reserves, who had watched the battle from a nearby hillside, then withdrew. Once the Zulus had found themselves unable to force a way in, they lay in the long grass on all sides, keeping up a heavy but inaccurate return fire. At last Chelmsford judged the moment right to send out his mounted men, who drove the Zulus away from the laager, and then in full retreat towards the river. In the aftermath of Isandlwana, feelings were running high among the British and the mounted men cut down exhausted and wounded warriors without mercy.

Colonel Northey was killed during the battle. There is a memorial to him in the cemetery, but his body was brought home to England at the request of his relatives. One young Zulu boy managed to penetrate the British line only to be sat upon by a marine; the lad later joined the Royal Navy. It was at this battle that officers first questioned the efficacy of the Martini-Henry rifle, as most Zulus had been killed within the 200-yard marker, although the British had opened fire at 600 yards.

THE BATTLE OF GINGINDLOVU

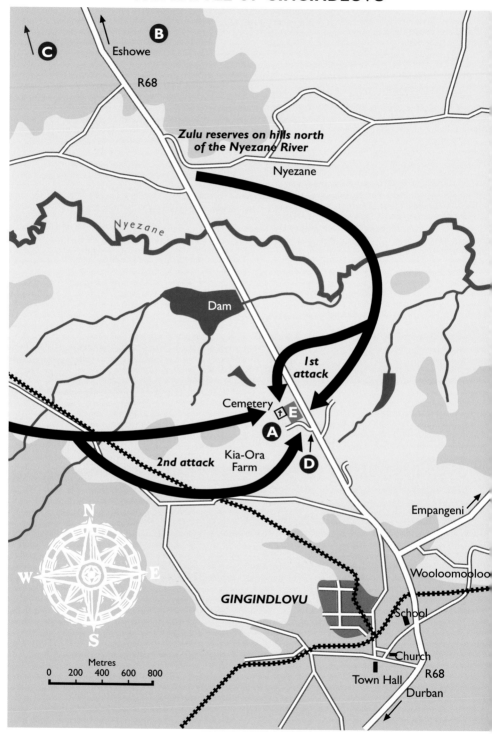

The Battle of Gingindlovu, as it became known, showed how much Chelmsford had learned from his mistakes at Isandlwana. There were no more open formations and no more exposed flanks. Instead, there was a solid concentration of men, which met the Zulu on every side, and in turn demonstrated the one great Zulu weakness – its inability to respond to concentrated firepower. Not that the Zulu attacks were not courageous. The first attack, on the front face, came so close that one Zulu commander was actually killed touching the Gatling, while other attacks reached within twenty yards before being driven back.

By mid-morning the battle was over. Rather than risk his entire column on the final leg to Eshowe, Chelmsford set out on the morning of 3 April with a light flying column, leaving the rest at the laager. The road lay up a steep incline, past the Nyezane battlefield, and the march proved gruelling on a hot day, but early in the evening the first troops reached Eshowe and were cheered in by the garrison.

Participants
Imperial: Commanded by Lieutenant General Lord Chelmsford. The Ist Brigade under Colonel Law included units from the Royal Artillery, Naval Brigade (HMSs *Shah* and *Tenedos*) 91st Highlanders, 3rd Regiment The Buffs, 99th Duke of Edinburgh's Regiment. 2nd Brigade under Lieutenant Colonel Pemberton included units from the Royal Artillery, Naval Brigade from HMS *Boadicea*, 57th West Middlesex Regiment and the 60th Rifles. Total: 3,390 white officers and men.
Colonial: 4th and 5th Battalions NNC. Total: 2,280 black troops.
Casualties: 2 officers and 9 men were killed, with 4 officers and 46 men wounded.
Zulu: The total Zulu force is estimated at 12,000, excluding an unknown number of reserves, and consisted of 6 amabutho under the command of Somopho, supported by Prince Dabulamanzi.
Casualties: Not less than 1,200 men; most were killed during the post-battle rout.

Points of interest
Ⓐ The cemetery. Colonel Northey's remains were taken to England for re-burial.
Ⓑ Fort Eshowe is 12 miles (20 km) to the north along the **R68**.
Ⓒ The battlefield of Nyezane is 10 miles (16 km) to the north along the R68 and is clearly visible to the north next to the road.
Ⓓ The battlefield memorial, next to the road/track junction.
Ⓔ The British Square.

Battle of Gingindlovu. *Illustrated London News*

Location: The nearest town is Gingindlovu, which has the usual facilities of an average-sized town. Gingindlovu lies on the **R102** and is 90 miles (150 km) north of Durban.

How to find it:

Route 1. **From Durban. Route 68.** Take either the **R102** or the **N2** motorway north from Durban. If travelling by motorway, take the first exit to Gingindlovu, which brings one onto the **R102**. Follow the signs to Gingindlovu. Remain on the **R102** avoiding the town centre. Within a few hundred yards, take the left fork to Eshowe, the **R68**. The battlefield is only

After the Battle of Gingindlovu. *Illustrated London News*

one mile (1.6 km) from Gingindlovu and is situated on the left side of the road. A battlefield sign, stone memorial and the name of the farm, Kia-Ora, mark the entrance. Take this turning off the main road and follow the signs to the cemetery, which is 100 yards along the track.

Route 2. **From Eshowe. Route 68.** Follow the **R68** southwards towards Gingindlovu until the route crosses the Nyezane stream. From this point the battlefield is only ³⁄₄ of a mile (1 km) further on and is situated on the right. A battlefield sign and the name of the farm, Kia-Ora, mark the entrance. Take this turning off the main road and follow the signs to the cemetery, which is 100 yards along the track.

Distinguishing features: The only obvious feature of the battlefield is the prominent leaning pine tree next to the battlefield. This tree can easily be seen from both directions and in early 2003 it was a good marker point. Sadly, so much has changed since the battle. The battlefield is located in sugar cane fields, however, the cemetery is usually well maintained. A reasonable view of the battlefield can be gained from the cemetery itself.

Recommendations
• Have a walk around the cemetery but do spray legs and ankles against ticks if walking around in long grass. It is not possible to explore the battlefield unless the sugar cane has been cut.
• Do not walk among newly planted cane without the permission of the farm owners.

Part Three

Re-invasion and Conquest of Zululand

Prior to the second invasion the British suffered further defeats at the hands of the Zulus at Ntombe and Hlobane in the north. At Hlobane the same amabutho that had triumphed at Isandlwana just two months earlier utterly defeated a large British mounted force under Lieutenant Colonel Buller. The following day, flushed with victory, they moved on to attack Colonel Wood's entrenched position at Khambula, only to suffer a serious defeat. In early April the Zulu force that had surrounded Pearson's column at Eshowe was defeated at Gingindlovu. At opposite ends of the country, the Zulus had been broken and their total casualties from those three battles numbered over 3,000 dead, with countless numbers wounded. All the strategic advantages that King Cetshwayo had won at Isandlwana were lost and the tide of war turned decisively against him.

The King tried to re-open diplomatic contacts with the British in a final attempt to discover what terms they would accept for peace, but both Chelmsford and Sir Bartle Frere needed a decisive victory to avenge Isandlwana. With the Zulu capacity to mount an offensive now broken, Chelmsford was able to mount a fresh invasion of Zululand.

Lord Chelmsford's plan

For the second invasion of Zululand, Chelmsford planned on making a two-pronged attack using two divisions. The first division would follow the coastline northwards into Zululand using troops from Pearson's Coastal Column, now under the command of Major General H.H. Crealock, an experienced officer whose younger brother, John North Crealock, was Chelmsford's Military Secretary. Chelmsford planned that the second Division would advance from the north-west, following roughly the line of the old Centre Column but avoiding the battlefield of Isandlwana, where the dead still lay unburied. This force was composed of troops fresh out from England. It was commanded by another new arrival, Major General Newdigate, although Chelmsford

*himself accompanied this column, and Newdigate, like Glyn before him, found himself
with little real opportunity to exercise his authority. A new cavalry division,
consisting of the 1st (King's) Dragoon Guards and 17th Lancers commanded by Major
General Marshall, was to be attached to the Second Division. Evelyn Wood's column
was re-designated the Flying Column. Its orders were to join with the Second Division
and advance in tandem with it to Ulundi.*

Chelmsford's advance began on 31 May and by this time he had become
increasingly resolved in his determination to bring the war to a conclusion by
any means. Where the soldiers met with any resistance they burnt Zulu
homesteads and drove off any cattle they found.

On 1 June a further disaster occurred when the Zulus killed the Prince
Imperial of France. The young prince had been confined to camp following his
over-enthusiasm for giving chase to Zulus without authority. On the morning
of 1 June he had persuaded Colonel Harrison to allow him to accompany a
small sketching party led by an experienced officer, Lieutenant Carey. During
a break from sketching the party made coffee in a deserted Zulu homestead,
only to be ambushed by a Zulu scouting party. The Prince and two troopers
were killed and Lieutenant Carey was subsequently court-martialled, and
found 'guilty', but this finding was not confirmed. With Isandlwana still fresh
in everyone's mind, the British press and public once again subjected
Chelmsford to enormous criticism. Carey's career was in tatters, although,
unbeknown to Carey, he had already been promoted to the rank of Captain.

At the end of June Chelmsford established camp on the banks of the White
Mfolozi River while a flurry of last-minute diplomatic activity by the Zulu
King took place, but Chelmsford was not moved by Cetshwayo's pleas.
Meanwhile, the decision had been taken in Britain to replace Chelmsford with
Sir Garnet Wolseley, who arrived in South Africa on 23 June. Chelmsford
desperately wanted to take 'battle honours' with a final victory, as did
Wolseley, who unsuccessfully tried to reach the front to take over command.
Wolseley sent Chelmsford a series of telegrams to stall the British advance,
which Chelmsford skilfully ignored.

At first light on 4 July 1879 Chelmsford led the Second Division and Flying
Column across the Mfolozi River towards the waiting Zulu Army. They
defeated the Zulus at Ulundi in a forty-minute battle dominated by the
Gatling machine gun. Ulundi was burned but King Cetshwayo escaped; he
was eventually captured on 28 August although some skirmishing continued
into September in the northern parts of the territory. The Battle of Ulundi was
taken to mark the end of major hostilities. Chelmsford handed over his
command to Wolseley and the British prepared to withdraw their army and
implement a plan for the settlement of Zululand.

Prince Imperial Memorial

Overview

Having lost the war with Prussia at the Battle of Sedan in 1870, Napoleon III was taken prisoner, while his wife, the Empress Eugènie, and their young son Louis, the Prince Imperial, fled to England. Napoleon was later exiled to England where he died on 9 January 1873. The Prince Imperial continued his interest in matters military and completed his education by attending the Woolwich Royal Academy where Artillery and Engineer officers were trained. He graduated seventh out of thirty-four officer cadets in 1875. Apart from occasional military exercises, Louis then began to languish. Being a French national, he could not carry a British commission. He applied to the Emperor Franz Josef to be able to join the Austrian Army, but was refused.

The Zulu War came as a gift to the young prince. He formally applied to the Duke of Cambridge for permission to go to South Africa and, after the direct intervention of his mother and Queen Victoria, permission was granted; he was allocated to Lord Chelmsford's staff as a civilian observer. It soon became apparent to Lord Chelmsford that Louis was irresponsible and headstrong, and, after several incidents of Louis breaking ranks to chase after Zulus, careful instructions were given to senior officers to curtail his impetuosity. On 1 June 1879 Louis persuaded Colonel Harrison to allow him to accompany a mapping patrol to reconnoitre the following day's campsite. Lieutenant Carey of the Quartermaster General's staff led the patrol of six troopers of Bettington's Horse, although for part of the journey they were initially accompanied by Major Grenfell, a senior staff officer, (he later became Field Marshal Lord Grenfell). The area of the proposed campsite was the river beyond Itelezi Hill.

Battle account

The party rode for eight miles (13 km) along the ridge towards the Ityotyozi Valley where Major Grenfell left the party to report to his new post at Itelezi Hill. At 12.20pm the party halted on a hilltop overlooking the river. Less than one mile (1.6 km) away, they observed an apparently deserted Zulu kraal next to a field of tall maize. Carey finished his map and the Prince Imperial gave orders for the men to off-saddle for a quarter of an hour. The prince then suggested that the whole party should descend into the valley to the Zulu huts where they could obtain water from the nearby river and make coffee. As the party descended the hill they were watched by a small Zulu scouting party who began to approach the group under cover of the maize field.

The kraal consisted of five huts next to the maize field; the ashes in the fireplace were still warm and a dog was seen nearby. The men off-saddled their horses and a guide was posted as sentry; a fire was lit and coffee was

137

L'AMBASSADEUR DE FRANCE

1951

1879   1979

1ᴱᴿ JUIN 1979
CENTENAIRE DE LA MORT DU
PRINCE IMPERIAL
CÉLÉBRÉ PAR L.L.A.A.I.I LE PRINCE
ET LA PRINCESSE NAPOLÉON
EN PRÉSENCE

The Prince Imperial Memorial with British graves behind. *Adrian Greaves collection*

Graves of Troopers Abel and Rogers, killed alongside the Prince Imperial.
Adrian Greaves collection

The lonely memorial of the Prince Imperial and British graves.
Adrian Greaves collection

brewed. The Prince and Carey discussed their maps and chatted in French, which Carey spoke fluently. At about 3.30pm the guide appeared and waved his hand towards the mealie field. Corporal Grubb interpreted for the guide and informed the party that the guide had seen a Zulu in the maize field. The Prince gave the order for the men to gather and re-saddle their horses, but it took some ten minutes before they were ready. Carey mounted his horse as the Prince gave the order to mount; at that moment a volley of rifle fire crashed out from the maize field, a distance of only thirty yards, and then the Zulus charged the group. Their horses were startled; they reared and began to bolt with the riders desperately trying to mount. Troopers Abel and Rogers fell severely wounded or dead, Carey controlled his horse and pointed it away from the kraal, from which it fled at a gallop, closely followed by the remainder of the party, or so Carey thought. The Prince tried to mount his horse by vaulting into the saddle but the holster strap he grabbed snapped under the strain. He fell heavily to the ground and, although dazed, managed to regain his feet as the Zulus closed with him. He ran towards a dry river bed and faced the Zulus; he drew his revolver and fired several shots before a spear struck him in the thigh. The Prince withdrew the spear to use as a weapon, but the Zulus overwhelmed him. He sustained seventeen assegai wounds, all to his front. The black guide was also quickly caught and killed.

Two hours later Lieutenant Carey reported to Lord Chelmsford that the Prince Imperial was dead. The immediate effect on the British establishment and the public was dramatic – as dramatic as the news of the defeat at Isandlwana. Carey was court-martialled and sent back to England under escort to await the result; but the findings were never confirmed. The British press championed Carey as an innocent scapegoat and he was released back to his own regiment, then serving in India. He died in 1883 while still serving in India.

Captain J. Carey 98th Regiment, of unfortunate history in Zululand, has, we regret to hear, died under mysterious circumstances in India, a victim of much persecution. Army and Navy Gazette

The body of the Prince Imperial was carefully transported to England for burial. For a full account of the death of the Prince Imperial, see *With his Face to the Foe* by Ian Knight. The subject is also covered in various Journals of the AZWHS.

Participants
The Prince Imperial, attending in his private capacity with the staff of Lord Chelmsford; Lieutenant Jaheel Brenton Carey, 98th Regiment, six Troopers of Bettington's Horse and a black guide.
Imperial survivor: Lieutenant Carey, 98th Regiment.
Colonial survivors: Sergeant Willis, Corporal Grubb and Troopers Le Tocq, and Cochrane.

Casualties: The Prince Imperial, Troopers Abel and Rogers, 1 Zulu scout.
Zulus: Mixed scouting party consisting of iNgobamakhosi and uMbonambi warriors.
Casualties: No known casualties.

Location: The site of the Prince Imperial memorial is in an isolated valley adjacent to the Ityotyozi River. (Jojosi River on modern road maps).

How to find it: As this site is difficult to find, it would be worthwhile taking a guide.
From Dundee. Take the **R68** eastwards for a distance of 27 miles (45 km) to the town of Nqutu. In the centre of the town, go straight on at the crossroads and take the dirt road towards Maduladula and Nondweni. You then have a choice of two routes.
Better road. Stay on this road for 12 miles (20 km) until reaching a T-junction, turn left. From this point, the Prince Imperial Monument is signposted. After two miles (3.2 km) take the next turn left towards Esigodini, which is signposted to the memorial. As the road crosses the river, the memorial is directly in front.
Rough road. After about 3 miles (5 km) you will see power pylons parallel to the road. At this point there is an unsigned dirt road to the left. Follow this route for about 5 miles (8 km). It crosses two streams before reaching the river. As the road crosses the river, the memorial is directly to the left front.

Distinguishing features: From about one mile away, it is possible to see an isolated clump of trees next to six Zulu huts.

Points of interest
➤ The memorial is set within a low walled cemetery. The stone that marks the actual memorial, known as the 'Victoria Cross', was erected by Major Stabb of the 32nd Regiment on the orders of Sir Garnet Wolseley. Curiously, a memo from Buckingham Palace, dated 28 May 1880 states, 'No orders have been given by the Queen to the Governor of any Colony to erect a cross to the late Prince Louis Napoleon'.
➤ The graves of Troopers Abel and Rogers are behind the Prince Imperial memorial.

Recommendations:
• This is an isolated site that can only be reached by motor vehicle. There is a site warden who will produce the visitors' book for signature.
• Visitors to the site, due to its isolated position, are rare and, as such, will attract much curious attention from the local children.
• Take a reliable and up-to-date local road map or a guide.

Ulundi, 4 July 1879

Overview

This battlefield marks the location of the final military defeat of the Zulu Army.

Lord Chelmsford's plan

Chelmsford began with the second invasion of Zululand on 3 June 1879, one day after the Prince Napoleon's body was found. There were two main Divisions invading Zululand, Chelmsford to the north and Major General Crealock's 1st Division along the coast. Crealock was so badly hampered by the rivers blocking his route and by his ponderous fortification of every bivouac that his column became known as 'Crealock's crawlers'. On 23 June, Lord Wolseley arrived in Durban to take over from Chelmsford, who avoided his signals, even his direct order not to engage the Zulus. By 2 July the 2nd Division was concentrated less than 5 miles (8 km) from Ulundi where they built Fort Nolela, sometimes mistakenly referred to as Fort Victoria. Wolseley telegraphed to Chelmsford, 'Concentrate your forces immediately, undertake no operations and flash back your moves. Astonished at not hearing from you.'

Chelmsford merely acknowledged receipt of the message.

King Cetshwayo made desperate attempts to sue for peace, sending pleas, the Prince Imperial's sword, Martini-Henry rifles collected at Isandlwana, ivory and placatory gifts of cattle but all were refused by Chelmsford. On the 3 July Lieutenant Colonel Buller was dispatched with a strong mounted force to reconnoitre a possible site for the final battle with the Zulus. Uncharacteristically, Buller was led into a carefully prepared Zulu ambush near the Mbilane stream where a number of soldiers were wounded and several were unhorsed from their mounts. Captain D'Arcy, Lord Beresford and Sergeant O'Toole went back into the fray to rescue their fallen comrades and received the Victoria Cross for their bravery. Private Raubenheim was killed in the action and his body was badly mutilated. On the day of the battle, the newly reconstituted 1/24th Regiment was held in reserve, two companies at Fort Marshall and five companies at Fort Nolela. The regiment was displeased at not being able to avenge their defeat at Isandlwana, but Chelmsford was fully aware that, being fresh replacements from the UK, they were inexperienced in warfare.

After the battle the Royal Artillery shelled Cetshwayo's homestead before it was sacked and burned. Contrary to expectations, there was, according to one officer, 'no treasure worth looting'. Bishop Colenso was more acerbic in his observations on the defeat of the Zulus; he wrote that 'the battle of Ulundi was not important to the Zulus'. It was the signal victory that Chelmsford so

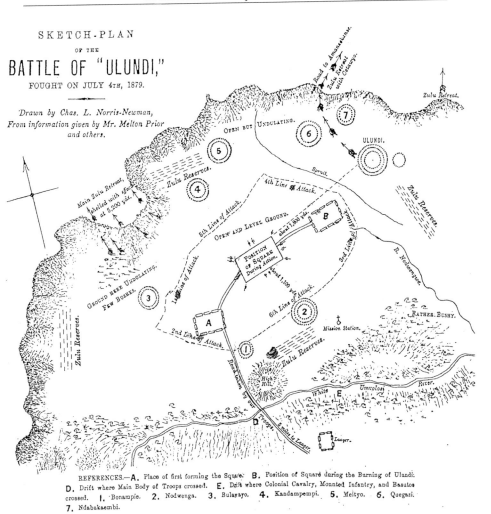

SKETCH-PLAN

OF THE

BATTLE OF "ULUNDI,"

FOUGHT ON JULY 4TH, 1879.

Drawn by Chas. L. Norris-Newman,
From information given by Mr. Melton Prior
and others.

REFERENCES.—**A.** Place of first forming the Square. **B.** Position of Square during the Burning of Ulundi. **D.** Drift where Main Body of Troops crossed. **E.** Drift where Colonial Cavalry, Mounted Infantry, and Basutos crossed. **1.** Bonampie. **2.** Nodwenga. **3.** Bulawayo. **4.** Kandampempi. **5.** Meityo. **6.** Quegazi. **7.** Ndabakaembi.

desperately sought and, with the battle won, the British began to withdraw from Zululand. On 24 July, as the last of Chelmsford's force were approaching Natal, the AbaQulusi Zulus again sought to attack the British; King Cetshwayo refused them permission. Skirmishing continued in the north into September but the battle of Ulundi is generally accepted as constituting the end of military operations. He remained a fugitive until he was finally captured on 28 August 1879. He was a prisoner of the British until 1883 when, at the request of Queen Victoria, he returned to Zululand.

Battle account

At 6am on the morning of 4 July 1879 the British set off from their overnight campsite around Fort Nolela and crossed the White Mfolozi River unopposed. Chelmsford duly ordered the advancing column to 'form square', and then, in a tightly packed column, the British moved towards a previously reconnoitred small rise in the middle of the Mahlabatini Plain. It was obvious to Chelmsford that the Zulus were reluctant to fight, but, by advancing his column towards King Cetshwayo's royal homestead, he successfully provoked the battle he so desperately sought to save his reputation. With the King's homestead in view three miles (5 km) distant, the Zulus began to form up in opposition to the advancing column, which then turned to face the advancing Zulus. The British gained the high ground and settled down to await the Zulu charge. The Zulus continued to show a reluctance to fight, so at 8.20 a.m. Buller and his mounted troops moved out of the square and provoked the massed Zulu ranks with several volleys of gunfire. The Zulus charged and Buller withdrew back into the square.

At about 9am the Zulu Warriors, already disheartened by previous losses, were disorganized in their attacks, which soon faltered under withering Martin-Henry volleys, fire from the Royal Artillery's 7-pounder and 9-pounder guns and from two Gatling guns. Although the Zulus managed to get to within thirty yards of the British line, they could not sustain their attack. The Zulu reserves watched the attack falter and began to leave the battlefield, which added to the growing confusion among the Zulu warriors. With the Zulu attack controlled, Chelmsford again ordered Buller and his mounted troops, along with the 17th Lancers, out of the square to harass the retreating Zulus. The route continued for another two hours and for several miles in all directions until most of the fleeing Zulus had either escaped or been killed.

The infantry, who carried a hundred rounds per man, kept up a fire like one continual blaze, but notwithstanding this the Zulus got to within fifty or sixty yards of us, and I could see them on one side breaking their assegais short for a final rush, so you can form some sort of an idea as to the sort of metal they are, but the 9-pounders put case into them at this distance, which did not seem to agree with them. NCO 17th Lancers.

The Zulus did not fight with 'the same spirit' at Ulundi as hitherto 'because they were frightened'. Mehlokazulu kaSihayo quoted by Norris-Newman 1880

In a final act, Chelmsford ordered the destruction by shellfire and burning of King Cetshwayo's royal homestead. With Chelmsford's fighting square still intact, orders were given for the column's dead to be buried and the casualties tended to, the column then marched on for half a mile to the Mbilane stream. After eating a midday meal, the column retraced its steps back to the camp near the White Mfolozi River. The final battle of the Zulu War had lasted just ninety minutes.

Before the Battle of Ulundi. *The Graphic*

On the march to Ulundi. *The Graphic*

Ulundi

4 July 1879 – Charge of The 17th Lancers

Artist, Jason Askew, Anglo-Zulu War Historical Society

The Battle of Ulundi. *The Graphic*

Participants

The total force amounted to 4,132 white troops and 1,009 blacks troops.

Imperial: Lieutenant General Lord Chelmsford, with the 2nd Division commanded by Major General Newdigate, commanded the column. The Flying Column (formally the Northern Column) was commanded by Brigadier General Sir Evelyn Wood. The 2nd Division included units of the King's Dragoon Guards, the 17th (Duke of Cambridge's Own) Lancers, Royal Artillery, Royal Engineers, the 2/21st Royal Scots Fusiliers, the 94th Regiment, and the 58th (Rutland) Regiment. The Flying Column also included units from the Royal Artillery, Royal Engineers, 1/13th Light Infantry, the 80th Regiment, the 90th Light Infantry, the Army Medical Department, Hospital Corps, Mounted Infantry and the Army Staff Corps.

Colonial: 2nd Bn. NNC, Shepstone's Horse, Bettington's Horse, Wood's Irregulars, Natal Pioneers, Transvaal Rangers, Frontier Light Horse, Baker's Horse, Natal Light Horse and the Natal Native Horse.

Casualties: 2 officers and 10 men were killed, with 1 officer and 69 men wounded.

Zulu: The total Zulu force was estimated at 20,000 warriors and consisted of elements of various amabutho under the command of Ziwedu, Cetshwayo's brother. He was supported by three battle-experienced indunas, Mnyamana Buthelezi (the Zulu Prime Minister), Zibhebhu Ka Mapitha and Ntshingwayo Khoza (commanded at Isandlwana).

Casualties: Not less than 1,450 dead warriors were found around the battlefield. Many of these would have been killed during the rout.

Location: The nearest town is Ulundi, five miles (8 km) away, which has all the usual facilities of a small town.

How to find it:

Route 1. **From Durban.** Take either the **R102** to Gingindlovu or the new **N2** motorway north from Durban. Take the first exit to Eshowe and Gingindlovu, which brings one onto the route **R102**. Follow the signs to Gingindlovu and Eshowe. On approaching the town of Gingindlovu, remain on the **R102** avoiding the town centre. Within a few hundred yards, take the left fork to Eshowe, the **R66**. Follow this road for a further 72 miles (120 km), passing through Eshowe and Melmoth until the high plain overlooking Ulundi is reached. Take the obvious right-hand turn off the **R66** towards Ulundi. Descending from the high plateau, the road crosses the White Mfolozi River and on entering the outskirts of Ulundi, take the right-hand turn that is signposted to Mangosuthu Buthelezi Airport and to the battlefield. Stay on this road for half a mile and the battlefield will appear on the left-hand side of the road. The domed building in the middle of the site indicates the battlefield. The British cemetery is at the eastern end of the fenced area.

Route 2. **From Isandlwana or Rorke's Drift. Route 68.** On joining the **R68**, head east towards Babanango, 40 miles (61km) and Melmoth, a further 25 miles (42km). On reaching the junction with the **R66** as you approach Melmoth, take the left turn towards Ulundi. The route leads to the high plain overlooking Ulundi. Once this is reached, take the obvious right-hand turn off the high ground towards Ulundi. Descending down a long hill, the road crosses the White Mfolozi River and, on entering the outskirts of Ulundi, takes the right-hand turn that is signposted to Mangosuthu Buthelezi Airport and to the battlefield. Stay on this road for half a mile and the battlefield will appear on the left-hand side of the road. The battlefield can easily be identified by the domed building in the middle of the site. The British cemetery is at the eastern end of the fenced area.

Distinguishing features: The most obvious feature of the battlefield is the domed memorial building in the centre of the battlefield. The shape of the British square is roughly marked out by the site's perimeter fence. Note the plaque on the wall in the domed memorial. For many years this was the only memorial to the Zulus who fell in the entire campaign.

Points of interest

❶ The battlefield memorial. The protected area is on the approximate location of Chelmsford's square.

❷ The route taken by Chelmsford's square.

❸ The British cemetery. This is at the far end of the battlefield square.

❹ The Ulundi Museum.

❺ The original site of King Cetshwayo's Royal homestead. Parts of it have been reconstructed in the original style.

❻ The site where the British column advanced to and had lunch – before returning to Fort Nolela.

❼ Where Buller's force was ambushed on 3 July, the day before the battle.

❽ Fort Nolela overlooking the White Mfolozi River.

Recommendations:

• Walk around the whole battlefield and visit the cemetery at the far end. The battlefield is very compact.

• After visiting the battlefield, continue for one mile (1.6 km) further along the dirt road, crossing the Mbilane stream, until you come to the Zulu Cultural Museum. Enter the museum compound with its large car park; tickets can be obtained from the orientation centre just inside the entrance gate.

• On the north side of the museum, visitors can walk round the original site of King Cetshwayo's homestead. The site of the massacre of Piet Retief and his men is only 12 miles (20 km) distant – see Mgungundhlovu.

After the Battle of Ulundi, bearing away the wounded. *The Graphic*

Ulundi Battlefield

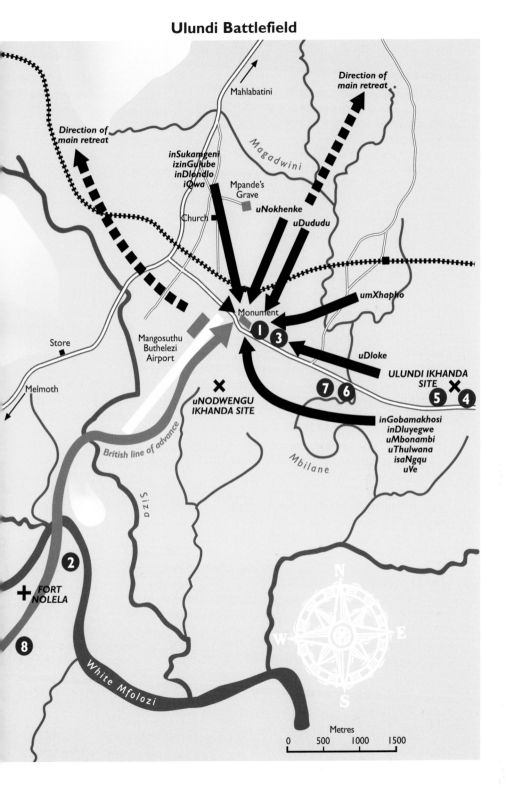

Post Ulundi

It fell to Lord Chelmsford's successor, Sir Garnet Wolseley, to oversee and then supervise the settlement of the defeated Zulus. They were informed that Zululand was to be divided into thirteen independent 'chiefdoms' each ruled by a Zulu chief selected and appointed by the British, each chief to have command under the overall supervision of a British 'resident'. The intention was to prevent any individual, of royal birth or otherwise, from ever reuniting the Zulus.

Cetshwayo was taken to Cape Town from where he frequently petitioned Sir H. Robinson to ask Queen Victoria to grant him an audience. He finally arrived in England in August 1882 and was presented to Queen Victoria at Osborne House on the Isle of Wight. Partly as a result of this meeting, steps were taken to return Cetshwayo to Zululand as King of the Zulus.

The chiefs were to abolish the formal Zulu military system and not obstruct any of their people who might wish to work in neighbouring territories. This requirement was especially destructive as it encouraged the migration of male Zulus to the diamond fields located to the north and west – and agricultural enterprise in the south. The Zulus were forbidden to import firearms or become involved in any form of trade that did not reach them through British-controlled Natal or the Transvaal. Capital punishment without trial was forbidden; land could not be sold or purchased without British permission and they were to keep the peace and apply the law according to the 'ancient laws and customs' of their people, so long as these laws did not offend the sensitivities of the British administrator. As a result of these unreasonable provisions, Zululand was plunged into a state of civil war as Zulu fought against Zulu, and more Zulu blood was spilled in the following period than in 1879.

Melmoth Osborn, an ex-Naval officer, was appointed as the British Resident Administrator, but the position lacked any real administrative or legislative authority, only diplomatic duties. It is possible that the 1879 settlement was deliberately designed to set Zulu against Zulu, the new borders of the country and the boundaries of the chiefdoms indiscriminately cutting across both the social and political groupings that had developed during the previous fifty years.

With regard to Cetshwayo's relatives, Wolseley gave instructions that members of the royal house should abandon their homes and move into Dunn's territory, an order that was simply ignored as Dunn had 'sold' his erstwhile friend and benefactor, King Cetshwayo, 'down the river'. Wolseley further instructed the appointed chiefs to collect royal cattle and firearms and deliver them to the Resident. Of all Wolseley's dictums, this one most irritated the Zulus; after all, cattle were virtually the currency of the Zulu economy. Both directly and indirectly, Cetshwayo owned most of Zululand's cattle, which made him the wealthiest man in the kingdom. His royal herds were easily recognized by their whiteness as belonging to the King and, due to their large number; they were distributed among many royal households. King Cetshwayo died under tragic circumstances in 1884, following the Civil War of 1883/4, possibly poisoned by his cousin, the great Zulu general Zibhebhu Ka Maphitha. He was buried in a remote area near the Mome Gorge, the last refuge of the Zulus, where the last great struggle of the infamous Bambata uprising took place in 1906.

Wolseley's instructions merely gave those newly appointed chiefs who felt sufficiently confident a golden opportunity to seize the King's cattle and plunder from those Zulus who had previously been loyal to Cetshwayo.

Zululand remained in turmoil until 1906 when the Zulu Rebellion took place.

Emakhosini and Mgungundhlovu

Emakhosini

Also highly recommended is the beautiful valley of Emakhosini, which means 'The Place of the Kings'. Note that the location is sometimes shown as Makoseni on modern maps. A good-quality dirt road runs along the Emakhosini Valley that runs between Babanango joining **Route 68** and towards Ulundi joining **Route 66**. From the earliest times, the valley and surrounding area were occupied by many Zulu royal homesteads and seven important Zulu kings are buried here, including Zulu, Jama, Senzangakona and Dinuzulu; the burial place of Dinuzulu is now a National monument. Earlier Zulu chiefs are believed to be buried here but the location of their graves is uncertain.

Piet Retief Memorial and King Dingane's Royal Homestead at
Mgungundhlovu. (On R34 between Vryheid and Melmoth)
At the junction of the **R66** with the **R34,** take the **R34** for 2.5 miles (6 km) towards Vryheid and then turn left towards Babanango. Take the next turning left indicating the memorial and graves of Piet Retief, the Boer leader murdered by the Zulus in 1838. The site is 2 miles (4 km) along the gravel road immediately adjacent to King Dingane's royal homestead, Mgungundhlovu, which should also be visited. There is an orientation centre there with excellent parking, picnic and toilet facilities. The most spectacular approach is from Babanango. Take the R68 towards Melmoth; after 2.5 miles (4km) take the dirt road towards Denny Dalton for 12 miles (20km). Do not take the turning to Denny Dalton. On reaching the R34 junction turn right. You will see the site indicated.

Retief's visit to King Dingane, Mgungundhlovu

On 5 November 1837 the famous Voortrekker leader Piet Retief and his party of some sixty Boers approached Dingane's royal homestead at Mgungundhlovu in order to seek permission to settle in Zululand. Retief must have been impressed; the homestead consisted of a settlement containing over 2,000 huts each capable of housing a number of people and with another 300 huts for Dingane himself, his wives and his senior Indunas. He was even more impressed by the eight days of celebration, feasting, dancing and displays which seemed to go on endlessly and which must have exhausted Retief and his party.

At the end of the eighth day Dingane suddenly informed Retief that he would be granted permission to settle where he requested, subject only to Retief first recovering cattle that had been stolen from Dingane by a rival chief, Sikonyela. Retief accepted the arrangement and returned to his settlers who, without his permission, had begun to spread out towards the Tugela River. Other trekkers, encouraged by the promising news, were enthusiastically following across the Drakensberg Mountains in the hope of bountiful grazing. Retief gathered seventy of his best fighting men to undertake the mission against Sikonyela and left the main party in the care of the youths and elderly Boers who remained, though without instructions for the remaining families to laager or prepare defensive positions.

Within the week they arrived at Sikonyela's homestead, and, on the pretext of presenting him with a bracelet, snapped the chief into handcuffs and held him prisoner while the stolen cattle were collected. Sikonyela was then released and Retief headed back to Dingane in optimistic mood and with the recovered cattle. Prior to Retief's return to Mgungundhlovu on 3 February 1838, missionary Owen had observed an unusual number of young warriors arriving and also recorded in his diary rumours that all was not well as Dingane was obviously annoyed that Retief had permitted Sikonyela to live. Retief immediately returned the stolen cattle to an apparently appreciative Dingane, whereupon the celebratory feasting began. For some days Retief and his men were obliged to watch the continuous entertainment until, on 6 February, following an impressive display of horsemanship and firearm salvoes by the Boers, Retief was finally called to Dingane. In the presence of Dingane's senior Indunas, Dingane allegedly gave permission for the Boer settlement; everything promised by the King was apparently written down and then translated back into Zulu for the benefit of the King by Thomas Halstead, Retief's interpreter. The Boers' belief, supported by Missionary Owen, is that the document was then signed by Dingane and witnessed by the three most senior Indunas before Retief placed it in his leather pouch for safety.

As Retief was about to depart he and his men were invited to one final feast. Not wishing to appear discourteous or impatient, Retief reluctantly agreed. The Zulu Indunas reminded Retief that it was impolite for anyone to enter the King's enclosure with firearms and Retief readily agreed, so all their firearms were stacked outside the enclosure next to their horses.

The feast commenced and hundreds of young warriors began a series of dances. Suddenly Dingane rose to his feet and a chilling silence descended on the multitude. Dingane called out 'Babulaleni abathakathi' (Kill the wizards). Zulu folklore reveals a little-known event that would partly explain Dingane's treatment of Retief. The Boers had ridden their horses round Dingane's sleeping quarters, (a forbidden area) under cover of darkness. When challenged, the Boers denied responsibility but could not explain the horse-droppings and hoof-prints. The Zulus possibly thought the Boers might attempt to assassinate Dingane. Before the unsuspecting Boers realized what fate held for them, they were seized, bound hand and foot with leather throngs and dragged several hundred yards to the far exit of the homestead to the hill of execution. Missionary Owen was watching the whole event through his telescope just as a warrior arrived at his house with a message from the King to the effect that Owen and his family need have no fear for their lives.

At the hill of execution some Boers had their arms and legs broken with knobkerries before being beaten to death. Retief was made to watch, including that of his twelve-year-old son, before he too was executed. Owen wrote that he fainted from the shock, as did his wife.

Also murdered were the thirty or so black servants who accompanied the party. Rumours still exist that a number of Boer women were with the party and that they too were murdered. There is no known evidence that this was the case. The Zulus unsuccessfully chased a native retainer named Lomana who was in Retief's party, but he escaped the slaughter and died near Weenen in 1909. Dingane decreed that no Boer, woman or child, should survive on his land. Owen's next record reveals that, within two hours, a large impi was gathered and almost immediately departed the King's kraal .

Disaster was about to befall the unsuspecting Boer families gathering in the area now known as Bloukrans and Weenen, (which can easily be found between the modern towns of Estcourt and Colenso); all were totally unsuspecting and eagerly anticipated Retief's return with the promised permission to settle. Under cover of darkness, Dingane's impi approached the sleeping Boer families and then launched their attack.

By dawn the mutilated bodies of 531 elderly men, women, and children were spread over an area of twenty square miles. A handful of distraught souls desperately clambered back across the Drakensberg Mountains to raise the alarm. Dingane had set the stage for Boer retribution.

The Boers indeed took their revenge under the command of the famous leader Andries Pretorius. History tells us that he inflicted a terrible defeat upon the Zulus at the Battle of Blood River on 16 December 1838.

The site of Blood River battle is also worth visiting. It is just off the R33 between Dundee and Vryheid.

Part Four

The Main Players

The British

Lord Chelmsford

Lieutenant General Frederick Augustus Thesiger, or Lord Chelmsford as he became following his father's death, had his reputation seriously damaged when his inadequately defended camp at Isandlwana was overrun and laid waste by Cetshwayo's impis. Despite his eventual success in defeating the Zulus and the strenuous efforts of his friends in high places to absolve him of blame, Chelmsford is generally regarded as an unsuccessful commander.

Born in 1827, he was of German origin. His background, despite lacking much wealth, was conventional for a Victorian gentleman. His education at Eton was followed by the purchase of a commission, initially into the Rifle Brigade, and then into the Grenadier Guards. He was a conscientious and diligent officer at a time when most officers did not take much interest in their military duties. He was subsequently promoted to the rank of captain and appointed ADC to the commander of forces in Ireland. In 1855 he joined his regiment in the Crimea and thus missed the Battle of Inkerman, in which the Guards played so crucial a role. He was designated to a succession of staff duties and ended his posting to the Crimea as Deputy Assistant Quartermaster General.

A further promotion brought him the lieutenant-colonelcy of the 95th (2nd Bn. Sherwood Foresters) and it was with his new regiment that he sailed for India in 1858. By the time they arrived the Indian Mutiny had all but been suppressed, but they were involved in mopping-up operations in Central India during 1859. Chelmsford's reputation as a competent staff officer resulted in his appointment as Deputy Adjutant General.

When General Sir Robert Napier was ordered to mount an expedition against King Theodore of Abyssinia in 1868, he chose Chelmsford to be his Deputy Adjutant General. In a well-organized and successful expedition, the Anglo-Indian force suffered few casualties despite the potential for disaster. Chelmsford emerged from the campaign with much credit, being mentioned in despatches and being made Companion of the Bath for his tireless staff work. He was also appointed ADC to the Queen and made Adjutant General of India. This period of his life was to be his happiest and most successful, for he also married the daughter of an Indian Army general who eventually bore him four sons. It was also at this time that he became friendly with the Governor of Bombay, Sir Henry Bartle Frere, a man who would have considerable influence on Chelmsford's life. After sixteen years service in India, Chelmsford was recalled home. With little in the way of family wealth, the prospect of expensive entertaining befitting an officer of his rank was a constant source of worry to him.

When he was offered the post of Deputy Adjutant General at Horse Guards, he felt obliged to decline and made known his wish to take a command again in India, where the cost of living was much cheaper. Instead, he was promoted to Brigadier General commanding the 1st Infantry Division at Aldershot pending a suitable overseas posting.

It was fate that the vacancy he accepted occurred in South Africa and was, coincidentally, his first independent active service command in thirty-four years. He was able to renew his association with Sir Bartle Frere, now the High Commissioner for South Africa, and to share Frere's vision of a confederation of southern African states under British control.

When Chelmsford arrived at the Cape in February 1878 the fighting against the Xhosa rebels was entering its final stages. His subsequent experiences against a foe that relied on hit-and-run tactics, rather than becoming involved in a full-scale battle, coloured his opinion of the fighting capabilities of South African natives. Chelmsford did, however, show himself to be a commander who did not shirk hard work, often riding great distances over rugged country in the effort to break any remaining resistance. He was a commanding figure with his tall, spare frame, pleasant features, usually hidden by a black beard and bushy eyebrows.

The Xhosa Wars finally petered out in May of 1878 and Chelmsford felt that he had acquitted himself well. His handling of troops had been exemplary and he even earned the grudging respect of the generally ill-disciplined colonial volunteers.

During the Zulu War he was critical of many of the officers and officials and openly wished they could all be like Wood and Buller. Significantly he was irritated by Colonel Anthony Durnford's role on the Boundary Commission once it found in favour of the Zulus and he was to find further fault in Durnford's actions in the days leading up to the Invasion. In one particularly stinging rebuke, Chelmsford actually threatened to remove Durnford from his command. One can see that, in the aftermath of Isandlwana, Chelmsford would have had little compunction in laying the blame for his defeat on a despised, and now conveniently dead, subordinate officer. He kept his emotions firmly under control, until the enormity of the events at Isandlwana nearly crushed him, for he had no confidant to whom he could unburden his feelings. He wrote to his wife but her support and sympathy took many weeks to reach him.

The letters he wrote to Wood reveal much about his state of mind. Seeming to suffer from bi-polar depression, Chelmsford fluctuated between confidence and despair. He and Frere obviously discussed the option of resigning and Chelmsford accordingly wrote both to the Duke of Cambridge and to Colonel Frederick Stanley, the Secretary of State for War. In his letter to the latter he reveals that he had contemplated being replaced as far back as June 1878! He wrote '...the strain of prolonged anxiety & exertion, physical & mental, was even then telling on me - What I felt then, I feel still more now.'

The result was the appointment in May of Lieutenant General Sir Garnet Wolseley as both High Commissioner for South Eastern Africa and Commander-in-Chief of the Forces in South Africa.

Adding to Chelmsford's woes were the relentless personal attacks on him by the newspapers, which blamed him for the loss of the camp, despite the clean bill given him by the Court of Enquiry, which he had specially convened. Affecting disdain for the newspapers and in particular the ever-present war correspondents, Chelmsford was deeply hurt and shaken by the vitriolic attacks on his reputation, attacks which further eroded his confidence. His friends advised him to retire on health grounds but, with Wood's decisive victory at Khambula and the arrival of several regiments of Imperial troops, Chelmsford seemed to sufficiently recover his determination to defeat the Zulus.

He personally chose to lead the column to relieve Colonel Pearson's besieged force at Eshowe. At Gingindlovu Chelmsford and his staff had displayed the Victorian officers' disdain of enemy fire by remaining standing to encourage the troops, many of whom were newly arrived raw recruits. The result of such foolhardy exposure was that, although Chelmsford was not hit, Crealock was slightly wounded in the arm and lost his horse, while Captain Molyneux had two horses killed. As they constituted the high command, it seems an unnecessary risk to have taken.

With Eshowe relieved, the ever-present spectre of the unburied remains at

Lord Chelmsford. *Ron Sheeley collection*

Isandlwana was the next priority. Besides soothing his conscience, Chelmsford had a much more practical reason for sending a large burial party: their role was to recover the precious wagons of the slaughtered Central Column which he urgently needed for the re-invasion of Zululand. As his forces and supplies built up, so Chelmsford's confidence appeared to return. Once the invasion was under way, he moved cautiously, laagering his camp every night, building forts to protect his lines of communication and scouting well ahead. Nevertheless, it was on one of these map-making reconnaissances that another misfortune befell the luckless commander. During a routine reconnaissance by a small patrol, which included the Prince Louis Napoleon, a group of Zulus opened fire on the party and, in the scramble to safety, two troopers were shot from their horses and the Prince was caught and slain.

When the news broke in the British newspapers, the shock was even greater than that of the Isandlwana massacre. Chelmsford could not reasonably be blamed for the Prince's death but, following all the previous disasters, his culpability was implied.

Chelmsford then received the news that he was to be replaced by General Sir Garnet Wolseley, both a blow to his ego and a spur to his intention of personally defeating the Zulus in a final showdown. In the event it was a close-run thing. Wolseley arrived just too late to prevent Chelmsford disobeying Wolseley's previous direct order not to attack Cetshwayo. Chelmsford proceeded to inflict a crushing defeat on the Zulus at Ulundi, which allowed him to hand over his command on a high note.

In any event, and wishing to return home as soon as possible, Chelmsford journeyed to Cape Town, where he received an enthusiastic reception by a population for whom Ulundi had eradicated the memories of earlier disasters. He sailed home on the RMS *German* in the company of Wood and Buller, his most effective and reliable commanders.

Opinion at home had polarized. Disraeli refused to receive the Commander who had cost the country so much and brought discredit to the Government. Some newspapers continued to pillory Chelmsford, popular songs mocked him and even some of his fellow peers were critical. But it was those who really mattered, the Horse Guards and Queen Victoria, who rallied to his support.

Chelmsford was showered with honours. His rank of lieutenant general was confirmed and the Queen used her influence to have him appointed Lieutenant of the Tower. He later became a full general and Colonel of the Sherwood Foresters and then of the 2nd Life Guards.

After his retirement, honours still came Chelmsford's way. Queen Victoria appointed him Gold Stick, an honour that was carried over when her son,

Edward, succeeded her. He also made the ageing general a GCVO.

On 9 April 1905, at the age of seventy-eight, Lord Chelmsford had a seizure and died while playing billiards at the United Service Club. So died a man with many admirable attributes but who was thrust into a position for which he was not intellectually equipped. Instead of being a long-forgotten Victorian general, his name is still remembered as the man ultimately responsible for the Victorian Army's greatest military defeat.

Sir Bartle Frere

Henry Bartle Edward Frere was born in 1815 into a family of fourteen. He was educated in Bath and in 1834 went out to work for the East India Company in the Bombay presidency. In 1842 he was appointed private secretary to the Governor of Bombay and, after a spell of leave in England and Italy, he was appointed Resident at Sattara (1847-49), a Native state south of Bombay, being present at its annexation and becoming the Commissioner for Sattara thereafter (1849-50). In 1850, at the age of thirty-five, he was promoted to be Chief Commissioner for the newly pacified, but still unruly, province of Sind, with responsibility for the strategically important Bolan Pass, a post he held for the next nine years. In 1856 he took sick leave and sailed for England, before returning to India in March 1857 in time to play an active part in the suppression of the Indian Mutiny. He served on the Governor-General's (or Viceroy's) Council (1859-62) and as the 'legendary' Governor of Bombay (1862-67) before returning to England to serve on the Indian Council (1867-77). Known as a leading 'India hand', 'the most outstanding figure of the ten years after the mutiny,' a keen geographer (President of the Royal Geographical Society, 1873) and sanitary reformer in active partnership with Florence Nightingale, his wide interests included participation in the anti-slavery movement. This prompted Lord Granville to send him out to Zanzibar in 1873 to negotiate an anti-slavery treaty and his success there raised him to the rank of Privy Councillor. The royal connection resulted in his being chosen to shepherd the Prince of Wales on the Indian Tour of 1876, before Carnarvon finally asked him to take on the job of Confederation in South Africa as Governor (1877-80).

Frere was not the swaggering imperialist bully that his most vehement denigrators suggest. Rather he was a conscientious servant of an Empire he believed to be benevolent and who feared that it was about to be tested in a global war against a far worse alternative, Russia. To that end, he believed himself justified in breaking up a rival Zulu empire, which he felt had no other rationale for its existence than war for its own sake, lest it strike at a vulnerable imperial station independently but simultaneously with Russian naval forces.

Sir Bartle Frere. *Ron Sheeley collection*

Had Disraeli been less of a genius, and failed to persuade the Russians to withdraw, Frere might well have been pardoned, the ruin of Zululand by Garnet Wolseley avoided, the First Boer War averted, and Confederation pushed through by a sympathetic and competent administrator going on to serve as its first Viceroy. What is certain, however, is that the fate of the Zulus was decided by reference to factors residing primarily outside South Africa rather than within it. The defeat at Isandlwana and his subsequent recall ended a brilliant career and he died, broken and protesting his innocence, in 1885.

For further information see AZWHS Journal No. 8.

Evelyn Wood

One field officer who did emerge from the shambles of the Zulu War with his reputation enhanced was the commander of Number 1, the Left Flank Column, Brevet Colonel Henry Evelyn Wood. One of the most highly

Colonel Henry Evelyn Wood. *Adrian Greaves collection*

decorated officers of the Victorian era, Wood's career was rich in incident and bravery. He was born on 9 February 1838 at Cressing, near Braintree, Essex, into a clerical family. His father, Sir John Page Wood, had been the Chaplain and Private Secretary to Queen Caroline and his maternal grandfather was an Admiral.

When he was only nine Wood was sent to the newly founded public school, Marlborough College, which at that time resembled Dickens' *Dotheboys Hall*. A near-starvation diet and a brutal headmaster eventually provoked a mutiny amongst the pupils, during which some masters were attacked and the hated headmaster had his desk set alight. Pleading with his parents to take him away from this unenlightened establishment, Wood applied to join the Royal Navy. At the age of fourteen, he passed his entrance examination into the Royal Navy, joined HMS *Queen* and two years later graduated to midshipman.

When war with Russia was declared in 1854, HMS *Queen* was part of the fleet that bombarded Sevastopol as the Allies began their year-long siege of the city. Short of heavy artillery with which to shell the Russian defences, the Navy was called upon to send ashore a Naval Brigade to man their guns in the trenches. Commanding the 21-gun battery was the charismatic Captain William Peel, son of the former Prime Minister, Sir Robert Peel. Wood and a fellow midshipman, Edward St. John Daniel, became devoted to Captain Peel and were appointed aides-de-camp. Despite the terrible weather of the winter of 1854-55, they were constantly on duty in the trenches. Peel later recalled that Wood did not miss a day's duty in nine months. It was this sustained exposure to the percussive effects of cannon fire that undoubtedly contributed to Wood's incipient deafness.

During an artillery exchange the thatch of a powder magazine was set alight and, as nobody dared approach, young Wood climbed on the roof and managed to stamp out the fire. Peel often mentioned his exploits in despatches.

The following summer the Allies attempted a number of abortive attacks on the Russian defences. On 18 June the British made a suicidal assault on the Russia stronghold, the Redan, during which they suffered heavy casualties. The seventeen-year-old Wood carried a scaling ladder and was the only one to reach the Redan, despite being twice wounded by grapeshot. Peel was fulsome in his praise of his young ADC and recommended him for a Victoria Cross. As his friend and rival, Daniel, had also been recommended for the same action, during which he had bound up Peel's wounded arm, Wood was turned down. Instead, he was awarded the Légion d'Honneur and the Order of the Medjidie.

Wood was sent home to recuperate from his wounds and reflected on his future career. When he had recovered, he decided, having tasted the excitement of fighting on land, to resign his commission in the Navy and to apply to join the Army. His outstanding service at Sevastopol gained him a cornetcy without purchase in the 13th Light Dragoons.

Upon joining this regiment, he was immediately posted back to the Crimea as part of the reinforcements to fill the losses incurred during the Charge of the Light Brigade. Unfortunately for Wood, he was struck down with both typhoid and pneumonia and was hospitalized at Scutari for five months. This was just the start of his life-long battle against sickness and accidents, for there has rarely been an officer who was so unfortunate with his health. During the next fifty years, Wood was inflicted with malaria, dysentery, sunstroke, neuralgia, deafness, toothache, eye problems and, to crown it all, ingrowing toenails.

Besides his Crimean wounds, he was further wounded by gunshot during the Ashanti War. His penchant for daring escapades led him to receive severe facial injuries after a giraffe, that he attempted to ride, trod on him. He suffered further injuries when he was scratched by a tiger, and broke his nose and collarbone when his horse deposited him against a tree during a foxhunt. At an age when he should have known better, Wood collided with a Hackney cab horse while attempting to ride a bike. The horse bit him and he carried the mark for the rest of his life.

By the time Wood had recovered, the Crimean War was over and he returned to England. Just a year later, in June 1857, he exchanged into the 17th Lancers, who were being sent to help quell the Indian Mutiny. It was in 1858, with the Mutiny over, that Wood won his Victoria Cross for attacking the camp of a band of robbers who outnumbered his small force by about 10-1. He killed several, put the rest to flight and rescued two captives.

Wood had been on almost constant service for two years when he fell sick and was invalided back to England. When he had recovered, he quickly moved up the promotion ladder and by 1862 was made a Brevet Major. He then exchanged into the infantry and joined the 73rd Regiment. This was but a step, for Wood was ambitious and he entered the Staff College, graduating in 1864. This was a period of learning for him for he held various staff jobs and cultivated influential contacts. One of his most valuable associations was with the Army's rising star, Garnet Wolseley. Wood impressed Wolseley with his energy, intelligence and infectious good humour. Despite Wood's rather hangdog looks and his hypochondria (he had good reason to worry about his health), he was a popular companion and became one of the original members of the 'Wolseley Gang'.

All through 1868 Wood suffered from stomach pains, and, because he was ill for so long, seriously considered leaving the Army and, using his knowledge of military law, attempt to qualify for the Bar. It was not until the next year that, following prescribed doses of opium, he recovered sufficiently to enable him to continue his duties.

By 1873 he was both married and had become a lieutenant colonel. When Wolseley was made commander of the British force sent to subdue the fierce West African tribe, the Ashanti, he chose Wood to be his Transport Officer and to raise a native regiment. The short hard campaign was successful and both Wolseley and Wood emerged as public figures. Mentioned in despatches and sporting a fresh wound, Wood was made Companion of the Bath and brevetted full colonel.

A series of staff appointments led to Wood being sent to South Africa in early 1878 commanding the 90th Light Infantry. The Ninth Frontier War, as this short-lived series of skirmishes was named, was a frustrating campaign, in which the British found it impossible to coax the enemy into fighting a pitched battle. Instead, they adopted a strategy of encirclement and piecemeal picking off of the hostile natives that gradually wore down the opposition. Wood and his regiment marched hundreds of miles, fought a few skirmishes and became campaign-hardened. Thesiger came to rely on the experienced Wood and the two became friends and confidants. Having pacified the Transkei, Thesiger and the High Commissioner, Sir Bartle Frere, then turned their attention to what they perceived as the next source of conflict, Zululand.

Wood persuaded Thesiger that the Field Force, called the Natal Column, should march to Natal rather than attempt the complications of sea transport. The Column marched 500 miles over rough terrain and crossed thirty-seven rivers. By the time they had reached Pietermaritzburg, all who had taken part were toughened by the experience and had learned to 'rough it'. Wood summed it up, 'a healthy climate, for, with proper sanitary arrangements and the absence of public-houses, the young soldiers improved out of recognition.' Wood and the 90th were sent north to Utrecht in the Disputed Territory on the Zululand Border. Sir Bartle Frere had appointed him as Political Agent for North Zululand and Swaziland and given him the task of enlisting support for the British from the Boer population. Only one Boer leader, Piet Uys, offered his service and he backed this up by bringing about forty of his family who acted as irregular cavalry.

During the last three months of 1878 Evelyn Wood was constantly on the move visiting the small settlements, recruiting support and obtaining wagons and draught animals for the planned invasion. He later wrote;

The incessant work, however, now began to tell on me, and my glands swelled as they had done when I was overworked in the Amatola Mountains, although for pleasure and on principle I played either lawn-tennis or polo for an hour or two every evening, the subalterns of the 90th being always available for a game.

From Midshipman to Field Marshal 1906

Chelmsford had originally intended that five columns would converge on Cetshwayo's capital at Ulundi but soon modified his plan to just three. Wood, who had the shortest distance to advance, jumped the gun and entered Zululand on 6 January, four days before the ultimatum expired. Crossing the Blood River, Wood's 2,500-strong Column marched ten miles to a flat-topped hill called Bemba's Kop where he built a fortified camp. His force was made up of eight companies of the 13th and 90th Regiments, six guns of 11/7th Battery, about 200 Volunteer Cavalry and 300 natives given the rather unflattering title of 'Wood's Irregulars'.

Ordered to delay his advance to allow the other two columns to catch up the extra distance, Wood's mounted Colonials, under the command of Redvers Buller, indulged in some highly successful cattle raiding. This was both profitable and useful as a diversion, especially for the Centre Column, as it kept the local Zulus occupied in the north. This ploy was to no avail, however, as a strong Zulu force overwhelmed Chelmsford's camp at Isandlwana.

On the night of 20-21 January Wood led the 90th and Buller's mounted troops into the Zunguin Mountains, collecting cattle and driving off about 1,000 Zulus. When they reached the eastern end they saw beneath them about 4,000 warriors drilling in the shadow of the formidable bulk of Hlobane Mountain. As they returned to camp on the evening of the 22nd the distant sound of guns from the south could be heard. This later proved to be Harness's 7-pounders firing at the wrecked camp when Chelmsford's men returned from their fruitless search for the enemy.

The following day Wood again led his men towards Hlobane and, after a brief skirmish, saw a large body of Zulus ascend to the safety of the mountain. At this moment Wood received the news of the Isandlwana defeat. The raiding party immediately returned to their base and Wood decided that he should find a more defensible base. He found this at Khambula Hill, where he had ready access to firewood and water. Here he received a note from an understandably shaken Lord Chelmsford in which he wrote:

You must be prepared to have the whole of the Zulu Army on your hands any day... No.3 Column, when re-equipped, is to subordinate its movements to your column.

Wood took this last statement to heart and he later incurred much resentment and jealousy during the Second Invasion.

The remnants of the Centre Column, who retreated to Rorke's Drift and Helpmekaar, and also Pearson's Coastal Column, who were now besieged at Eshowe, spent many miserable weeks on the defensive. Only Wood's Column was intact and he continued to make his presence felt by taking cattle, burning crops and destroying kraals.

He pulled off something of a propaganda coup when Cetshwayo's brother, Hamu, unconditionally surrendered to him with some 6,000 followers. This would have made any advance towards Ulundi considerably easier were it not for that thorn in his side, Chief Mbilini. This renegade Swazi chief and his men had recently killed eighty soldiers of the 80th Regiment as they slept in camp on the bank by the Ntombe River near Luneburg and were known to have moved to the southern slopes of Hlobane Mountain. Wood knew that he would have to deal with Mbilini as Hlobane lay in the path to Ulundi.

Wood had misgivings about attacking Hlobane, although he knew its threat had to be neutralized. Buller, with a mounted force of 400 men, was enthusiastic, not only to defeat Mbilini, but also at the prospect of capturing so many head of cattle and the prize money they brought. Chelmsford had requested that Wood should make a move on 27 March to tie in with his plan to march on Eshowe a few days later. Wood responded to Chelmsford's request in a note in which he wrote;

Buller has started, and at 3pm I follow, to try to get up the Inhlobane at daylight tomorrow. I am not very sanguine of success. We do not know how steep the Eastern end may be, but I think we ought to make a stir here, to divert attention from you, although, as you see by our last reports, it is asserted that you have only Coast tribes against you, and that all Cetewayo's (sic) people are coming here.

The debacle that followed left a question mark about Evelyn Wood's state of mind for he ignored standard military practice and had no control over the fighting. He adopted a 'floating' form of command, which meant he followed at a distance and was quite unable to influence events. But luck was on Wood's side. Because Hlobane was a largely Colonial affair and, as there were no war correspondents with Wood, it did not receive much press coverage in Britain. His mishandling of the ill-managed assault on Hlobane was conveniently swept under the carpet and overshadowed by the events of the following day at Khambula. His handling of his firepower was effective and he timed his counter-attacks to perfection. Typically, he even managed to get involved in the fighting on the front line.

The war then came to an end and Wood looked forward to returning to England. For his services, he was awarded the K.C.B., although promotion would have to wait. Wood showed his appreciation of his men when he treated his long-serving escort to dinner at the best hotel in Pietermaritzburg.

Back in England, Wood attended numerous dinners in his honour and was a guest of both the Queen and Disraeli. He also gained promotion to Major General, the youngest to have attained that rank. After six months of being feted, Wood was on his way back to South Africa on a highly unusual and emotional mission.

As a personal favour, the Queen asked Wood to take charge of the pilgrimage of the Empress Eugènie who wished see where her son had been slain. Among the small entourage was the Honourable Mrs Ronald Campbell, the widow of Wood's staff officer and friend. The party then returned to England at the end of July.

Wood was not finished with South Africa for he was sent out again within six months at the outbreak of the First Anglo Boer War of 1881. Soon after he arrived, General Sir George Colley, the Army Commander, was killed with many of his men, when the Boers overran their position on Majuba Hill. As a result, Wood was sworn in as Acting Governor of Natal and Administrator of the Transvaal. He became unpopular in the Colony and among his fellow officers when, acting under the instructions of the British Government, he negotiated a peace settlement with the Boers that ended the war.

At the end of 1881 Wood left South Africa for the last time. Although the rest of his career was long and filled with interesting and responsible appointments, his days of campaigning were over. By the time he retired Wood had attained the rank of Field Marshal.

Colonel Redvers Buller

When satirists lampoon a typical overfed, red-faced block-headed Victorian general, they probably have in mind a picture of General Sir Redvers Buller. In his sixties, and reluctantly in command of British forces at the outbreak of the Anglo-Boer War, he did, indeed, cut an archaic and risible figure. He was ponderous in both speech and build and his rather piggy eyes were set in a crimson jowly face dominated by a large grey walrus moustache. He had a short fuse and a spectacular temper. He was also stubborn, lacking in energy and unsuccessful, which led to his being replaced by his hated rival, General Frederick Roberts. Sadly this lasting impression of Buller conceals what an exceptional and inspiring leader he had been twenty years earlier in the Zulu War.

Born in 1839, Buller was the second of seven sons and four daughters born to a West Country squire and M.P. The family home of Downes, near Crediton, Devon, was a large well-run estate and the family was a close, self-contained unit, greatly influenced by their warm-hearted mother. His father, in contrast, was an undemonstrative and distant figure. The young Buller grew up as a country boy who enjoyed mixing with the estate workers and gained a firm grounding in carpentry, smithy work, animal husbandry and other rural skills that later often surprised his soldiers.

After a brief stay at Harrow, he moved to Eton where he was regarded as a clumsy country bumpkin and an undistinguished pupil. He lived for the holidays so he could work on the estate and indulge his passion for riding and hunting. His happy childhood, however, was shattered during the Christmas holidays of 1855. He and his elder brother, James, had accompanied their beloved mother on a shopping expedition to Exeter and were waiting on the station platform for the train to return them to Crediton. Suddenly his mother collapsed with a lung haemorrhage. Too ill to be moved, she lay in the waiting room attended by Redvers until she died. A further tragedy occurred just six months later when his favourite sister, Julia, also died. The Bullers, despite living in the country, were not a robust family and sickness was to claim another sister and his elder brother.

With his brother James due to inherit Downes, Redvers decided on a career in the army, despite the family having no great military connections. In 1858 he was commissioned into the 60th Rifles, one of the elite British regiments. Accident prone, Buller nearly ended his new career before it began. Helping with some forestry in the estate woods, he badly hacked his leg with an axe. So severe was the wound that the doctor recommended amputation, but was deterred by Buller's vehement protestations. Although the injury gave him a limp for the rest of his life, it did not affect his skill in the saddle.

His first posting was to India and he arrived just as the last pockets of mutineers were being hunted down. From India he was posted to Hong Kong and took part in the Second Opium War against China in 1860. Unlike most of his contemporaries, he had a conscience, believing that the war was unjust and he annoyed his fellow officers for many years by refusing to wear the campaign medal. A souvenir he did take from the China War, however, was a kick in the mouth from a frisky horse, which left him a speech impediment for the rest of his life.

At this time he was described by a contemporary as 'a raw and self-willed young man, with perhaps no great interest in his profession'. His next posting changed that for ever. Buller's battalion was sent to

Colonel Buller.
Adrian Greaves collection

170

Canada, and he soon relished the beauty of its wilderness. He also became greatly influenced by his commanding officer, Colonel R.B. Hawley, who saw great potential in his protégé and encouraged him to perfect his soldiering skills. These came to be noticed when the 60th formed part of the Red River Expedition of 1870. Under the command of the senior staff officer in Canada, Colonel Garnet Wolseley, Buller was given the chance to shine and he took the opportunity with both hands. Although the campaign did not involve any fighting, Buller's energy and handling of his men contributed greatly to its success. Most importantly, it brought the young Buller into the favoured circle of officers that surrounded the ambitious Wolseley.

Three years later Buller further enhanced his reputation in the foetid jungles of West Africa where he acted as Wolseley's Intelligence Officer in the Ashanti War. This gave him his first experience of handling spies, interpreters and volunteers. He also met the 'gentlemen of the press' and started a lifelong hatred of the profession. For their part, they were generous in their praise of him. One, Winwood Reade of *The Times*, perceptively wrote of Buller, 'his talents are best displayed on active service'.

The campaign left him with a brevet majority, a CB and a dose of malaria, which was to torment him for the rest of his life. He returned to Downes to recuperate and while he was there his brother James died. Now squire of Downes and a wealthy man, Buller was tempted to retire from the Army and devote his life to managing the estate. But by now he had begun to enjoy soldiering, especially under the reforming influence of Wolseley, and he chose to remain a soldier. His next overseas appointment was to accompany Major General the Hon. Frederic Thesiger, the new Army Commander in South Africa. When they arrived in early 1878 the Ninth Frontier War was being fitfully fought in what was known as British Kaffaria, to the south of Natal. Almost immediately Buller was given his first independent command, the 250-strong Frontier Light Horse. This could have been a poisoned chalice, for the volunteers were an unruly mixed bunch made up of British deserters, sailors, bar-flies, failed miners and border toughs. As he wrote in a letter to a sister, ' I fear there is not much credit to be got out of being associated with them, but I will do my best'.

In a short time, by dint of example, encouragement and hard discipline, Buller turned this unlikely rabble into a cohesive and effective force. An example of how he dealt with insubordination was illustrated by his handling of an abusive trooper who was drunk on parade. Pretending to ignore the incident, Buller led the unit out on patrol. After a few miles on the empty veldt, he ordered the offender to dismount and to walk back to camp. At this time Buller's appearance was described as tall and wiry. He dressed like his men, in brown cord breeches, high leather gaiters, a flannel shirt, a many-pocketed jacket and a wide-brimmed hat with a red puggree. The whole ensemble was hung with bandoliers and ammunition pouches. The favoured weapons were Snider or Martini-Henry carbines, bayonets and revolvers, but no swords. Buller led by example and proved he was as tough as they were. The Frontier Light Horse were involved in a few skirmishes, one of which resulted in an officer and six troopers being killed, but mostly they were on long and fruitless searches for the elusive enemy.

> *If we were lying in the rain, so was Buller. If we were hungry, so was he. All the hardships he shared equally with his men.*   FLH member.

The 9th Frontier War had petered out by the end of May and in September Buller was ordered to take the FLH north to the disputed territories that lay between the Boer republic of Transvaal and north-eastern Zululand. There they joined Colonel Hugh Rowlands', expedition against the belligerent Pedi tribe under the leadership of Sekhukhune. After a long and weary march, through a drought-blighted country, Buller was disgusted when Rowlands called off the advance within sight of Sekhukhune's stronghold.

Buller did not have to wait long before he saw action. When the British provoked a war with the Zulus, Thesiger, or Lord Chelmsford as he had become, appointed Buller as commander of all mounted troops in Wood's Column. In addition to the Frontier Light Horse and the Imperial Mounted Infantry, which consisted of regular British infantrymen who could ride, there were six other units. These were the Natal Native Horse, Baker's Horse, Transvaal Rangers, Kaffrarian Rifles, Border Horse and the Burgher Force. The last-mentioned was commanded by Piet Uys and was a forty-strong all-Boer unit, of whom most were related to its commander. During the period that Buller was acquainted with Uys, he developed a strong respect and sympathy for the Boers, which he carried into the Anglo-Boer War. This led Buller to be accused of being soft on the Boers and may go part of the way to explain his lack of ruthlessness during his attempt to relieve Ladysmith.

It is also worth mentioning that this unit would not accept payment for their service, but relied on their share of the Zulu cattle they could rustle. The Natal Native Horse were well-disciplined and steady troops, the Border and Baker units were both commanded by former regular British officers and were made up of generally reputable volunteers. The Kaffrarian Rifles were recruited from the Transvaal and were entirely German and Dutch volunteers. The Transvaal Rangers were the unit that drew the most adverse comments. Recruits were variously described as 'a forbidding lot of mixed Hottentots and scum of the diamond fields as never collected together outside a prison wall', and 'if they fight as well as they thieve, they will be of great execution amongst the Zulus'.

All in all Buller was in overall command of some 600 diverse and individualistic men of many nationalities. It speaks volumes that he welded them into a cohesive command that acquitted itself with some distinction during the War. After the defeat at Isandlwana Chelmsford's column retired to Natal until reinforcements arrived. Wood's command had not been involved in the First Invasion and was strongly encamped just inside the Zulu border at Khambula.

From here Buller and his command made frequent raids against Zulu kraals in the neighbourhood with the express purpose of capturing cattle and claiming prize money from the authorities. It seems probable that Buller's motive for wanting to mount an expedition against the formidable Hlobane Mountain was less about neutralizing the hostile Mbilini and more about capturing the considerable cattle herd that was grazed on the high plateau. In any event, the ill-conceived raid turned into a first-class disaster, with Buller emerging as both villain and hero.

Although his superior, Colonel Wood, had been present on the periphery of the battle, Buller had effectively been in command and was responsible for what was the second worst defeat after Isandlwana. His bravery was not in question and he had effected a withdrawal that had saved many of his men. When it came to look for scapegoats for the disaster, the Army was not about to sacrifice a man like Buller. Instead, the unpopular Lieutenant Colonel John Russell, who had pulled his men away from the bottom of Devil's Pass at a critical moment in the retreat, shouldered much of the blame.

With only a few hours rest, Buller was again involved in a battle. The main impi present at Hlobane was, in fact, on its way to attack the well-prepared camp at Khambula. At about 1 pm the Zulus were observed getting into position to attack in the classic head and horns formation. In order to break up this formation before it was completed, Buller led out his volunteers to incite the Zulu right horn to attack. At a distance of only two hundred yards from the Zulus, they dismounted and fired a volley at the massed ranks. This had a two-fold effect. The Zulus immediately charged and most of the volunteers' horses became spooked, with the result that many of the cavalry only just escaped with their lives as they tried to mount their panicked mounts. Amongst these was the disgraced Colonel Russell, who was saved by Lieutenant Browne, 24th Regiment, attached to the Imperial Mounted Infantry. For this act Browne won the only Victoria Cross awarded for this battle.

Despite his disdain of the press, the newsmen recognized that Buller was newsworthy and built him up as 'The Bayard of South Africa'. Archibald Forbes accurately described Buller as, 'a stern-tempered, ruthless, saturnine man, with a gift of grim silence'. He further penned a rather purple-tinged account of Buller.

Leading his men at a swinging canter, with his reins in his teeth, a revolver in one hand, and a knobkerrie he had snatched from a Zulu in the other, his hat blown off in the melee, and a large streak of blood across his face, caused by a splinter of blood from above, this gallant horseman seemed a demon incarnate to the flying savages, who slunk out of his path as if he had been – as indeed they believed him – an evil spirit, whose very look was death.. Archibald Forbes

As Wood's column was marching from Khambula to rendezvous with Chelmsford's main force, Wood and Buller were riding ahead when they spotted an officer galloping towards them.

'The Prince – the Prince Imperial is killed', the officer blurted out.

Buller demanded, 'Where – where is the body? Where are your men, sir? How many did you lose?'

When the distraught officer, Lieutenant Carey, was unable to give a clear reply, Buller lost his temper, saying accusingly, 'You deserve to be shot, and I hope you will be. I could shoot you myself.'

Once the facts were learned and Buller cooled down, he was more sympathetic towards Carey, no doubt recalling his own experience with the headstrong Frenchman who had regularly disobeyed orders.

By 3 July the column went into laager just five miles short of Ulundi. Buller and his men were sent forward to select a suitable position for the British to occupy in the coming battle. Having chosen a possible site, Buller's men were ambushed by some 3,000 Zulus, who were hidden in long grass. Handling his men well, Buller extricated his command with units covering one another as they fell back. Seven men were killed and three Victoria Crosses won in this copybook withdrawal. The following day the Zulu impis were broken after just thirty minutes. Buller's horsemen repeated their Khambula tactic of riding out to provoke an attack and then, when the Zulus retreated, were let loose to pursue and kill.

No one had seen more action or ridden greater distances than had Buller. The bloodletting had also taken its toll and he was weary of killing. Exhausted and feverish, Buller also suffered from veldt-sores, which so crippled his hands that his writing was permanently affected.

A grateful nation was not prepared to let him convalesce quietly at his Devon home. He was promoted to colonel and ADC to the Queen and given the CMG. He was also summoned to Balmoral, where his sovereign pinned the Victoria Cross to his tunic. This was in recognition of his valour for rescuing at least four unhorsed men at Hlobane, but he could have won it many times over for other brave acts. For the record, after the 24th Regiment, who were awarded nine VCs, the men of Buller's Mounted Irregulars won six Crosses.

Although Redvers Buller went on to higher command and a knighthood, the greatest achievement of his career was to be found in the Zulu War, where he took command of unpromising material and moulded them into the most effective unit to emerge from the conflict.

Colonel Richard Thomas Glyn

The Anglo-Zulu War was a brief conflict that enhanced few reputations but damaged many. Colonels Evelyn Wood and Redvers Buller emerged with credit, while others like Lord Chelmsford and Colonel Cecil Russell lost their former standing through their questionable competence and actions.

Other participants were badly affected by what they experienced, both physically and mentally. In an age when mental trauma was misunderstood, there was little sympathy or understanding for those who broke under the strain of witnessing the savagery of warfare. In an institution like the Army, it

Colonel Richard Thomas Glyn. *Courtesy Major Everett, 24th Regimental Museum, Brecon.*

was expected that emotions should be kept on a tight rein, especially among the senior officers; the 'stiff upper lip' syndrome prevailed. It is well documented that Chelmsford underwent a period of severe depression in the aftermath of Isandlwana. Colonel Hassard, Officer Commanding Royal Engineers, had such a severe nervous breakdown that he was replaced. Colonel Pearson, the defender of Eshowe, was invalided home suffering from mental and physical exhaustion. Of all the senior officers who suffered in such a way, none felt greater anguish than the commanding officer of the 1/24th Regiment, Colonel Richard Thomas Glyn.

Born 23 December 1831 in Meerut, India, he was the only son of R.C. Glyn, an officer in the Honourable East India Company. On his return to England, a conventional country upbringing produced an expert horseman and a fanatical huntsman. Despite his short stature (he was just 5ft 2in) Glyn was physically strong and keen to pursue a military career. When he was nineteen his father purchased him a commission in the 82nd (Prince of Wales's Volunteers) Regiment, later the 2nd South Lancashires.

After several years of duty in Ireland, Glyn and his regiment were sent to the Crimea and arrived on 2 September 1855, just six days before the fall of Sebastopol, thus missing any fighting and becoming part of the Army of Occupation until 1856. It was in this year that he married Anne Clements, the daughter of the former Colonel of the Royal Canadian Rifles. Their honeymoon period was cut short when Glyn's regiment was rushed to India to become part of Sir Colin Campbell's force that relieved the besieged force at Lucknow in mid-November 1857. Just a few days later the 82nd received a drubbing at Cawnpore from rebel forces and sustained many casualties. Glyn was then promoted to captain and soon gained much experience in the hard and brutal suppression of the Mutiny.

Like many officers, Glyn found post-Mutiny India an agreeable place to serve, particularly enjoying the opportunities to indulge his passion for hunting. Anne joined him and they set about producing a family of four daughters. He advanced up the promotion ladder by purchasing his majority in 1861. In 1867 he purchased the Lieutenant-Colonelcy of the 1/24th Regiment, then stationed at Malta. In 1872 the regiment was transferred to Gibraltar, where Glyn was promoted to full Colonel. Even here he was able to hunt across the border into Spain, which was about the only excitement to be had in this peaceful outpost.

After three pleasant but uneventful years the Regiment was relieved to have a change of posting. At the end of November the Glyns and most of the 1/24th embarked on Her Majesty's Troopship *Simoon* and, thirty-five sailing days later, the ship dropped anchor in Table Bay, Cape Town. Glyn's appearance at this time could be described as 'bristling' with his full wax-tipped moustache and short aggressive-looking stature, he looked as if he was on the point of exploding with rage. This appearance, however, belied his true personality. He had a steady and unflappable temperament, though somewhat unimaginative and lethargic. He was fortunate to command some very able officers, including Henry Pulleine who could be relied upon expertly to administer the regiment's day-to-day running.

By 1876 Southern Africa was a cauldron of small states and territories, of which the Cape Colony was the richest and largest. To the north lay the diamond-rich territory of Griqualand West, which was in a state of ferment and on the verge of rebellion. The Cape Government ordered Colonel Glyn to take his regiment and restore the appointed civil authorities. The march to Kimberley was long and arduous, crossing mountains and the dreary dry Great Karoo plain. Keeping up a steady pace through the heat of the African days, the 1/24th took two months to cover the seven hundred miles. When they arrived, they found that their presence alone was enough to stifle the rebellion and there was little more to do than march all the way back to the Cape. One positive aspect of the long march was that the regiment was now physically hardened and ready for the tough campaign that was looming to the north-east.

In the meantime there was more than enough time for recreation in the form of hunting. As the fox does not exist in southern Africa, the nearest equivalent quarry was the black-backed jackal. Colonel Glyn, as Master of the Hunt, kept a full pack of hounds and three hunters. He appointed his three Irish subalterns, Daly, Hodson and Coghill, as Whips. They exercised the pack three times a week and sometimes went hunting for up to ten days at a time. Besides hunting, Glyn and his officers organized small game and partridge shoots.

The Colonel is good a little man as ever breathed has what amounts to monomania, 'unting being 'is 'obby.   Lieutenant Coghill

While it was undeniably true that Glyn enjoyed his hunting, it was common knowledge that he craved male companionship as an escape from his all-female household. His wife, Anne, had become that most formidable of women, 'The Colonel's Wife', and she gave her easy-going husband little peace. His officers viewed Glyn with affection and the Glyns regarded the regimental officers as part of their own family. Neville Coghill was a particular favourite and it is not inconceivable that he was looked upon as the son Glyn never had.

The pleasant round of socializing came to an end with problems in the Transkei, east of Cape Colony. Sir Bartle Frere ordered the 1/24th to this trouble spot and appointed Colonel Glyn as Commander in the Transkei, with the rank of Colonel of the Staff and Brevet Brigadier-General. In a frustrating campaign that involved three columns sweeping the country, the Xhosa foe was seldom persuaded to stand and be shot at. They finally made a determined stand at a stream called Nyamaga, where, on 14 January, they were routed by Glyn's men. Another fight took place at Centane in February where the Xhosa were again beaten by the superior firepower of the British. By keeping the Xhosas on the move, the British wore down their will to resist. Despite this successful campaign, General Cunynghame was removed from overall command and Lieutenant-General Frederick Augustus Thesiger was appointed in his place. There was little for the new Commander to do except to keep the Xhosa on the move until they submitted in the summer of 1878.

The Regiment had performed well and duly received the thanks of the Governor. Colonel Glyn received high praise from both the Duke of Cambridge and Sir Bartle Frere and, in a more tangible form of gratitude, he was made a Companion of the Bath. Under Glyn's command the 1/24th had gained a reputation for good behaviour in the towns where they were stationed. They were also highly experienced at campaigning in South Africa and were already designated to be the army's backbone in the next step in Frere's expansionist plan. The feeling among the Governor and the military was that the subjugation of the Xhosa was little more than a prelude to a confrontation with the far more formidable Zulus.

Glyn and his regiment were ordered to Pietermaritzburg in Natal where the Regimental Headquarters were established. Sir Bartle Frere also left Cape Town and took up residence at the nearby Government House where he could more effectively connive with Chelmsford and keep at bay his opponents in the Natal government. As war with the Zulus became inevitable, Coghill asked Glyn to find him a place on his staff as soon as Sir Bartle Frere would release him.

The build-up of forces in Natal coincided with the ending of the long drought and the following torrential rains made the assembling and dispersal of the invasion forces along the frontier difficult. It was on 30 November that Colonel Glyn bade farewell to his wife and daughters and, to the accompaniment of the band, led his Regiment out of Pietermaritzburg towards the desolate post of Helpmekaar. Enduring constant heavy rain and deep mud, the Column took a week to cover the one hundred miles to the Biggarsberg Plateau overlooking the Buffalo River valley and the frontier with Zululand.

Colonel Glyn had been given command of Number 3 Column which became known as the Central Column. Assembling stores and additional manpower, Helpmekaar grew into a sprawling encampment of tents, huts, wagons, livestock and stores. Glyn had a staff that were largely strangers to him and were newcomers to South Africa. His Principal Staff Officer was the contentious and egocentric Major Cornelius Clery, who had originally served in this capacity with Colonel Evelyn Wood's Number 4 Column (the Left Flank or Northern Column). He had been transferred at Lord Chelmsford's request, probably to ensure that the easy-going Glyn kept to his task.

Clery, ever critical of his superiors, described Glyn as 'a guileless, unsuspicious man, very upright and scrupulously truthful, yet a slow, not to say lethargic temperament'. He undoubtedly was contrasting the relaxed unambitious Glyn with the energetic and talented Wood.

Nonetheless, Glyn was experienced in campaigning and relished the coming invasion. It therefore came as great blow to him when Chelmsford and his staff, instead of establishing an independent force headquarters, attached themselves to Glyn's Column. Chelmsford, ever the considerate gentleman, sought to assure Glyn that he would not interfere in the running of the column. In practice this did not work. With two staffs, each jealous of the other and, in Chelmsford's case, high-handed and arrogant, there was considerable friction. Clery and Chelmsford's Military Secretary, Lieutenant-Colonel John Crealock, both lacked diplomacy but possessed vitriolic tongues which further strained relationships between the two camps. Crealock dismissed Glyn by saying, 'do not expect anything (of him). He is a purely regimental officer with no ideas beyond it.'[1]

Glyn and his staff were effectively relegated to mere figureheads. Clery caustically remarked that 'Colonel Glyn and his staff were allowed to work the details – posting the guards, etc., and all the interesting work of that kind'. This usurping of his command caused Glyn to become disinterested and withdrawn, for it was not in his nature to object or challenge any orders. He may well have felt intimidated both by Chelmsford's status and his height. (The tall, lanky General towered over his diminutive Column commander.) Clery again: 'He (Glyn) was scarcely ever seen or heard of, the more so as he got anything but encouragement to interest himself in what was going on.'[2]

Throughout the Zulu War the tone in Chelmsford's dealings with Glyn is one of impatience and some antipathy. Glyn had wanted to fortify both Helpmekaar and Rorke's Drift in accordance with Chelmsford's instructions, but he was overruled. On arrival at Isandlwana, Glyn gave instructions for the layout of the camp, but Chelmsford felt that it would take a week to entrench the camp and some of the wagons were scheduled to return to Rorke's Drift for further supplies. Chelmsford also considered that the position of the camp had such a commanding view into Zululand that the Zulus could not possibly take the British unawares.

Instead, Chelmsford decided personally to lead four companies of the 2/24th, most of the mounted men and four out of the six guns to tackle the enemy. In a somewhat belated effort to smooth Glyn's ruffled feathers,

Chelmsford offered him the command of the force.

At four o'clock on the morning of Wednesday 22 January Chelmsford led Glyn's Column out of Isandlwana and marched towards the south-east to join Major Dartnell who believed he had found the advancing Zulu Army. The Zulus were not to be found as they were attacking Isandlwana. It was only that night that Chelmsford and Glyn discovered the remains of the British camp.

In order to spare his men further distress, Chelmsford ordered a return to Natal before dawn. The British expected to find that Rorke's Drift had been razed to the ground and its occupants slaughtered, especially when they passed the returning Zulu force that had attacked Rorke's Drift. The Zulus made no move to attack Chelmsford's force which was a relief as his men were exhausted from the events of the previous twenty-four hours. Chelmsford and Glyn found instead that the defenders had put up an effective defence and had inflicted many casualties, which explained the subdued behaviour of the Zulu Warriors. Pausing only to congratulate the defenders, Chelmsford and his staff rode off to Pietermaritzburg to report the disaster. Colonel Glyn, in a complete state of shock at the loss of his regiment, was left to fortify Rorke's Drift.

Fearing that the Zulus would attack at any time, Glyn had a strong perimeter built around the camp and made everyone move inside. No tents were allowed except for the Rorke's Drift survivors, who were provided with the only large groundsheet for protection, the remaining garrison being crammed into the small defended area, which was soon churned into a quagmire. Without tents, blankets or change of clothing and cold rain falling steadily, the men began to suffer badly. Rotting stores and poor sanitation together with a monotonous diet contributed to the low morale that afflicted everyone. All medical supplies had been destroyed when the Zulus set fire to the hospital and the camp sick list, which included Lieutenant Chard, grew steadily.

The grieving Colonel Glyn withdrew into his shell of despondency and took little interest in the misery around him. Without doubt he was displaying all the symptoms of a breakdown. Not only did he feel bereaved by the loss of his regiment, he also expressed the feeling that he should have been with his men as they fought for their lives, a common enough emotion among survivors.

It was not until 4 February that a patrol led by Major Wilsone Black discovered the bodies of Coghill and Melvill on the Natal bank of the Buffalo River. A further search found the Queen's Colour in the river some half a mile downstream. A cairn of stones was piled on the bodies and the colour was taken back to Rorke's Drift. Glyn was moved to tears when he received the flag and learned of the fate of his favourite young officers.

At the end of February conditions had become so bad that a new fort was built nearby and named after Lieutenant Melvill. Helpmekaar was also fortified, but in both instances conditions continued to be grim. From the latter site it was possible, with the aid of a telescope, to observe the battlefield of Isandlwana. The vultures wheeled overhead for weeks and the ground became white with bleaching bones. The first casualties of Isandlwana to be properly interred were Coghill and Melvill on 14 April in a ceremony attended by Glyn. While the isolated Glyn was suffering both mentally and physically at Rorke's Drift, Lord Chelmsford and his followers were attempting to play down their role in the disaster. In a subtle piece of responsibility shifting, Chelmsford stated that, 'Colonel Glyn was solely responsible' and 'that Colonel Glyn fully and explicitly accepted this responsibility cannot, however, affect the ultimate responsibility of the General-in-Command'. This attempt to share the blame with Glyn rang hollow, as it was generally known that Glyn had little say in matters. Chelmsford's staff contributed to the growing controversy by saying that it was Glyn's failure to entrench the camp that caused it to be overrun. As he was commander of the Central Column, the blame should be firmly laid at his door.

It was Major Clery who silenced this tactic by producing Chelmsford's note to Glyn stating that the ground was too rocky to dig and, as the camp was soon to be moved, hardly worth fortifying. Anne Glyn, recovering from the terrible news, was incensed at the attempts to blame her husband and was outspoken in her criticism of Chelmsford. Glyn himself seemed too numb to do more than briefly give the facts without comment to the Board of Enquiry. Chelmsford then turned his attention to Colonel Durnford as the conveniently dead scapegoat.

As the months passed, so reinforcements began to reach South Africa and Chelmsford could put his new invasion plans into effect. Despite his antipathy towards Glyn, Chelmsford appointed him to command the First Infantry Brigade, which comprised of the 2/21st, the newly re-constituted 1/24th, 58th and 94th Regiments. These were all 'green' and untried soldiers. While on the march into Zululand, the nervous night guards of the 58th precipitated a furious firefight with their own men, which expended much ammunition but fortunately no loss of life.

After several delays, the second invasion got underway on 31 May when Glyn led his brigade across the border. Within a day Chelmsford was further devastated by the news that Louis Napoleon, the Prince Imperial, had been killed while on a patrol led by Lieutenant J.B. Carey. A Field Court Martial was convened and Colonel Glyn was appointed President. The court listened to the evidence regarding the culpability of Carey and found him guilty, but did not publish its findings, preferring to refer the matter to Horse Guards. The advance into Zululand towards the capital of Ulundi continued at a snail's pace. Chelmsford, ever mindful of Isandlwana, had fortified supply depots built along the route. He was also careful to laager and entrench his camp each night. Eventually they were within sight of Ulundi. Much to the disappointment of the 1/24th, they were ordered to remain guarding the camp by the White Mfolozi River, while the rest of the brigade advanced on Ulundi. Glyn did take with him eight officers of the old 1/24th and they were with him in the huge square upon which Cetshwayo's army was finally destroyed.

For the 24th the war was over and they began the long march back to Pietermaritzburg, where the Glyns were reunited. Then they travelled to the encampment at Pinetown, where Colonel Glyn had the pleasant duty of presenting the Victoria Cross to Surgeon Major James Reynolds (Rorke's Drift) and Lieutenant Edward Browne 1/24th (Khambula).

Finally, the 24th embarked on the troopship *Egypt* and set sail for England on 27 August. Because of mechanical problems, the journey took four weeks to complete. During that time the redoubtable Anne Glyn used her needlework skills to repair the tattered Queen's Colour. On their arrival at Gosport, the Duke of Cambridge, who expressed his sorrow that so few of the old soldiers of the 24th had returned home, greeted them. In May 1880 Glyn relinquished his command of the 1/24th and took charge of the Brigade Depot at Brecon. The following year the Regiment was given the new title of The South Wales Borderers.

In 1882 Richard Glyn was promoted to Major General and appointed a KCB. He eventually retired as a Lieutenant General and lived at Mortimer in Berkshire. A sad and stooped little man, Glyn's remaining years were overshadowed by the memory of his lost family on the rocky slopes of Isandlwana. In 1898 he was honoured with the title of Colonel of the South Wales Borders. It was in this capacity that he saw off his old Regiment as they went off to South Africa again, this time to fight the Boers. Within a few months of their departure, he died on 21 November 1900 and was buried in the family grave at Ewell, Surrey.

Colour Sergeant Frank Bourne

It is fair to say that most people fascinated by the Anglo Zulu War had their initial interest fired by the film *ZULU* and for many the outstanding character in this film was Colour Sergeant Bourne, as portrayed by Nigel Green.

The real Frank Bourne was born on 27 April 1854. His family were farmers at Balcombe, a Sussex village between Haywards Heath and Crawley. Because he was the youngest of eight sons and bottom of the pecking order, he felt there was little chance of inheriting the farm. The prospect of spending the rest

Colour Sergeant Bourne and family. *Ron Sheeley collection*

of his life within the narrow environs of a rural community did not appeal to this intelligent and active youth, so, despite his father's attempts to prevent his son leaving the farm to join the army, with all the stigma that such service implied, young Bourne travelled to the nearest recruiting centre at Reigate and volunteered on 18 December 1872. He was just eighteen.

His army records describe his physical appearance as being 5ft 5 inches tall, dark complexion, grey eyes and brown hair. In his own words, he was painfully thin and hardly an imposing figure. In fact he was like many of the recruits of that time, short and underweight. In January 1873 he was posted to the 2nd Battalion 24th (Warwickshire) Regiment. Bourne thought that the Sergeant Major must have had a sense of humour for he was put in A Company, traditionally the Grenadier Company and manned by the tallest soldiers. The 2/24th had served in India and Burma since 1860 and were due for a spell of home service and it was during this period that Private Bourne learned his new trade. He was keen, abstemious and, rare for that period, literate; then aged twenty-one, he was rewarded with promotion to Corporal in 1875.

After years of routine duties in postings such as Dover Castle, it must have been something of a relief for Bourne and his comrades to be posted overseas.

The regiment travelled to Portsmouth where they embarked on the troopship *Himalaya* on 1 February 1878 and set sail for South Africa. Their sister battalion, the 1/24th, had been there since 1875 and was active in the final Frontier War. The Second Battalion was being sent to help stamp out the last resistance in Griqualand.

Upon arrival, Bourne rapidly ascended the promotion ladder. Between 7-27 April 1878 he was promoted Lance Sergeant, Sergeant and then Colour Sergeant of B Company. Although hostilities had all but ceased, the men of B Company, led by Lieutenant Gonville Bromhead, were involved in light skirmishing around Mount Kempt and remained there for several weeks until a general amnesty was proclaimed at the end of June.

By the end of the campaign Bourne, in common with his comrades, now sported a heavy growth of beard and wore a uniform that had seen rough service.

In July 1878 the battalion was sent into camp at Pietermaritzburg in Natal. Here they prepared for the war they knew was coming with neighbouring Zululand. After three months they were sent fifty miles closer to the border, to Greytown. Here they were encouraged to take part in all kinds of athletics, including a daily mile run before breakfast. In December, as they prepared to march to Helpmekaar, so the rains came. The seventy-four-mile march was one the soldiers would never forget.

After five days they finally reached Helpmekaar, which had mushroomed into the main assembly point for the Central Column. Troops, stores, livestock, wagons and ordnance covered the desolate plateau. As the invasion date approached, so the column descended to the crossing point at Rorke's Drift, where an advanced store depot and hospital were established.

On the 12 January 1879 Bourne, accompanied by Sergeants Galagher, Smith, Windridge and Wilson, climbed to the summit of the Shiyane Hill from where they had a magnificent view into Zululand. From here they could spot the distinctive shape of Isandlwana that, in the days to come, was to dominate the rest of their lives. The sergeants had taken to regularly climbing the Shiyane for signs of the column's progress. It was on the late morning of the 22nd when they heard the distant sound of artillery fire coming from the direction of Isandlwana. They strained to see the ten miles to Isandlwana but could see nothing of note through the damp haze; they nevertheless felt it worth reporting to Bromhead. It took another ninety minutes for the first panic-stricken survivors to reach the post and the news they brought was mind-numbing, that a Zulu impi was on its way to Rorke's Drift.

It would have been Bourne's first duty to supervise the taking down of the Company's bell tents, a recognized military drill, to give a clear field of fire. Rifles were stacked and ammunition placed within the perimeter. Bourne was further occupied with posting lookouts on the higher ground and, lastly, leading a skirmishing line to intercept the advancing Zulu force.

It was not until May that the first of the eleven Rorke's Drift Victoria Crosses were presented, to be followed several months later by five awards of the Silver Medal for Distinguished Conduct (DCM). One of the latter was Frank Bourne who was also offered a commission, a rare honour in Victoria's Army. Having no income other than his sergeant's pay, he was unable to afford the considerable cost of becoming an officer and felt obliged to decline the offer.

There followed months of frustrating inactivity as the Battalion waited at their camp near Durban for an available ship. In January 1880 they embarked and sailed for their next posting, Gibraltar. It was here, in 1882, that Frank Bourne married his wife Eliza, who was subsequently to bear him five children. During this time he was promoted to Quartermaster-Sergeant of the battalion.

In 1887 Bourne had one more overseas posting when his regiment was sent to Burma to join the Field Force led by Sir Garnet Wolseley. They spent most of their effort in marching through the jungles of Upper Burma in pursuit of elusive guerrillas without bringing them to battle. By 1890 the region was more or less at peace.

The army seems to have been determined that Bourne's talents should be rewarded and he was appointed Honorary Lieutenant and Quartermaster in May 1890. Eighteen months later he left his Regiment to take up the post of Adjutant at the School of Musketry at Hythe in Kent. Here he remained until his retirement in 1907 with the rank of major.

His reputation was such that the legendary Lord Roberts appointed him as an assistant to the Society of Miniature (Small-Bore) Rifle Clubs. This was during the period when quasi-military pastimes like shooting, The Boys' Brigade and The Scouts became very popular with the nation's youth.

With the outbreak of the First World War, the sixty-year-old Bourne volunteered his services once more. He was appointed Adjutant for the School of Musketry, this time in Dublin. When he again retired at the end of the war, he was promoted to the rank of Lieutenant Colonel and awarded the Order of the British Empire. A photograph shows him wearing his full dress uniform and displaying his South African War Medal (bar 1878-79), Indian General Service (bar Burma 1887-89) and his Distinguished Conduct Medal.

He then retired to live in a modest house in the centre of Dorking. Although there was no veterans' association, he was persuaded to attend the Northern Command Military Tattoo at Gateshead in 1934. To a tumultuous ovation, he appeared in the arena with the only other living Rorke's Drift survivors, Alfred Saxty, William Cooper, John Jobbins and Caleb Woods.

In December 1935 he made a BBC radio broadcast for a series entitled 'I was there'. It generated enough interest for three hundred and fifty people to write to Bourne. It says something of the man that he replied to every one of them.

At the very end of the Second World War, Frank Bourne peacefully passed away on 8 May 1945, VE Day, aged ninety-one years, and was buried at Elmers End Cemetery. Thus ended the life of a remarkable and modest man, a true hero.

Major Warren Richard Colvin Wynne R.E. Architect of Fort Tenedos and Eshowe
Warren Wynne was born on 9 April 1843 in County Louth, Ireland. He was educated at New Cross Royal Naval School where he distinguished himself by winning numerous prizes, especially for classics and mathematics. He was equally successful at the Royal Military Academy, Woolwich, and passed out in fourth position, which entitled him to a commission in the Royal Engineers. He was accordingly gazetted to the Corps on 25 June 1862, aged nineteen. To place his success in context, each course began with 200 aspiring officer cadets, but, due to the rigorous training, often ended with no more than twenty-five to thirty successfully completing the course. With regard to other notable cadets, the Prince Imperial had been placed seventh out of thirty-five and Chard was eighteenth out of nineteen.

Wynne's initial posting was to Gibraltar and towards the end of his first year he was appointed to the position of Acting Adjutant. His next posting was to Guildford and then to nearby Reading as a surveying officer for the Ordnance Survey and for the next few uneventful years he was directly responsible for contouring many of the detailed Ordnance Survey maps of Berkshire, Hampshire and Sussex. In December 1878 he was posted to Shorncliffe as a Captain in command of the 2nd Field Company that was under orders to proceed to South Africa for service in the impending invasion of Zululand.

At this stage of his career Wynne's promotion had not been spectacular, promotion in the Corps relied on seniority and not merit, resulting in him spending twelve years as a Lieutenant. He was, however, highly unusual in having been married twice, firstly to Eleanor (died 1873) and then to Lucy, eldest daughter of Captain Alfred Parish, R.N.R. Perhaps the Corps were not too concerned about their junior officers marrying but it was, after all, common service lore that 'While Captains might marry, Majors should and Colonels must; but Lieutenants definitely should not'. Nevertheless, Wynne's letters home reveal that he was a man equally dedicated to his career and family, being the proud father of three sons.

Wynne was given one day's notice to report to Shorncliffe where he found his new command in some turmoil and in the midst of preparations for their departure to South Africa the following morning. Fortunately Wynne had two excellent and experienced subalterns, Lieutenants Courtney and Willock, who rendered their new commanding officer every assistance. At 7.15 the following morning, Wynne, and his 2nd Field Company marched off to the railway station for transfer to Gravesend and embarkation on the *Walmer Castle*. The *Walmer Castle* was one of a fleet of vessels, all bearing the suffix 'Castle', which were owned by the Currie family and their Company, the 'Castle Line'. This line originally served the Cape route, and in peacetime was assigned to carry passengers and the Royal Mail. Several sister ships of the *Walmer Castle* had been engaged by HM Government to transport men and supplies to South Africa; these included the *Dunrobin, Dublin* and *Edinburgh Castle*.

After a few days rest Wynne and his men continued their voyage in the *Walmer Castle* towards Durban where they arrived on 3 January 1879. On 7 January Wynne and his men departed Durban to join Colonel Pearson's column heading for the main supply depot near the Tugela River, which marked the Natal border with Zululand. Their march was uneventful, apart from the constant rain and associated problems of getting their laden wagons across numerous flooded rivers and streams. They arrived at Fort Pearson on 12 January where Wynne was briefed on his future role, to build a fort on the far side of the river. This fort, on Zulu territory, was intended for use as both a defensive fort and store area to supply the coastal column as it advanced further into Zululand.

Wynne crossed into Zululand the following afternoon and promptly conducted a survey to locate a suitable site for his fort. There were two forts already in existence on the Natal bank; Fort Williamson had, though, been abandoned in 1870. Fort Pearson was perched on the top of a hill and was both on the wrong side of the river and far too small for the volume of supplies needed for the invasion. Wynne's orders were to build a fort some 600 yards from the river to be named after HMS *Tenedos*. He must have been reasonably relaxed about the task being undertaken in enemy territory, as initially his men were unarmed. Wynne and his men worked tirelessly and by late on 17 January, the fort was virtually finished. Wynne was then detailed to accompany Pearson's column on the march to Eshowe.

On 22 January Wynne was supervising his men crossing the Nyezane River when a large party of Zulus attacked the column. This was the first action he was to experience; he extended his men into an open line and was relieved when two companies of the Buffs joined his inexperienced Engineers. The whole group then moved forwards until the Zulus fled. On their arrival at Eshowe Wynne was tasked with fortifying the Norwegian mission house for the column.

Chelmsford then sent Colonel Pearson a letter cancelling all previous orders and instead instructed him to take whatever action Pearson considered appropriate under the circumstances. Aware that his column was now isolated some thirty miles inside Zululand, Pearson responded by calling a meeting of his senior officers to discuss their predicament, namely, whether to stay and fight or retreat to Fort Pearson. Wynne was strongly in favour of holding Eshowe, as otherwise the Zulus would have had an easy victory. He also pointed out that the fort would provide an ideal base for operations against the Zulus while the General reorganized his army. Wynne's argument carried the day and defensive work was renewed with increasing vigour. The Zulus surrounded Eshowe and effectively trapped Pearson's column. Wynne was probably suffering as severely as anyone else; Captain MacGregor wrote that 3 officers and 22 men had died by the 28 March.

Fleet Surgeon Norbury of HMS *Active* and his staff were now working extremely hard. The Mission Station had by now been converted into a hospital, but it could not cope with the volume of patients and medical supplies were soon exhausted. An inventive man, Surgeon Norbury then used the fort's veterinary medicines and, when these were used, he created his own medicine from tree bark and herbs from around the fort. On 3 April the siege of Eshowe was lifted and the following day saw the sick transferred back to Fort Pearson. There can be little doubt that Wynne suffered terribly from this wagon journey along the rough track. On 9 April 1879, his birthday, Captain Wynne succumbed to his illness and died.

Wynne unknowingly achieved his promotion to Major one week before he died. His neatly tended grave can easily be found at the Euphorbia cemetery overlooking the remains of his fort, Fort Tenedos, and the Tugela River estuary. The 2nd Field Company served throughout the remainder of the Zulu War, with Captain Courtney in command.

The Zulus

King Cetshwayo. *Cetshwayo ka Mpande Zulu* 'The Slandered One'
Cetshwayo was born in 1830, the son of King Mpande and his wife, Ngqumbazi. The year 1856 saw a trial of strength to succeed the ailing King Mpande when Cetshwayo defeated his brother Mbulazi at the battle of Ndondakusuka. In 1861 he was recognized by Sir Theophilus Shepstone as the *de facto* leader of the Zulus and was crowned King in 1872. Cetshwayo became the ruler of a powerful nation with an available force of fighting men numbering some 30,000. He was a strict ruler who resuscitated the military discipline established by his uncle, Shaka.

Cetshwayo resisted the Boer encroachment onto his land and even threatened military action against them; he was deterred by pleas from the British who suggested that a Boundary Commission would settle the matter. Meanwhile, the British planned an invasion of Zululand that took place in early 1879. King Cetshwayo was always opposed to military confrontation with the British and he used his diplomatic skills in a final attempt to prevent conflict, but these overtures were rejected by the British who were set on war. Even as late as the days leading to the Battle of Ulundi, he sent a large number of his favourite white cattle, the *Inyoni kayiphumuli*, to Lord Chelmsford as a peace offering. If was a futile gesture and the cattle were turned back by the King's front-line warriors, the Khandempemvu, who resisted the handing over of this national treasure.

Following the British victory at Ulundi, King Cetshwayo fled to the Ngome forest where he was eventually captured. He was taken to the Cape where he remained until he was taken to England in 1882. Due to the intervention of Bishop Colenso, King Cetshwayo formally requested permission to meet Queen Victoria in order to outline his claim for reinstatement as King of Zululand. On 14 September 1881 permission for the visit was telegraphed to Sir Hercules Robinson, the High Commissioner in South Africa.

The King's visit was delayed by officials in South Africa, worried by the implications of his return to authority in Zululand. Nevertheless, King Cetshwayo arrived in London the following August where he was enthusiastically received by curious Londoners. On 14 August he met Queen Victoria at Osborne House on the Isle of Wight and then had further discussions with officials in London.

Queen Victoria urged her government to facilitate Cetshwayo's repatriation and he was returned to South Africa to await permission for his return to Zululand. He had to wait until 7 December and the news shocked him; two large swathes of Zululand had been disposed of. One was an area to be known as the Zulu Native Reserve under the control of John Dunn and Chief Hlubi while the other area had been allocated to Chief Zibhebhu, a former rival of the King. Cetshwayo reluctantly signed the agreement and in the following January was permitted to return to the site of oNdini (Ulundi) with a view to rebuilding his shattered nation. Meanwhile Zululand was in turmoil; the country had been thrown into disorder by the British administrators who had divided the country into thirteen chiefdoms. His former general, and cousin, Zibhebhu, chief of the Mandhlakazi Zulus, eventually attacked the King and his followers on the 2 July 1883. Cetshwayo's new homestead was burnt to the ground and, wounded, he was forced to flee to Eshowe where he sought protection from the British Resident Commissioner. He died – some believe he was poisoned following a meal – on 8 February 1884 and, for political reasons, he was buried in an isolated part of the Nkandla Forest at Nkunzana near the Mome Gorge. The grave is visible from the Bhobhe Ridge.

Without doubt the Zulu people regarded Cetshwayo as a great king. Certainly he was highly intelligent and, following his capture by the British, he impressed all those who met him, including Queen Victoria.

Zibhebhu ka Mapitha Zulu

Zibhebhu was the son and heir of Mapitha, a cousin of King Mpande. He succeeded his father in 1872. He was one of the chiefs who initially counselled King Cetshwayo to accept the British ultimatum in 1878. However, once war was declared, he fought heroically for King Cetshwayo at both Isandlwana and Ulundi. It was Zibhebhu who led the Zulus down the Fugitives' Trail and some Zulus believe that it was Zibhebhu who killed Coghill and Melvill.

Zibhebhu was one of the Zulu commanders at the battle of Ulundi and, the day before the battle, he personally led a small Zulu skirmishing party that fired on the British while they were bathing in the White Mfolozi River. The British pursued the warriors and Zibhebhu almost led the British, led by Colonel Buller, into a carefully prepared ambush.

It was Zibhebhu's responsibility to muster the King's cattle for the British after the war, an act that resulted in him being alienated by the King's relatives. Perhaps for his assistance to the British, Zibhebhu was granted one of the new thirteen chiefdoms that constituted Zululand. After the restoration of King Cetshwayo, one of the King's chiefs, Ndabuko, sent an impi to attack Zibhebhu; the attack failed and a few months later Zibhebhu retaliated by attacking King Cetshwayo's oNdini homestead. The bloodbath of this battle resulted in more than fifty of Cetshwayo's senior men being killed, including Ntshingwayo and Sihayo. The King was wounded and fled to the Nkandla Forest.

Following the King's death, Zululand was in turmoil; Cetshwayo's son, Dinuzulu, sent an impi to attack Zibhebhu. Well-armed Boers assisted the impi and Zibhebhu was defeated, causing him to flee to Eshowe. He later returned to his home area, but hostilities continued; Zibhebhu was finally defeated at Nduna Hill and was again force to flee for his life. He received protection from the British and eventually returned to his home area in 1898.

Without doubt, Zibhebhu was a most able Zulu general and, although later despised by the House of Shaka for his attacks against them, he was beloved of his people. After the Zulu War he became a staunch ally of the British. He fathered over 200 children and had many wives, although he restricted his warriors to two wives each. He resented obese men and warriors who were out of condition would be sent on very long journeys. He died in 1905 and is buried at Bangonomo.

Map of the thirteen Chiefdoms, post Zulu War

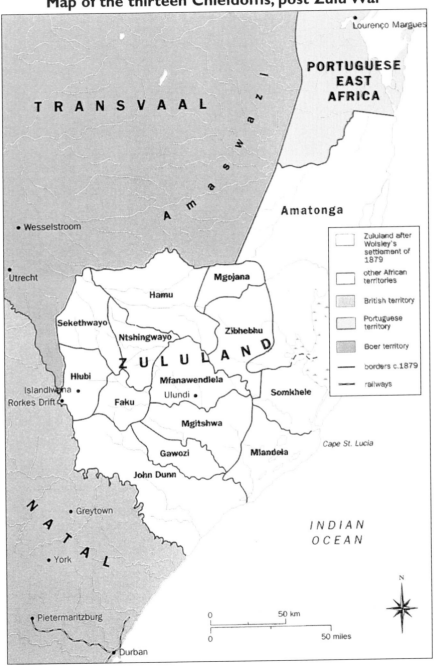

Dabulamanzi kaMpande

Prince Dabulamanzi was the youngest brother of King Cetshwayo. He was a friend of John Dunn and it was Dunn who taught Dabulamanzi to use firearms. At the age of forty, Dabulamanzi commanded the reserve at Isandlwana and, immediately following the battle, took his force across the Mzinyathi River into British-held Natal in contravention of the King's order. He then commanded, on horseback, the Zulu force that attacked Rorke's Drift. On his return to Ulundi, Dabulamanzi escaped his brother's wrath by claiming a victory and within months was appointed to lead the Zulu Army at the battle of Gingindlovu where he sustained light injuries.

Dabulamanzi was present when King Cetshwayo was dying at Eshowe. It was to Dabulamanzi that King Cetshwayo spoke concerning his young son, Dinuzulu.

There is my child; look after him for me. Bring him up well for I have no other sons. Dinuzulu is my only son. This is your task Dabulamanzi, to look after my child. James Stuart Archive, quoted in Rope of Sand by Prof. John Laband p. 368.

Dabulamanzi was murdered by Boers on 22 September 1886.

Ntshingwayo kaMahole

Ntshingwayo was Chief of the Khoza and at the outbreak of the Zulu War he was both a friend and an important member of King Cetshwayo's inner circle of advisors. Although in his 70s, he was appointed to lead the Zulu Army and he commanded at both Isandlwana and Khambula. While directing the Zulus at Khambula he allowed the two attacking horns to attack the British position out of synchrony. The two horns were unable to liaise with each other, a fact that led to their defeat. Post-war, he was appointed to one of the thirteen chiefdoms. He was killed during the battle between the followers of King Cetshwayo and Zibhebhu during the Zulu Civil War in 1883.

Mnyamana kaNgqengelele

Mnyamana was the chief of the Buthelezi tribe and at the time of the Zulu War he was King Cetshwayo's prime minister. He accompanied the Zulu force, on behalf of Cetshwayo, which attacked the British at Hlobane and Khambula. After the British victory at Ulundi, Cetshwayo fled to Mnyamana's homestead in northern Zululand before going into hiding.

Mavumengwana kaNdlela

Chief of the Ntuli, he shared command at Isandlwana with Ntshingwayo. He was also present at the Battle of Gingindlovu. His father, Ndlela, had risen to prominence under King Shaka due to his ability as a warrior, and became senior commander to Shaka's successor, King Dingane.

Godide kaNdlela

Godide was an elder brother of Mavumengwana, and at the age of seventy he commanded the Zulu coastal force that unsuccessfully tried to ambush Pearson at Nyezane.

Somopho kaZikhala

Somopho was the senior commander of the Zulu force that surrounded Pearson at Eshowe. It was his force that was defeated at Gingindlovu by Lord Chelmsford.

Prince Mbilini waMswati

Prince Mbilini was an exiled member of the Swazi royal family, having tried to seize the Swazi throne in 1865. He took up residence in northern Zululand in 1866 and swore allegiance to King Cetshwayo. He led the daring raid that defeated the British at Ntombe River. In another skirmish he sustained a head wound but this did not discourage his activities. On 4 April he led a large force to harass the homesteads of Africans loyal to the Luneburg settlers but was chased by a mounted patrol led by Captain Prior and Private Bowen of the 80th Regiment. Mbilini was shot in his shoulder and the round passed through his body, exiting below his waist. He died of his injury a few days later before he could reach his base at Hlobane. Until his death, Mbilini was feared by the British for his aggressive raiding. He was arguably the most talented guerrilla leader to fight for the Zulus during the war.

Mehlokazulu Ka Sihayo

Mehlokazulu was the son of Chief Sihayo who controlled that area of Zululand immediately opposite Rorke's Drift. He rose to fame when he pursued two of his father's wives who had engaged in extramarital liaisons and then fled to Natal for safety; the two wives were brought back to Zululand and executed within sight of the Mission Station. It was for this incident that the British sought punitive compensation and later used as an excuse to invade Zululand. After the Zulu War he was taken as a prisoner to Pietermaritzburg where he was interviewed extensively about the campaign. He gave a number of statements that have given historians valuable source material concerning the campaign. During the unrest that followed the Zulu War, Mehlokazulu sought sanctuary in the northern Nqutu region from which he fermented serious unrest towards the British and the new chief, Chief Hlubi, who had been appointed by the British to rule Mehlokazulu's former territory. Conditions across the land deteriorated to such an extent that by 1906 rebellion and uprisings broke out across Zululand. It was during the British pacification of the area, in the battle of Mome Gorge, that Mehlokazulu was killed.

Memorials in Zululand

There are battlefield memorials and cemeteries at the following battlefield sites:
• Rorke's Drift – British and Zulu. Remember, there are two British cemeteries; the other is on the far side of the river.
• Isandlwana – British and Zulu.
• Ntombe River – British.
• Prince Imperial Memorial – Prince Imperial and British only.
• Gingindlovu – British.
• Nyezane – British.
• Ulundi – British and Zulu.
• Helpmekaar – British.
• Fugitives' Drift – British only, to Lts Coghill and Melvill.
• Khambula – British.
• Hlobane – the only graves that can still be found, with difficulty, are those of Campbell and Lloyd. A guide will be needed to find them, as they are neglected and hard to find. There is no other memorial or cemetery, although this battle was a major defeat for the British in which they, and the Zulus, suffered many casualties. At the base of Devil's Pass are the remains of Piet Uys memorial, sadly vandalized.
• Eshowe – British cemetery.
• Fort Pearson – British.

Visitors to the above sites should be warned that, apart from Isandlwana, Fugitives' Drift and Rorke's Drift, most of the sites have suffered damage and vandalism in recent years. The South African Government body with responsibility for the battlefields and cemeteries is AMAFA. They can be contacted at – *Amafa, PO Box 523, Ulundi 3838.*

Difficult to find graves

The route to King Cetshwayo's grave
King Cetshwayo died on 8 February 1884. Visitors should be aware that this grave is very definitely off the beaten track and is located in a remote part of Zululand. To reach the grave, one must travel between Eshowe and Nkandla and then turn off into the extremely remote area south and east of that road. All the tracks are unmarked and it would be foolish to attempt going there without a reputable guide, preferably a Zulu speaker. There is a Zulu caretaker who lives close to the site and will approach you and guide you to the grave itself. Every respect should be shown, hats should be removed and people should speak softly.

The authors at King Cetshwayo's grave. *Adrian Greaves collection*

The 'track only' route to King Cetshwayo's grave. *Adrian Greaves collection*

Fort Chelmsford

This fort was built on the hill overlooking the Nyezane River. Today, the site is occupied by Fort Chelmsford Farm although the memorial, to all the British soldiers who died of disease at the fort, can be found on the far side of the main road, just to the south of the farm. If in doubt, call at the farm for directions.

Fugitives' Trail

From Isandlwana, in the direction of Fugitives' Drift, the route taken by the battle survivors is littered with whitewashed cairns for a distance of about one mile. The first cluster of cairns is clearly visible from the battlefield car park. If venturing down the trail, the services of a guide are recommended as the correct route is criss-crossed by cattle tracks.

Fort Newdigate

During a skirmish with Zulus on 5 June 1879 Lieutenant Frith of the 17th Lancers was shot and killed. He is buried on the site of the fort and his grave can be found in the open pastureland near to the site on the opposite side of the road.

Fort Marshall

The site of a small British cemetery containing unknown graves and the grave of Lieutenant Pardoe of the 1/13th regiment. He died of wounds received at the Battle of Ulundi while being transferred from the battlefield.

KwaMagwaza

Lieutenant James Henry Scott-Douglas, who was ambushed and killed at KwaMagwaza, Zululand, on 30 June 1879, was the eldest son of Sir George Henry Scott-Douglas.

On the morning of 30 June he was employed with his signalling party at Entonjaneni: before noon a mist came on which obscured the sun and prevented the working of the heliograph, and shortly afterwards an urgent message arrived from Lord Chelmsford to Sir Garnet Wolseley. Lieutenant Scott-Douglas, with his orderly, Corporal Cotter of the 17th Lancers, immediately set out to carry it to Fort Evelyn, twenty miles (40 km) distant.

They were surprised by a body of some five hundred Zulus who were marching to join Cetshwayo at Ulundi. Lieutenant Scott-Douglas was able to discharge five shots with his revolver, and then fell pierced to the heart by an assegai. His body was found some days afterwards by Brigadier General

Wood, lying near to that of Corporal Cotter, who had also stood his ground most gallantly: the two were buried, with military honours, side by side, in graves marked by crosses and sheltered by a luxuriant growth of indigenous plants.

This tiny isolated cemetery is well worth the small detour involved.

Location:
From Melmoth. The tarmac road to KwaMagwaza is only 2 miles (3.2 km) south of Melmoth (which is 25 miles (40 km) north of Eshowe) and is signposted from the **R66**. Follow the KwaMagwaza road for 5 miles (8 km) to the mission station. The cemetery lies about 100 yards off the roadway up a track to the right (north) of the mission station.

Zulu War Medals for Gallantry

The Victoria Cross
The Victoria Cross was born out of the carnage and muddle of the Crimean War. The idea of an award for supreme gallantry, regardless of rank, was first suggested by the then Secretary of War, the Duke of Newcastle, and soon taken up by the Prince Consort. Queen Victoria took a keen interest in her new award and it was her wish that the motto read FOR VALOUR. The design of the medal was largely decided by the royal couple and the simple cross could in no way be described as ostentatious. Even the dull crimson ribbon was decidedly low-key. Once the royal design had been approved, the first medals were struck from the bronze cut from cannon captured at Sevastopol. On 26 June 1857 the first investiture took place in Hyde Park, where the Queen presented her own award to 62 officers and men from both the Army and Navy. So was born the most coveted, exclusive and democratic award for gallantry of any country.

The Distinguished Conduct Medal
This medal was instituted in December 1854 for other ranks only. Before this date there had been no way of rewarding outstanding acts of bravery by ordinary soldiers and, in the rush of jingoism that accompanied the outbreak of the Crimean War, the press and the public demanded some form of recognition for their heroes. Moving with unusual speed, the Horse Guards produced the DCM, which carried with it a gratuity of £15 for sergeants, £10 for corporals and £5 for privates. Many of these medals, such as the Crimean War medal, were issued to men actually serving at the front and were worn by them in the trenches before Sevastopol.

Like most medals of this period, it was designed by William Wyon. The obverse showed the young Queen Victoria's diademed head, while the reverse had the inscription, FOR DISTINGUISHED CONDUCT IN THE FIELD. The medal was made of silver with a scrolled silver suspender, which hung from a ribbon of red with a dark blue centre stripe. The result was aesthetically pleasing and generally well received.

The awarding of this medal, however, has a history of inconsistencies. For instance 770 were awarded during the Crimean War but only 10 for the Indian Mutiny, while 2,026 were issued for the Boer War, but just 87 for the Sudan.

The Zulu War saw as many as 23 Victoria Crosses awarded compared with just 14 DCM's. One wonders why only 5 DCMs were awarded for the Defence of Rorke's Drift when there were so many acts of gallantry displayed. Indeed, one could argue that some of the Victoria Crosses awarded for this action probably merited the DCM instead. But then other motives were at work to lessen the impact of Isandlwana on the British public. The Rorke's Drift recipients of the 'Silver Medal', as it is sometimes known, were Corporal Francis Attwood, Army Service Corps, Gunner John Cantwell, Royal Artillery, the celebrated Colour Sergeant Frank Bourne 2/24th and Private William Roy 1/24th who was one of the brave defenders of the hospital. The fifth was Corporal Michael McMahon, Army Hospital Corps who subsequently had his award taken away for theft and desertion.

There were two native recipients, Sergeant Simeon Kambula and Troop Sergeant Major Learda, both of the well-regarded Natal Native Horse. The former received his for saving life at the Mfolozi River, while the latter received his for a similar act at the Battle of Khambula. They were not, however, the first black recipients of the DCM, as is generally believed. Several members of the West India Regiment won this distinction for gallantry during the British Honduras campaign of 1872 and the Ashanti War of 1873/74. Private John Power, 1/24th, was attached to the Mounted Infantry, escaped from Isandlwana and won his medal for three separate actions in Griqualand West in September 1878, and at Khambula and Ulundi in 1879. Two recipients, Colour Sergeant James Philips of the 58th and Gunner William Moorhead RA, received their medals for the Ulundi action. As the Zulu attack was defeated by overwhelming firepower before they could get anywhere near the British, one wonders what distinguished conduct these men could have displayed within the security of the British square.

The Battle of Khambula provided three DCMs, all for rescuing fallen comrades under fire. Private Albert Page of the 13th, for instance, ran from the lines to bring in a wounded native from the cattle kraal. Corporal Edward Quigley RA brought in a wounded soldier of the 90th.

The first medals presented to Europeans serving in locally raised regiments were awarded to Corporal William Vinnicombe and Trooper Robert Browne of the Frontier Light Horse for bravery during the Hlobane débâcle. The latter also served as Colonel Redvers Buller's orderly and no doubt Buller's sponsorship smoothed the way for his award. As with the Victoria Cross, the award of the DCM was haphazard and reliant to a large extent on influential witnesses who were prepared to champion the candidate's cause.

Another favoured recipient at Hlobane was Private Alexander Walkinshaw of the 90th, who was Colonel Evelyn Wood's bugler/orderly. He risked his life under fire to retrieve a book of prayer from the saddle bag on a dead horse so that his commander could conduct the rather bizarre burial, under fire, of Captains Campbell and Lloyd at the base of Hlobane mountain. At the end of the war Walkinshaw transferred to the 58th so that he could remain in South Africa and later took part in the disastrous First Boer War of 1880/81. His DCM was a long time in being issued and he was finally presented with it in 1882.

During the First Boer War the number of DCMs awarded was twenty, but, unlike the Zulu War, the campaign was not afforded the recognition of a medal or even a bar.

Medals in Campaign Order

Isandlwana, 22 January 1879
Victoria Cross. Private S. Wassall 80th Regiment.
Note. In 1907 two further awards were made to Lieutenant Coghill and Lieutenant Melvill of the 24th Regiment who died after crossing back into Natal from Isandlwana. At the time of the Zulu War there was no provision for posthumous awards.

Rorke's Drift, 22 January 1879
Victoria Cross. Lieutenant J.R.M. Chard RE; Lieutenant G. Bromhead, 2/24th Regiment; Surgeon J.H. Reynolds, Army Medical Department; Acting Commissary J.L. Dalton, Commissariat and Transport Department; Corporal W.W. Allen, 2/24th Regiment; Corporal F.C. Schiess, Natal Native Contingent; Privates F. Hitch, A.H. Hook, R. Jones, W. Jones and J. Fielding (alias Williams) of the 2/24th Regiment.
Distinguished Conduct Medal. Colour Sergeant F. Bourne, 2/24th Regiment; Corporal F. Attwood, Army Service Corps; Wheeler J. Cantwell, Royal Artillery and Private W. Roy, 1/24th Regiment.

Note: Corporal M. McMahon of the Army Service Corps was also awarded the medal but it was subsequently withdrawn following his conviction for theft and desertion.

An interesting postscript concerning Chard's Victoria Cross occurred in 1999. Stanley Baker, who played Chard in the film *ZULU* acquired Chard's pair of medals at auction in 1972. Although the campaign medal was genuine, the Victoria Cross was catalogued as a copy and, as a consequence, Baker paid the comparatively modest sum of £2,700 for the pair. On Stanley Baker's death, the Cross changed hands three times until it ended up, lodged for safety, with Spinks of London who decided to check the nature of Chard's 'copy' medal; its metallic characteristics were tested by the Royal Armouries. The test results were compared with those of the bronze ingot kept at the Central Ordnance Depot, from which all Victoria Crosses are cast. The tests revealed that the 'copy' had come from this same block and there was no doubt that it was the genuine article. No price can be put on this authenticated VC belonging to such a famous recipient.

With the exception of Robert Jones's medal, all the VC's belonging to the men of the 24th are now on display at the Regimental Museum in Brecon.

Ntombe River, 12 March 1879
Victoria Cross. Sergeant A.C. Booth, 80th Regiment.
Hlobane 28 March 1879
Victoria Cross. Brevet Lieutenant Colonel R.H. Buller, 60th Rifles; Major W. Knox-Leet, 1/13th Regiment; Lieutenant H. Lysons, 90th Regiment; Private E. Fowler, 90th Regiment.
Distinguished Conduct Medal. Corporal W.D. Vinnicombe, Frontier Light Horse; Trooper R. Brown, Frontier Light Horse; Private J. Power, 1/24th Regiment; Bugler A. Walkinshaw, 90th Light Infantry.

Khambula, 29 March 1879
Victoria Cross. Lieutenant E.S. Browne 1/24th Regiment.
Distinguished Conduct Medal. Troop Sergeant Major Learda, Natal Native Horse; Acting Sergeant E. Quigley and Private A. Page, 1/13th Regiment.

Mfolozi River, 3 July 1879
Victoria Cross. Captain Lord W.L. Beresford, 9th Lancers; Captain C.D.D'Arcy and Sergeant E. O'Toole, Frontier Light Horse.
Distinguished Conduct Medal. Troop Sergeant Major S. Kambula, Natal Native Horse.

Ulundi, 4 July 1879
Distinguished Conduct Medal. Colour Sergeant J. Phillips, 58th Regiment
and Gunner W. Moorhead, Royal Artillery.

South Africa Campaign Medal
The South Africa Campaign Medal, to give the Zulu War Medal its correct title,
was given to all who were involved in the war effort and covered the period
from 25 September 1877 to 2 December 1879. The original design was by
William Wyon RA and was the same as the 1853 medal issued to
participants in the Frontier Wars, for three separate campaigns during the
years 1834-35, 1846-47 and 1850-53. The medal is a silver disc measuring
35.5mm (1.4") diameter. The authority for the medal came from a Royal
Warrant dated January 1880 which was followed by a further two Royal
Warrants. This was followed by a General Order No. 103 published in
August 1880. Due to its ambiguous drafting, a further clarifying G.O. No.
134 was issued in October 1880. The medal obverse shows the diademed
head of a young Queen Victoria with the legend VICTORIA REGINA. The
'young Queen' design first appeared on medals as early as 1842 and was
still used nearly forty years later on the 1879 medal. One might wonder why
this should be when the other campaign medals of the 1870-80 period show
a matronly head of the Queen. The probable explanation is cost. Some
36,600 medals, all struck by the Royal Mint, were issued and as there was
already a die for the South African War Medal, it was a fairly simple matter
to mint a further quantity.

The reverse was designed by L.C. Wyon, (a son of W. Wyon RA). Beneath
the words SOUTH AFRICA is the graceful illustration of the lion
symbolizing Africa and is usually wrongly described as stooping to drink
from a pool in front of a protea bush. In fact, the artistic effect should convey
submission. One Under-Secretary hoped that 'the lion doing penance will
not be taken for the *British Lion'*. In the exergue (the space below), the date
'1853' was substituted with a Zulu shield and four crossed assegais. The
recipient's name and unit were stamped or engraved on the rim in capital
letters. After months of deliberation, Queen Victoria finally approved the
ribbon of watered pale orange with two wide and two narrow dark blue
stripes, which symbolized South Africa's parched terrain and many
watercourses.

Also issued for fitting to the medal was a date bar or clasp. Of all the medals
ever issued, that for the Zulu War presents the most bewildering number of
permutations. Date bars for 1877, 1877-78 and 1877-79 were issued to members
of the Colonial forces who fought against the Gcalekas. There was a separate
1878 bar for operations against the Griquas, also for Colonial forces only. There

were also bars for 1877-78-79 and 1878-79 and the Imperial regiments like the 3rd, 13th, 24th, 80th, 88th and 90th were entitled to fix these to their medals, as were N Battery 5th Brigade Royal Artillery, the principle being that the year(s) on the clasp convey all the operations in which the recipient may have engaged in. The 1879 bar was issued to all who took part in operations in Zululand. For those who remained in Natal 5,600 medals without a bar were issued, with the largest number in this category being awarded to the sailors of H.M ships *Euphrates, Himalaya, Orontes* and *Tamar.* Curiously, all participants at Rorke's Drift were awarded medals with bars, although a number of the recipients never crossed the border into Zululand.

Lieutenant Curling's South African Campaign medal.
Adrian Greaves collection

Zulu Awards

Bravery necklaces, or iziqu
These were necklaces made of small blocks cut from willow sticks and then threaded into a necklace or bracelet. They were highly prized by Zulu warriors and their history goes back to the time of King Shaka. The iziqu awarded for the battle of Isandlwana were so highly regarded that they were still being worn by the recipients when survivors were photographed in the 1930s.

Bronze armbands, or ingxotha
Although not specifically awarded for bravery, the king awarded these decorated bronze bands to men of high standing. In effect, they were status symbols and recognized as tokens of the king's favour. A king would rarely issue more than a dozen during his reign; once awarded, they were worn on the right arm.

References

1 Journal No. 4 December 1998, p.9, *Anglo Zulu War Historical Society*
2 Ditto.

Acknowledgement

The authors acknowledge the generous assistance of Brian Best with the text relating to Glyn, Buller and Zulu War medals.

Appendix A

The Efficacy of the Martini-Henry Rifle
and its Ammunition

It is generally accepted by most historians of weapon systems that the Martini-Henry rifle, carried by all regular infantry battalions in Zululand in 1879, was one of the most efficient weapons of the nineteenth century. It was robust, accurate and simple to use, and while it was undoubtedly prone to overheating during bouts of extended firing, most of the problems that ensued were attributable to the ammunition it employed, rather than the rifle itself.

Indeed, the weapon is still a firm favourite with gun collectors and shooters today. In ideal conditions – lying prone on a range, with ammunition laid out beforehand – the modern marksmen might hope to achieve a rate of fire of twenty aimed rounds in a single minute, with a hit rate as high as eighty per cent on a target 200 yards away. Such is the regard with which the rifle is held that it has influenced many of the debates concerning the battle of Isandlwana. In particular, the optimum rate of fire has often been used to support the theory that the 24th Regiment must have run out of ammunition during the battle, and that this was a crucial element in the British defeat. If the Martini-Henry was so rapid and so accurate, runs the argument, then surely the only way in which the Zulus could have penetrated the zone of British fire was by some failure on the part of that fire.

In fact, such conclusions are based on profound misunderstandings not only of the capabilities of the Martini-Henry itself, but of British tactical doctrine in the 1870s, and of the reality of battlefield experience. Conditions in the field were so unlike ideal conditions on the range that the two are largely incomparable.

The Martini-Henry was introduced into the British Army from 1874, replacing the Snider. The Martini-Henry was in fact the first purpose-built breech-loader to be issued throughout the Army; the Snider was essentially a hybrid, being a conversion of the old muzzle-loading Enfield rifle. The regulations for training troops in the use of their weapons were laid out by the War Office in a published manual of *Musketry Instruction Manual.* Prior to the Anglo-Zulu War, the last *Musketry Instruction Manual* had been published in 1874, with the result that troops fighting in 1879 had been trained according to principles which had evolved with the Snider in mind. A new edition of the *Musketry Instruction Manual* was published in 1879 that amended some aspects in the light of practical experience in the field with the Martini-Henry. All the troops who fought in Zululand would have been trained according to earlier editions, however. Subsequent editions of the manual added greater detail on training techniques, and embodied aims and objectives that were the result of experiences in the field across the period of the Anglo-Zulu War.

These manuals come as something of a surprise to anyone inexperienced in the use of weapons in the field. So, far from encouraging a rapid rate of fire, their emphasis is upon slow, controlled and accurate fire. As a result, the actual practices employed at Isandlwana and elsewhere, coupled with the reality of combat situations, produce strikingly lower rates of fire than has often been supposed. The implications, in terms of both ammunition expenditure and casualty expectations, are of the greatest significance.

The 1884 edition of the *Field Exercise Manual* – which described how troops should deploy and fight at tactical level – summed up the mechanics of infantry fire as it prevailed throughout the period in which the Martini-Henry was employed. Its instructions begin with a stern warning that sets the tone for of its theoretical approach,

In action Musketry Fire is the main element. It cannot be left to individual initiation without its degenerating into a useless expenditure of ammunition.

The duty of directing the musketry falls on the company commanders in the fighting line; that of regulating the fire, on the section commanders, under the direction of the company commanders.

The Captain points out the objectives to be attacked, and the nature of the fire to be employed. He directs the general advance of his company towards the particular point to be reached, leaving the section commanders the necessary initiative in carrying out his orders. He carefully watches the direction of the fire of the various sections, and endeavours to keep it under control so long as control is possible.

The Section Commander, having pointed out the portion of the object on which the sections should aim, will name the distances for which elevation is to be used, the number of rounds to be fired, and the description of fire.

The direction and control of fire requires, on the part of the company and section commanders, calmness and decision, skill in judging distance, a quick

perception in estimating the importance of various objectives, together with a complete knowledge of the advantages and disadvantages of the varying formation of the ground, and of the curve of the trajectory of the rifle at the different ranges.

There were two types of fire employed by British infantry in action, volley fire and independent fire. Volley fire – in which a group of men, usually a section or a number of sections – fire at the same time at a given target was best used against an enemy *en masse*. Although the constraints of the manoeuvre mitigated against individual accuracy, volleys had a devastating psychological effect on the target, which was often as damaging as the actual casualties they caused. The sudden crash of the volley created the impression in the minds of those on the receiving end that it was more destructive than it actually was, and this in itself often caused attacks to falter. Independent fire – in which the soldier picked his own target and fired when ready – often caused more casualties, but among nervous soldiers could lead to a much higher rate of fire with a greater degree of wastage.

It is interesting to note that in the 1874 regulations the soldier was required to load his rifle on the command 'ready', and on the command 'present' was to bring it to the aim, pause for a time equal to three beats of slow time – to steady himself – and then fire. No word 'fire' was given. If the situation changed during those crucial seconds, if the target was moving into cover for example, the soldier was still expected to fire, and the effectiveness of his shot could be greatly reduced. From July 1879 – presumably as a result of experiences in Zululand – Army Orders added the command 'fire', and this was incorporated into the 1882 edition of the *Field Exercise Manual*. This allowed those directing the fire to select the most opportune moment to actually fire, and to relieve individual soldiers of the obligation of firing by rote.

Throughout this period, the emphasis in British tactical doctrine was upon producing a rate of effective fire. By carefully pacing the rate of fire, commanders stood a far better chance of achieving their tactical objectives through a higher rate of hits. In the heat of battle, a natural nervousness encourages soldiers to fire as quickly as possible in the hope that this will discourage an enemy attack. Under such circumstances, aimed fire can soon be abandoned, and changes in the formation and distance of the target can be overlooked, so that the exact opposite of the desired effect can occur. By blazing away rapidly, the troops might cause fewer enemy casualties, and encourage rather than discourage attacks. Moreover, it has been noted on a number of occasions that the black powder charge of the Boxer cartridges employed with the Martini-Henry rifle produced a large quantity of dense white smoke when expended. This was particularly true when volley fire was used in close formations. On a still day one or two volleys would be sufficient to obscure the target, and any subsequent volleys, if not properly controlled, would be fired blind. One reason for slowing the rate of fire was therefore to allow the smoke to clear. It also allowed officers to see the effect of their fire and to change targets or adjust ranges if necessary.

The general principle embodied in British military practise was therefore that slow fire was more likely to be effective fire.

Sadly, there are no references in the training manuals of the late 1870s as to the rate of fire that was expected of infantry companies in the field. However, the *Musketry Instruction Manual* for 1887 – when the Martini-Henry was still in use – offers some rates of fire for field practices that are deeply revealing. These rates were a reflection of what the rifle might achieve under ideal conditions. So far from the 18 or 20 rounds of modern myth, it was noted that,

One minute will be allowed for each of five volleys, counting from the first command 'Ready'... . It should distinctly be understood that the section commander is under no obligation to fire five volleys; on the contrary, it would be wiser to fire only four volleys if he thinks the results would be better.

Even field training days would be ideal compared to battlefield conditions, where realistic rates of fire against a moving target, were probably no better than 2-3 rounds at extreme range by volley, and 4-5 rounds at closer ranges. Independent fire might be as high as 6-7 rounds and 9-10 rounds respectively.

As to effectiveness, the 1884 manual stated the ranges at which a trained soldier might be expected to hit the target 'without wasting ammunition',

- At 200 yards, a man partly sheltered or lying down.
- At 300 yards, a man standing or kneeling.
- At 450 yards, a mounted man.
- At 500 yards, fire may be opened on a thin line of skirmishers, with intervals of about 5 paces between each man.
- At 600 yards, on a thicker line with 3-pace intervals.
- At 800 yards, on skirmishers with less interval, or on a company at 'open files'.

The same manual advocated fire on targets of varying degrees of density up to 1,400 yards, where it might cause damage 'on Battalion Columns and on compact bodies of Artillery or Cavalry'.

If these rates of fire and effectiveness were expected of British troops in training in 1879, how viable were they in the field? One reason why officers were particularly keen to control the pace of fire of their men was a realistic appreciation of how inexperienced some of them might be in action. This was particularly true of the later stages of the Anglo Zulu War, when battalions of reinforcements rushed out to Zululand were brought up to strength with recruits, some of whom had not completed their basic musketry training. In any case, the perennial War Office worry about expense meant that many troops being despatched to the field had fired only a handful of rounds in practice. Some fired more rounds in their first action than they had in several years of peacetime manoeuvres. As Major Bindon Blood put it,

> *Thus it came about that our battalions landed in Zululand full of incompletely trained men, a great proportion of whom had never fired a round of ball cartridge, while many had never fired a round of blank, before they embarked. I put it thus because great trouble was taken on the voyage in the instruction of the recruits on board the transports, so that in the harbour of St Vincent for instance, where our ship anchored for about twenty-four hours, the bullets were frequently heard singing somewhat unduly near our ears! And the same thing happened also at Simon's Bay.* [1]

The results, when the reinforcements found themselves in action for the first time, were predictable, and were a salutary lesson to their officers on the importance of maintaining strict fire control. At Gingindlovu Captain Hutton of the 60th Rifles commented pertinently that

> *After the first volley, which could hardly have been expected to have done much execution, since there were but a number of darting figures at irregular intervals to aim at, I ordered my men to go on firing very steadily. A few showed signs of firing wildly, but a smart rap with my stick soon helped a man recover his self-possession.* [2]

Even so, John Dunn, the professional hunter and 'white Zulu' who accompanied the British force as an intelligence officer, thought the standard of firing very poor. He noted that their officers failed to order them to adjust their sights as the range closed, and he 'was much disappointed at the shooting of the soldiers. Their sole object seemed to be to get rid of ammunition or firing as many rounds per minute at anything, it didn't matter what'.[3]

By contrast, it should be noted that the 24th at Isandlwana were, in Smith-Dorrien's memorable phrase, 'no boy recruits, but war-worn matured men, mostly with beards, and fresh from a long campaign in the old colony where they had carried everything before them'.[4] As Frere had put it, they were 'old, steady shots', who were well used to their weapons, and had used them in action on several occasions before. Nevertheless, it is significant that their officers were still exercising strict fire control; the survivor, Captain Essex, recalled that in the opening stages of the action, he assisted Lieutenant Cavaye in pointing out targets to the men, and urging them not to waste ammunition.

Clearly they were placing their shots carefully, since Essex observed that they 'were as cheery as possible, making remarks to one another about their shooting'.[5] Smith-Dorrien thought that 'they lay on their position making every round tell'.

If the 24th were firing slowly and carefully, then how many shots did they fire during the battle? Clearly, this is crucial to any calculation regarding ammunition expenditure, but the answer will never be known. We simply do not know when individual companies opened fire and for how long they fired continuously. Tempting as it is to imagine that the 24th opened fire the moment the Zulus appeared and fired at a consistent rate throughout the battle, this simply would not have happened. As the evidence above indicates, officers exercising good fire control would have directed the men to fire at the best targets; with the Zulus moving rapidly and making good use of cover, there would inevitably have been times when they were obscured. Individual companies probably ceased firing for several minutes at a time, as circumstances changed about them. When Mostyn's and Cavaye's companies first opened fire on the Zulu right horn, it was at long range, and the rate of fire would have been moderate or even slow – the need to place shots was more important than the need to pour in the volume of fire necessary to break up an imminent attack. Moreover, any movement among the companies themselves obviously led to a break in firing. Essex thought that Mostyn's company had only been in action on the ridge for about five minutes – and Cavaye's, by implication, rather longer – when it was ordered to withdraw to the foot of the heights. Contemporary estimates of time are notoriously unreliable, especially in a battle like Isandlwana when the trauma of subsequent events serves to confuse the memory, and on balance it seems likely from other sources that Mostyn and Cavaye were in action on the heights for rather longer. Nevertheless, it is worth noting that Essex says these companies were running low on ammunition by the time they reached the bottom of the ridge and that he was prompted to organize a re-supply. Certainly, if they had been in action for twenty minutes, firing an average of two rounds a minute – not an improbable rate, given the factors already mentioned - they would have used up rather more than half the rounds with which they had begun the battle.[6]

It should be noted, however, that the actual expenditure in battle was usually surprisingly low. The optimum rates quoted in the manual were only desirable during the last stages of a determined attack, when it was necessary to break up a charge before it struck home. When firing at longer ranges, a slower rate of fire was distinctly preferable. At Gingindlovu – where the fire was less disciplined and therefore more rapid than at Isandlwana – Captain Hutton observed that 'the average number of rounds fired per man was rather under seven; that of the marines next to me was sixteen'. In his autobiography, Evelyn Wood noted that at Khambula – a battle where the intensity of the Zulu attack arguably matched that at Isandlwana – 'the Line Battalions were very steady, expending in four hours an average of 33 rounds per man'.[7] At Ulundi, the average was 10 rounds expended in half an hour. Colonel C.E. Callwell, in his wide-ranging review of colonial warfare first published in 1896, provides a number of examples of rates of fire with Martini-Henry rifles from outside the Zulu campaign. At the battle of Charasia in the 2nd Afghan War, 'the 72nd fired 30 rounds a man, being heavily engaged for some hours'.[8] At Ahmed Khel it was only 10 rounds per man, while at El Teb and Tamai in the Sudan – both battles in which the enemy launched extremely determined attacks – 'the troops most committed fired about 50 rounds a man'. By contrast, French troops at the battle of Achupa in Dahomey fired about 80 rounds a man in two hours, using a magazine rifle with a much faster rate of fire – a statistic that Callwell considered 'remarkable'.

These steady rates of fire were the product of the deliberate policy encouraged by official training manuals, where slow fire was regarded as effective fire. At Ulundi, the war correspondent Melton Prior noted with some disdain that Lord Chelmsford met a particularly determined Zulu attack with the order 'Men, fire faster; can't you fire faster?' and contrasted this with Sir Garnet Wolseley's maxim 'fire slow, fire slow'.[9] The measured volleys of the 24th at Isandlwana can be compared favourably to the experience of Private Williams of the 1/24th, Colonel Glyn's groom. Williams was in the camp at Isandlwana as the Zulu attack developed, and together with several officers' servants, began to fire from the edge of the tent area at the distant Zulus. This was independent fire, with no one to direct it, and Williams noted that 'we fired 40 to 50 rounds each when the Native Contingent fell back on the camp and one of their officers pointed out to me that the enemy were entering the right of the camp. We then went to the right ... and fired away the remainder of our ammunition'.[10] Note, however, that even under these conditions, Williams' 70 rounds lasted him throughout most of the battle.

Before leaving the question of the effectiveness of Martini-Henry fire at Isandlwana, it is worth noting that Smith-Dorrien's comment that the 24th were 'making every round tell' should be taken as a tribute to their reliability rather than at face value. This is particularly important, because an unrealistic assessment of the potential destructiveness of rifles on the battlefield can distort our reading of events. Clearly, if the 24th did indeed hit their targets with every shot, the 600-odd men of the 24th in the firing line would have killed the entire Zulu Army in 34 volleys! In battles across history – the more so in recent times, with modern rapid-fire weapons – the ratio of shots to hits is always high. The level of accuracy expected on the firing range was not attainable in the field, where even the strongest nerves could be unsettled by the tension of battle, and where the enemy was not only a moving target, but firing back. At Isandlwana the Zulu attack was carried out in open order, making good use of the ground, and the warriors only drew together during the final rush. When caught in the open, the 24th's volleys were devastatingly effective, but the Zulus naturally sought to avoid this situation. It is no coincidence that the attack of the Zulu centre stalled when it reached the protection of the dongas at the foot of the iNyoni ridge. Having found cover under heavy fire at close range, the warriors found it difficult to regain the impetus of their attack and mount an assault up an open slope into the teeth of the 24th's fire. It has been estimated that at long ranges (700-1400 yards) volley fire was no more than 2% effective. At medium range (300–700 yards) it might rise to 5% effectiveness, and at close range (100–300 yards) 15% effectiveness.[11] Given the amount of smoke produced by close-range fighting in any battle, and the effects of adrenaline generated by the proximity of the enemy, even that figure might be optimistic. It is interesting to note that at Gingindlovu, if Hutton's estimate of the number of rounds fired by the 60th Rifles is correct, then 540 men fired over 5000 rounds; he noted afterwards the just 61 dead were found within 500 yards of their line, in the most destructive fire-zone. Although more undoubtedly fell at longer ranges, and an incalculable number were wounded – several times the number killed – this figure suggests a ratio of 80 shots to kill one Zulu. At Khambula, using Wood's figure as a basis, some 1200 infantry fired nearly 40,000 rounds of ammunition, killing up to 2000 Zulus – a rather better ratio of 20:1, reflecting the greater experience of the battalions involved. In both cases, numbers of the enemy were killed by artillery fire, and many more in the pursuit, so the proportion of kills attributed to the infantry should be further adjusted downward. Taking the war as a whole, it probably took between 30 and 40 shots on average to kill one Zulu, although a number of those shots might have inflicted wounds and incapacitated the victims.

And therein lies an important truth about the effectiveness of battlefield fire. Killing the enemy was not the sole objective. Discouraging his attacks, breaking up his formations and causing him to retire were the tactical necessities, and it was necessary to kill only a small proportion of the enemy involved to achieve them. To withstand prolonged and accurate Martini-Henry fire was a terrifying experience that even the bravest warrior could not endure indefinitely. It inevitably sapped morale, and led to a growing reluctance to maintain an attack. As Hutton noted at Gingindlovu, heavy fire could drive off an attack even when the number of casualties was relatively low, simply because it created an impression of impenetrability. 'After a short while,' he wrote, 'the enemy, unable to make any headway against our fire, gradually withdrew.' This effect tended to be cumulative; at Isandlwana, the Zulu Army, still fresh with enthusiasm to defeat the invader and confident of victory, was prepared to endue the 24th's fire to a remarkable degree. Later, however, when the cost of the victory became apparent, there was a growing reluctance to face the fire on quite the same terms, so that by the time of the Battle of Ulundi, some British observers noted that the Zulu attacks sometimes faltered and hung back. Certainly, at that battle several Zulu veterans recalled that the noise and concussion of British fire at close range was in itself awe-inspiring.

Perhaps the most famous example of the fire being effective without being unduly destructive is at Rorke's Drift. Here the defenders fired off nearly 20,000 rounds in ten hours, killing some 600 Zulus – an average rate of fire of rather less than 15 rounds per man per hour, with a kill ratio of 33:1. The circumstances here are of the greatest importance, of course; after the initial attacks were met by volley firing, most of the fire would have been independent fire, at ranges so close that they effectively constituted hand-to-hand combat, or directed against an enemy concealed by natural cover. Moreover, much of that firing would have taken place with the bayonet fixed – which seriously affected accuracy – and in circumstances where careful aiming was difficult. After two or three hours, night fell and all firing was carried out in the dark, lit at best by the flames of the burning hospital. Under such circumstances, the low rate of kills to shots is not surprising, but the British fire could hardly be considered ineffective. On the contrary, it was particularly effective in its primary objective after dark – that of suppressing the enemy, and discouraging his attacks. Every time Zulu chants or shouts of command suggested that an attack was imminent, the defenders poured fire in that direction. Although the number of hits was undoubtedly minimal, it was often sufficient, by that stage of the battle, to prevent the attack from developing.

In the final analysis, a realistic appreciation of the battlefield capabilities of the Martini-Henry, and the tactical doctrines which underpinned its use, is essential to any analysis of the events of 1879. Yet if the rate of fire was much slower, and its destructiveness much less than popular myth suggests, it should be remembered that it was still a highly effective weapon that was greatly admired by the men who used it. As Hutton put it, 'We all had the utmost confidence in our rifles, which were at that time the most perfect weapons in the world'.

Acknowledgement

My thanks to Adrian Whiting, the Armourer of the Die-Hards re-enactment group and a keen Martini-Henry shooter, for helping to disentangle the various relevant training manuals, and for allowing me some practical experience of the weapon.

References

1 Blood, Sir Bindon, *Four Score Years and Ten*, 1933.
2 Hutton's account appeared in the *Army Quarterly*, April 1928 and in Frank Emery's, *The Red Soldier*.
3 Dunn's account, *The Red Soldier*.
4 Smith-Dorrien, Horace, *Memories of Forty-Eight Years Service 1925*.
5 Essex. Letter to *The Times*, 2 April 1879.
6 70 rounds per man; 20 in either pouch on the front of the waist belt and 30 in the black expense pouch or 'ball bag'.
7 Wood, Sir Evelyn, *From Midshipman to Field Marshal*, 1906.
8 Colonel C.E. Callwell, *Small Wars and their Principles and Practise*, 1896.
9 Prior, Melton, *Campaign of a War Correspondent*, 1912.
10 Williams' account Norman Holmes, *The Noble 24th*.
11 Whitehouse, Howard, *Battles in South Africa*, 1987.

Author's note

I recently came across this interesting comment made by Dr Adrian Goldsworthy in his book *Cannae* published by Cassell.

> *Modern studies suggest that relatively few soldiers, even in the best-trained units, actively aim at and seek to kill the enemy in combat, most firing their weapons wildly and some not even firing them at all. Certainly the ratio between the number of rounds fired and the number of casualties inflicted on the enemy in the well-documented combats of the last few centuries has been staggeringly low, usually at least several hundred to one.*
> Dr Adrian Goldsworthy, Cannae

The noted Zulu War author, Ian Knight, generously contributed this appendix article.

Bibliography

Adams, Jack, *The South Wales Borderers,* London 1968.

Atkinson, C.T., *The South Wales Borderers, 24th Foot 1689-1937*, Cambridge 1937.

Bancroft, J.W., 1991. *The Zulu War, 1879: Rorke's Drift,* Tunbridge Wells, Spellmount Ltd.

Clarke, Sonia, *Invasion of Zululand,* Brenthurst, South Africa, 1979.

Coupland, Sir Reginald, *Zulu Battle Piece Isandlwana*, Collins 1948.

Crook, M.J. *The Evolution of the Victoria Cross,* Midas Books, 1975.

Cunynghame, Sir A, *My Command in South Africa*, Macmillan 1879.

Dodds, Glenn, *The Zulus and Matabele,* Arms and Armour, 1998.

Emery, Frank, *The Red Soldier*, Ball Paperbacks, Johannesburg, 1977.

French, The Hon. Gerald, *Lord Chelmsford and the Zulu War*, Unwin, 1939.

Greaves, Adrian, *Fields of Battle – Isandlwana,* Cassells, 2001.

Greaves & Best, *The Curling Letters of the Zulu War*, Pen & Sword Books, 2001.

Greaves, A, & Knight, I, *A Review of The South African Campaign of 1879*, Debinair 2000.

Gon, P. 1979. *The Road to Isandlwana,* London. *A note on firearms in the Zulu kingdom with special reference to the Anglo-Zulu War 1879. Journal of African History* (4): 557-570.

Hamilton-Browne, *A Lost Legionary in South Africa,* Werner Laurie, 1911.

Hayward J. B. & Son. *Medal Rolls 1793-1889 of the 24th Foot, South Wales Borderers,* Hodder, *Heroes of Britain*, Cassell, 1880.

Holme, Norman, *The Silver Wreath.*

Hurst, G.Y. *The Volunteer Regiments of Natal and East Griqualand*, Durban, 1945.

Knight, Ian, *With his Face to the Foe,* Spellmount 2001.

There Will Be An Awful Row At Home About This, Shoreham, 1987.

The Sun Turned Black, Watermans, 1995.

Laband, John, *The Field Guide to the War in Zululand*, Lord Chelmsford's Zululand Campaign, Alan Sutton Publishing, 1996.

Fight us in the Open, Shuter and Shooter, S. Africa.

Laband, Thompson and Henderson, *The Buffalo Border 1879*, University of Durban, 1983.

Laband, J. & Thompson, P., *Kingdom in Crisis. The Zulu Response to the British Invasion of 1879*. Pietermaritzburg: University of Natal Press. 1992.

Lloyd, W.G., *John Williams, VC*. Glamorgan, 1993.

Lummis, M., MC, *Padre George Smith of Rorke's Drift*, Wensome, 1978.

Mechanick, F., 1979. *Firepower and firearms in the Zulu War of 1879*. Military History Journal 4 (6).

Montague. C.E., *Campaigning in South Africa*, Blackwood 1880.

Morris, Donald, *The Washing of the Spears*, Cape, 1996.

Morris and Arthur, *The Life of Lord Wolseley*, London, 1924.

Mossop, George, *Running the Gauntlet*, Thomas Nelson, 1937.

Paton, Glennie & Penn Symons, *Records of the 24th Regiment*, London 1892.

Swiss. A.H., *Records of the 24th Regiment*, London, 1882.

Trollope, Anthony, *South Africa*, 1878.

War Office, *Précis of Information concerning Zululand*, London, 1895.

Army Medical Reports, 1878.

Narrative of Operations Connected with the Zulu War of 1879, London, 1881.

Précis of Information, 1879.

Wilmot, A, *The Zulu War*, London, 1880.

Wood, Sir Evelyn, *From Midshipman to Field Marshal*, Methuen, 1906.

Worsfold, W.B., *Sir Bartle Frere: a Footnote to the History of the British Empire*, 1923.

Newspapers, Journals and Periodicals of 1878/1879

The Illustrated London News, London.

The Graphic London

The Natal Witness, South Africa.

The Natal Times, South Africa.

The Times, London.

Punch, London.

The Natal Mercury, South Africa.

The Natal Colonist, South Africa.

Standard, London.

Daily News London.

Parliamentary Papers

Parliamentary Papers 1878–1906 (C.2222–2295).

Journals

Journals 1–12 of the Anglo Zulu War Historical Society.

Index